THE CATHOLIC CRISIS

THE
CATHOLIC
CRISIS

THOMAS F. O'DEA

BEACON PRESS   BOSTON

Copyright © 1968 by Thomas F. O'Dea

Library of Congress catalog card number: 68-14707

First published by Beacon Press in 1968

First published as a Beacon Paperback in 1969

Beacon Press books are published under the auspices
of the Unitarian Universalist Association

Printed in the United States of America

CONTENTS

PREFACE TO THIS EDITION

THE reception of the encyclical of Pope Paul VI on birth control testifies to the breakdown of two long-standing pillars of popular Roman Catholicism: mistaking fear of sex for spirituality, and mistaking subservience to authority figures for membership in the *laos theou*. Like all genuine cases of mistaken identity, these two, so important functionally in the Catholic milieu, were based upon the failure to distinguish between what are really close family resemblances. The problems and paradoxes of spirit and flesh are, of course, as real as ever, and the functionality and legitimacy of authority remain vital to all human communities. Yet the confusions had to be cleared up. Men searching for communion in a time of the widespread breakdown of community were bound to seek new possibilities in the relations of man and woman; men struggling to achieve secular maturity in a post-traditional society found it difficult to accept the pronouncements of an episcopate many of whose members showed signs of considerable immaturity in both the secular and religious spheres. It was these two areas of contemporary Catholic concern that the recent encyclical brought together.

What has to come often comes in forms that please no one. Jacques Maritain's recent response to the new situation in the Church is more interesting in this respect than is credited by his critics. Maritain was long a leading Catholic thinker and at the same time a "man of the left," a combination which most American clergy (though illiterate in French history) could not forgive; he did more to enlighten American

Catholics than any two dozen figures we might name. Now he finds what he helped to bring about in the Church appalling to behold. He remains an intellectual giant in his latest book (a fact that points up the true dimensions of some of his critics), and a sensitive human being. He has been around long enough not to be beguiled by any modish cities — either the heavenly one of the 18th century philosophers in France or the secular one so recently discovered in America. It is difficult to read *The Peasant of the Garonne* without profound sympathy for his position. But he is wrong — dangerously wrong. He seeks to constrain the movement of the human spirit within the limitations of a single philosophical universe and to understand the great historic crisis of Catholicism within that universe. We need a new mode of being a Catholic and a man of the revolution, and we now know the revolution to be vaster than imagined by Maritain. There are many helpful hints in his works, but Maritain's mode itself seems no longer serviceable. Working out a new mode will not be easy. It will require a new understanding of both the revolution and Catholicism, and that will not be achieved by enthusiasm uninformed and unrestrained by ideas.

I am myself academic enough (to introduce a word likely to be suspect among both the young enthusiasts and their older clerical adversaries) to think that when it comes to solving problems, speech is superior to swinging one's arms about, and that within the province of speech itself, conversation is better than shouting. Between the enthusiastic shouting of the young and the dour dictatorial pronouncements of the old one is given little choice. It is indeed distressing to see an aged prelate, obviously out of touch with the revolution in which we have been embroiled since the 18th century, disciplining "his" priests in the attempt to proscribe public discussion of theological issues of the greatest personal implication for "his" people. It is equally distressing to see younger men and women, presumably informed and intelligent, discover the revolution in which we have been involved for two centuries, and for which we are farther than ever removed from the capacity to propose significant aims and policies, and respond to it as though it were the night of August 4, 1789.

Some have called what we are experiencing a crisis of authority. Authority, looked at empirically, is indeed a moral matter. It rests upon the conviction that it is right and just, fitting and proper, that those who rule should rule and those ruled be ruled. Such acceptance rests upon the conviction that the authority institution is part of the nature of things and that it ultimately derives from God. If this is the case with civil authority, how much more is it the case with ecclesiastical authority. This century has experienced a continual rebellion against established authority. Behind it stand events crucial to the development of modernity, the English regicide of the 1640s, the French regicide of the 1790s, the liberal and revolutionary movements of the 19th century, and the increasingly critical insistence of modern thought. From the rising in Petrograd in 1905 to the putsch in Lima in 1968, revolutions, putsches, and *coups d'état* have been commonplace. Faith that the powers that be are ordained of God, however formulated in the various cultural idioms of the world, has been largely eroded.

That authority crisis has now become a fact within the last bastion of Western religious authority — within the Roman Catholic Church. Hierarchs must now tolerate what most rulers outside the iron curtain and some inside it must put up with, public opinion. Although one can feel strong sympathy for Bishop Helmsing and his sentiments, one recognizes that the *National Catholic Reporter*, whatever its breaches of taste at times, has done the American Church the greatest service of any agency or institution in this century. It has provided leadership for the crystallization of an articulate and intelligent Catholic public opinion in the United States. Bishops in America and Stalinist bureaucrats in the Soviet

Union have this much in common, they have long preferred to rule without interference from that inconvenient animal.

There are hopeful signs here and there that some may now be trying to understand public opinion. The period from the issuance of *Pascendi Gregis* and the *Lamentabili* decree until the pontificate of John XXIII was characterized by strict discipline within the clerical estate. The Church appeared more authoritarian and more monolithic than ever. The typical American chancery, in addition to being plagued by practical problems, was marked by a combination of integralist phobias and government by crony. That appears to be the case insofar as one can penetrate into that last contribution of Renaissance princes to the Church — government in secret. To the bishops this time seemed to be another minor peace of the Church; to others it appeared to bear an uncomfortably strong resemblance to what in political structures would be identified as absolutism.

The authority crisis is a severe one, but it is only a symptom of a more fundamental and indeed more severe crisis — a crisis of meaning and direction. This crisis of meaning is both a part and a consequence of the long-term revolution in which we are involved. What is this revolution? It is a political revolution which has in the last two centuries caused the passing of old forms of power and subordination, and has brought often chaotic experimentation and casting about to find new principles and powers likely to effect human safety and happiness. It is a social revolution which finds large numbers of people in the condition President Wilson attributed to the people of Europe in 1918, "a revolutionary state of mind. They do not believe in the things that have been practiced upon them in the past, and they mean to have new things practiced." The submerged majority of mankind is surfacing in a historical earthquake causing older institutions to crack and crumble. It is a philosophical and intellectual revolution in which ancient and new truths alike are subject to the severest scepticism. Long-accepted definitions of man and his condition appear obsolete. Not only the content but the forms and modes of thought and expression of the past are alienated from meaningful resonance with the hearts and minds of many of our contemporaries. It becomes then a crisis of ultimate meaning — a religious crisis.

In our time Kant's questions — "what should I believe? what ought I to do? what may I hope for?" — have become issues of daily life, no longer merely the stuff of philosophical dialogue. The contemporary world is undergoing a profound process of moulting; it is shedding the older cultural forms in which it expressed its sense of what man is and what is his destiny. It is not simply that Christianity — a minority point of view among the influential people in Western society — is in crisis, but that those surrogates and substitutes which took the places vacated by Christianity find themselves in crisis as well.

Secular liberalism, though still a valuable political and intellectual attitude, provides at best antepenultimate guidelines for the conduct of public life, in government, in education, and in the community. The emancipation to which it once looked forward appears today as simply formal in character, a negative proscription of interference with the rights of others. Socialism, the last ardent expression — albeit in secularized form — of Christian and Jewish apocalypse outside the context of small and marginal holiness sects, was in deep crisis by the end of the 19th century; the rise of Stalinism in the 1930s signaled its end as a spiritual phenomenon with a significant future. The university is also in a state of crisis. I do not refer here principally to the demonstrations which are only surface symptoms of a general malaise among the literate and semiliterate and too easily become playthings for the immature and the irresponsible. I refer to the deeper causes of that general malaise, to our vast inability when confronted with the matter of developing in our day a creative

humane education capable of providing intellectually sophisticated and morally responsible leadership in the face of
modern predicaments.

The foundations of the world are shaken. But this must
be seen as sober fact, not apocalyptic sign. The drift of revolution appears irresistible. That drift, nevertheless, has brought
violence and chaos which in turn have produced tyranny. It
is no wonder that the "irresistible" drift frightens many.
Opposites are analytically and empirically closely related,
being two aspects of the same phenomenon. They rise and
fall, act and react, in relation to each other. It is the responsibility of intelligent men to seek to direct and constrain those
historical forces now beyond human control in directions
beneficial to human welfare. The history of the last several
decades has littered the world with dead men's bones as a
testimony to the horrors which revolution and counterrevolution can bring down upon mankind.

In the midst of all of this the Catholic Church at best
remained on one side unable to relate itself effectively to the
course of events, at worst allying itself with counterrevolution
and identifying its own aims with its illusions. It went along
throwing aside or losing by desertion those of its sons and
daughters whose concern with this grave situation threatened
to bring about a new and realistic confrontation of the actual
conditions of the Church and the times. Through all of this
the spiritual depth of the Catholic faith and the richness of
the Catholic tradition were not destroyed. They were con-
strained and distorted, or simply remained embedded in
obsolete folk beliefs and values. The Catholic sense of the
importance of the spiritual, of the immediacy of God, and
of the reality of the Church mediating man's relation to
God — all of these remained. These factors were the source
of those spiritual energies which brought into being recent
and present attempts at reform and renewal.

Because of a number of historical and contemporary

factors, the second Vatican Council heeded the advice of its reformers and began to reappraise and renew the life of the Church and to face the contemporary crises in depth. This book presents an analysis of the historical circumstances and the contemporary conditions which influenced this outcome. It probes the basic issues revealed by the Council debates and decisions and examines their implications for the condition of the Church and the world at this serious point in our history. It raises questions which demand much further study. It attempts to make a serious contribution to the great effort necessary in the Church if Christianity is not to vanish as an important spiritual force in the world.

It is doubtful that many bishops at Rome understood the scope of the transformation they were initiating. Surely they did not comprehend how great were the elements of discontinuity implicit in their decisions. In this book, again, we attempt to examine the problems of continuity and discontinuity which lie beneath all of the conflict within the Church in our time and to which none of us sees anything resembling a solution. Once removed from the press of conciliar demands and the stimulus of world attention, back in the familiar provincial atmosphere of their own dioceses, most bishops sought to apply brakes. But life is a fountain, not a kitchen tap, and the movement for reform and renewal just cannot be turned off. Their abysmal ignorance of history leaves many bishops unprepared to understand. Some try to apply the old authority, but it proves quite ineffective in the new conditions. Is it any wonder that Catholics show more trust in the theologians who disagree with the pope than in the bishops or the curia as the interpreters of what is really involved in Catholic faith and morals? These theologians gave leadership and inspired hope by their performance at the Council. Look at the record of episcopal leadership in America and indeed in the world in this century! Consider the long uninspiring record of papal leadership before the accession of

John XXIII. Is it any wonder that both priests and lay people now refuse to be defined as out of the Church by uncomprehending bureaucrats after having been told by the Council that the Church is a pilgrim people? Faced with this situation, some bishops, themselves raised on anti-modernist oaths, now talk about loyalty oaths for the lower clergy! At the same time many liberals in their sincere searching bear poor testimony to their cause in their fascination for novelty itself and by their failure to remember the seriousness of the present revolution.

If the bishops and older clergy do not grasp what is happening, the newer liberals, clerical and lay, show signs also of a lack of apprehension. Enthusiasm too frequently substitutes for solid intellectual performance; protest and a fascination with novelty take the place of efforts to understand. Many of those who think of themselves as the "new breed" seem utterly unaware of the depth and thoroughness of the revolution in which we find ourselves. Not seeing that, they fail to grasp how considerable — indeed at times overwhelming — are conservative reactions which seek to hold back impetuous forward motion in directions which none of us understands. They overlook the strength of outright reactionary forces seeking to restore the past. Both sides need to take the measure of the crisis and recognize that the times call not simply for protest, polemic, and authoritarian pronouncement, but for solid intellectual substance, for serious efforts at understanding supported by learning and scholarship.

Not only must the world be understood — this complex and dynamically changing modern world which is not to be understood easily — but the Catholic heritage must be understood as well. The conservatives think they are "preserving the Catholic faith." The challenge is not to preserve faith but to transmit and comprehend the Catholic heritage — the profound religious tradition of the Catholic Church. That heritage will not be preserved by being quarantined in second- and third-rate colleges or by the construction of a spiritual ghetto, standard policy almost completely unquestioned until a decade ago. That heritage will be preserved by serious study and critical evaluation by Catholic scholars. One is inclined to stress this because one has the distinct impression that the young do not always comprehend seriousness while the older clergy never comprehend freedom. It is only by such study that the Catholic heritage will become a real factor in spiritual life in our time and that men will be able to find in it the bases for the discovery of faith.

In education — in science and the humanities — the whole idea of what teaching means has undergone a tremendous revolution in the centuries since Trent and even in the decades since the first council of Baltimore. Is it not clear to all intelligent men that the whole concept of teaching and the teaching office of the Church must be reexamined in that context? The problems involved in formulating the content of faith have been transformed by changes in the modern mentality brought about by developments in science, history, and the study of languages and cultures. Is it not clear to all intelligent men that the whole notion of doctrine needs reexamination in that context? Charges of unorthodoxy, accusations of abandonment of Christianity, and countercharges and accusations against the establishment and its benighted views will be unhelpful in dealing with these issues.

Let everyone face certain facts of life. There will have to take place bold and far-reaching changes, transcending anything that has yet been achieved by any denomination if Christianity is to survive as a large-scale spiritual force. In this book we have examined the relevance of the post-conciliar situation in the Church and the world with respect to the possibility of such changes. There will be required what many will see as "a revision of doctrine." Such revisions have taken place before — most impressively in the transformation from the apocalyptic form of the faith of the Church in the year 30 to the sacramental formulation and expression in the year 200. Making Christianity relevant now to man's history in the making involves forms of participation in history — and modes of understanding such participation — which simultaneously place the Christian within history and enable him to transcend it. Working out what that means will involve a process of rethinking and reorganization which will probably occupy the better part of the next century. During the long interim period which we are now entering, a new provisional way of handling dogma, doctrine, and discipline must be worked out. If this is not done, the misunderstandings of the Reformation period will be reenacted once more and thinking men forced out of the Church. Facing the fact that the dynamic character of this transition contains implications beyond the grasp of even the wisest among us and that accomplishing the transition will require much diversity, much trial and error, is it not possible to develop a flexible pluralistic unity for this period of necessary reexamination, experimentation, and reformulation?

Open discussion and disagreement are a necessary part of this process. That was true in the creative ages of theology in the past; it is equally true today. The way important things are stated and the angles from which we approach them are never settled once and for all. At most there is settlement within the confines of one civilization or one epoch. But we live at the end of an epoch and at a time when our own civilization in severe crisis is brought into confrontation with the peoples and cultures of Asia and Africa. The analogies for our age should be sought in neither the Middle Ages nor the Renaissance, but in the first centuries of our era. For this process to go on it is necessary to preserve unity and brotherhood. These are not sufficient conditions for its success, but they are necessary ones.

I am not pleading for an end to conflict. Conflict is necessary to life and to all forward motion in human communities. It was the mistake of post-Tridentine Catholicism, building upon the less fortunate aspects of its medieval heritage, to seek to repress internal conflict about grave and serious issues. Conflict is inevitable, but let it be conflict about serious matters. It should involve on all sides the effort to understand, informed by the search for knowledge about what is fought over. Conflict is a form of dialogue, but that aspect of it is largely vitiated if a narrow and dogmatic partisanship prevails. And that will be the case unless Catholic unity is preserved and Catholic conversation developed. Seriousness of purpose and of content must be supported by reciprocal respect and a sense of decorum. I believe that the pope and also the bishops should be criticized publicly by all serious men who disagree with them. There can no longer be a clerical sanctuary from intellectual evaluation of performance and position by friend or foe in a world such as ours. Yet I am not edified (nor, to use the word more accurately, is the Church) to see the pope berated as though he were a retired Air Force general running for public office. The Church has since Trent suppressed all genuine revisionist scholarship and thought; by so doing it has postponed its needed reappraisal and reform and at the same time guaranteed that that painful and prolonged process has now to take place in the fierce glare of publicity inherent in the communications systems of the modern world. The clergy must now learn to put up with what they unwisely put off for so long.

But both clergy and laity, both the bishops and the dissenting priests, both the pope and the liberal bishops, both the hierarchy and the theologians, both the conservatives and liberals, both the cosmopolitans and the locals — in a word everybody in the Church — must make a central fact of their consciousness a recognition that unless ecclesiastical order and ecclesiastical freedom are combined in the coming period of time ecclesiastical unity will be broken. Order and freedom can be combined only if those in authority recognize the genuine newness of the situation and show the necessary flexibility. Above all they must learn to tolerate much which their background prepares them to suspect. When conservatives see the prospect of such openness and freedom as threatening, as they will not be able to help from doing, then let them remember that the consequences of disunity will be dire. Let the liberals who seek relief from their frustration by shocking the conservatives be aware of the same thing. For if Catholic unity is lost, then the Catholic old guard will retreat more and more into an obscurantist Catholicism with no relevance to the vast religious and value problems of modern men and might perhaps become identified with questionable forms of political reaction. The excommunicated and deserting liberals, cut off from the larger community, would vanish in two generations as a serious religious force in the modern world. Let those liberals who beguile themselves with the prospects of a "separated liberal Catholic Church" bear this in mind. Catholicism in America has the opportunity to carry forward the renewal started at Vatican II into a religious renewal of great significance to the crisis of Western man. It can do this only by encouraging its liberal forces and working together with its ecumenical brethren for a Christianity no longer obscurantist, no longer reactionary, no longer clutching its definitions. It has the opportunity to help men discover the good news of its message, but in order to do so it must seek to cleanse itself of the dross accumulated in its unfortunate historical encounter with modernity. It must now reconcile itself to modernity, but not at all by capitulating to secularist vanities and superficial fads. The times are indeed serious; they call for judgment, for patience, for critical intelligence. Too frequently both the conservatives and the liberals lose sight of this.

It is encouraging to read a contemporary Catholic writer who exhibits sympathy both for priests who marry and for those of conservative liturgical tastes who want Latin masses and Gregorian chant. For indeed the Church must not only find unity in diversity as Pope Paul has urged, but it must find and preserve unity with dissent. The Church lives in a pluralist world and it must itself become a pluralist community. Uniformity is no virtue in itself and it is impossible in our day. One suspects that it has always been a pseudo-ideal. Experimentation in brotherhood; unity with dissent; flexibility and the capacity for compromise: only with these can the Church become a community for the vast variety of the sorts and conditions of men within its ranks.

This volume is intended as a contribution to the pluralistic Catholic dialogue of our day. It is an attempt to analyze with the conceptual tools of the social scientist the historical situation of the Catholic Church before and after the Council, and to examine the basic issues that now confront the Church as it stands hesitant before the great historical challenge of the time. It is presented as a work not of polemic and debate but of scholarship in the conviction that relevant scholarship is more important than ever and will in the long run prove most practical.

THE CATHOLIC CRISIS

I

INTRODUCTION

THE Roman Catholic Church is a unique religious phenomenon. It is the largest of the Christian communions and indeed the most "catholic" of them judged in terms of its geographical dispersion and its accommodation to a diverse set of historical and social circumstances. It possesses a historical and theological uniqueness. It continues in our day the structure and tradition of the medieval Church, and its dogmatic and theological positions stand in unbroken continuity with the Fathers of the early Church. An understanding of the religious condition of this vast and ancient organization cannot but be of the first importance for the understanding of the contemporary religious situation as a whole.

Moreover, the Catholic Church has just emerged from one of the most important councils of its long career. Vatican II undoubtedly represents a great watershed in Catholic history, and its consequences will be felt for several generations. Many of them are beyond the capacities of our prevision at this time. Nevertheless, certain outlines reveal themselves, certain issues become visible, and certain tensions stand disclosed. These appear to be of diagnostic significance for an understanding of the future course of Catholic development. We shall attempt to analyze these elements of the current Catholic picture and to estimate their significance for the future.

The present situation in the Roman Church is interesting for an additional reason. It is in important respects diagnostic of the position of Christianity as a whole in the contemporary

3

world. The Second Vatican Council represents more than a massive effort for renewal and *aggiornamento* on the part of Roman Catholicism. It was that, and that in itself is of very great significance. But the more profound meaning of the event can be grasped only by viewing it in its full ecumenical context. Not only did non-Catholic observers play a large part in the informal theological discussions that surrounded the Council meetings and not only did non-Catholic world opinion have a tremendous, if hidden, effect upon Council decisions, but the updating efforts which came to fruition in the Council represent the precipitate of a long history. Within the Catholic Church again and again in the last century and a half, significant minorities have advanced proposals for renewal and reform. They brought forth proposals for radical reconsideration of the way the Church had up to then been meeting the challenges, problems, and dilemmas of its encounter with modernity. To have the Church take a fresh look, to have it abandon its defensive posture, to aid it in confronting the new world that was coming to be—such were the aims of these minorities, who were so frequently discouraged and repressed by ecclesiastical authority.

Thus the Second Vatican Council represents a continuation of developments that had been going on for over 150 years. It marks the fruition of insights of long standing. There is one great difference, however, whose significance needs only to be pointed out. Whereas in the previous efforts at *aggiornamento* such proposals came into conflict with and were usually suppressed by the authority of the Church, they were now adopted by the Church assembled in General Council and promulgated with all the legitimacy and even splendor of the papal approval.

This rootedness of the "new" stand of the Vatican Council in the past points to an even more notable dimension of the total ecumenical setting of the Council. It points to the fact that the insights of the Council were present in the Church before the Council. But, equally important, the great efforts

4

made now by Catholicism toward a more adequate confrontation with the world represent the second great attempt by
Christianity to face modernity and adjust itself to the challenge of today's conditions.

Protestantism has tended to divide into two major tendencies, two significant groupings, in the last century and a
half. One of these tendencies clung to a premodern understanding of the scriptures and of theology and stubbornly
refused to make a conscious accommodation to the requirements of science and modern thought. The more impressive
Protestant phenomenon of this period, however, is that which
we designate roughly under the label "liberal Protestantism."
Central here were the biblical research and the theological
and historical studies of German Protestant scholars. This
movement attempted to understand Christianity anew and
to reinterpret it in a way its new interpreters thought would
render it understandable and acceptable to the age in which
they lived.

The Second Vatican Council itself and the vast ferment
it has inspired in Catholic circles—the aspirations for renewal
and reform—represent a second major attempt to bring the
Christian religion into a relevant relationship with the evolving
modern world, characterized by science, technology, the
demise of traditional social and political entities, the vast
expansion of knowledge, rapid communications, and a new
valuation of secular activity.

The great Protestant effort and its counterpart in present-
day Catholicism are modern versions of a kind of activity long
to be seen in the history of the Church. In all periods it has
been the task of Christian thinkers to restate the Christian
faith so that their contemporaries would find it meaningful.
This task requires a confrontation with the leading ideas of
the age.

The early apologists were faced with the challenge of pagan
philosophy; Thomas Aquinas by that of the Averroism of the

medieval universities; Butler by that of deism. All of them by the skillful use of contemporary philosophical ideas restated the historic Christian faith in such a way as to win a hearing for it in their own time. But more than that, it may be said also that all of them made contributions of permanent value to theological thought, because they themselves won a deeper understanding of Christian truth through their work [52:3, 4].

In this sense, there is ample legitimate precedent in the Christian tradition for what liberal Protestantism did and for what is now attempted by postconciliar Catholicism.

Such a course, though necessary, is fraught with danger. To Macquarrie this danger is threefold.

Preoccupation with a secular philosophy and the employment of it in the interpretation of the Christian faith may easily lead to the distortion of Christian teaching through the over-emphasis of those elements in it which happen to be specially congenial to the philosophy concerned. Or again, ideas quite foreign to Christianity may slip into its theology while masquerading under the guise of traditional Christian terminology. At worst, there may be a plain accommodation of the Christian faith to the prevailing philosophical fashion of the age [52:4].

The Protestant rethinking of Christian meaning in the light of historicism, science, and biblical research stands as one of the great achievements of the Western mind. Liberal Protestant scholarship and theology and its successor phenomenon, neoorthodoxy, did indeed probe aspects of the Christian faith to win a deeper understanding of it in important respects. But it may also be asserted that Protestantism did not escape the dangers suggested by Macquarrie. There is alas some truth in the allegation that Liberal Protestantism often succeeded in reversing the miracle at Cana, transforming the wine of Christian faith into the water of scholarly opinion. These Protestant efforts too often won contemporaneity at the price of vitality. As a consequence, they can hardly claim to have made Christianity relevant to the age.

Conservative Protestantism on the other hand—so-called fundamentalism—tended to become sectarian, overliteralist, and superficially verbal. Often it occupied itself and expended its energies in defensive reactions to the modern world.

Within Catholicism as it emerges into the postconciliar epoch are tendencies which resemble in general character and stance both of these Protestant responses. Up to the time of the Council, the liberal groups constituted the weaker party and one whose legitimation rested upon weak supports. Liberal efforts were often the target of conservative attack and of authoritative censure. Yet such tendencies continued to exist and, if not to prosper, at least to grow. In the years following World War II, European Catholicism saw a kind of intellectual renaissance once again, which, coinciding with the rise of an articulate lay Catholic intelligentsia in the United States, found meaningful resonances in this country. To some observers, however, it seemed a repetition of what had happened in Europe after World War I. Then, too, there was a stirring, intellectual and social, among the Catholics of the continent. So shrewd an observer as the late Paul Tillich suggested that this renaissance would come to little of significance [86].

Writing over three decades ago, Tillich said, "Wherever there are movements which might develop into real revolts against Counter-Reformation Catholicism they are tolerated only so long as they are of value for purposes of propaganda. As soon as they become dangerous to the centralization and the absoluteness of the church they are destroyed. When and how this fate will come upon the romantic Catholicism of our time cannot be predicted. But it is certain that unless romantic Catholicism calls a halt to its development in time this fate will visit it also" [86:187].

It was Tillich's opinion in the early 30s that the postwar

Catholic renewal would be made use of by the Roman Curia, then in full control of Church management, for apologetic purposes and, to the extent that it was useful for such purposes, it would be tolerated. If it became significant beyond that function, if it seemed to promise or presage real efforts toward internal change in the Church, Tillich thought, the renaissance would be repressed.

The war interrupted these developments, but also it stimulated them in important respects. Following World War II, continental Catholic theologians were affected by a greater familiarity with and involvement in philosophy, sociology, history, and science. They came under the impact of the postwar reaction to the Europe which two wars had created. Under these influences, Catholic theologians continued and expanded the Catholic renaissance. The effect of contemporary thought and of contemporary realities on these men is apparent. Roger Aubert speaks of their interest in three significant and quite timely areas: "the theology of earthly realities, the theology of history, and the theology of the Church." But, he pointed out, even more striking than the topics of this new concern was the "new spirit" that inspired it.

> This has two different and at first sight somewhat paradoxical aspects: the desire to draw fresh vigor from contact with the source material—chiefly the Bible, but also the writings of the Fathers of the Church and the documents of the liturgy—and the desire to make the Catholic presence felt in the world by firmly confronting the Christian message with its aspirations [2:66–67].

In the 1940s Pope Pius XII had issued an encyclical on biblical studies and their place in the Church. This was generally considered to be a great victory for genuine scholarship over the suspicions and strictures of the conservatives, although some conservatives thought it so liberal that they never really accepted it. Also, during the war and immediately thereafter, liberal political statements came from Rome, as, for example, in the 1942 Christmas message of the same pontiff. But by the 1950s the effects of the conservative hostility to the new developments were becoming apparent. It looked as though Tillich's earlier prediction might soon be realized. Says Roger Aubert,

> From 1950 onward the reaction against some imprudent measures, against developments regarded as too precipitate and compromises felt in high places to be injudicious, brought a spate of admonitions on points of doctrine (the encyclical *Humani generis*, a number of warnings related to moral questions, increased activity of the Index and the Holy Office, and the matter of the progressive catechism in France), on pastoral subjects (particularly with reference to the worker-priests), and in the political and social field (concerning the "progressive Christians" and even the advocates of an "opening to the left") [2:53].

Our earlier references and characterizations of conservative and liberal Protestantism were of course greatly oversimplified. They reduced to a more or less clear-cut dichotomy a range of tendencies. The same thing must be said with respect to contemporary Catholicism. It is too easy to make pat distinctions and, once having made them, to take them too literally. Yet, despite the variation and range of tendencies involved, there are in fact two main tendencies here exhibited.

What is particularly important about the new Catholic efforts at updating is that they take place within a unified ecclesiastical body, within an as yet unbroken community of faith and tradition. Protestantism, in its earlier attempt to make a relevant relationship to modernity, broke apart into groups increasingly out of communication with each other. If Catholicism is to succeed in this second chance, it will do so only by preserving its own unity, for only a unified body can provide the setting for genuine dialogue among the various tendencies and perspectives which are found in this great historic process. It has been recognized on all sides that

ecumenical dialogue between Catholics and others outside
the Roman Church is an important prerequisite for success in
this matter. Such cross fertilization of thinking is of the first
significance. Equally crucial is the maintenance of ongoing
dialogue between the groups within Catholicism itself. Indeed,
it is of great consequence that "liberal-conservative" dialogue
within the Catholic body be raised to the highest possible
intellectual level. (The most interesting work in this respect
is Jeremiah Newman's *Change and the Catholic Church* [61].
Based upon a considerable knowledge of contemporary
sociological theory, it is solid and conservative and worthy of
careful attention.)

When we examine the position of the Roman Catholic
Church today, what discloses itself to us is this: Catholicism
stands as representative of and surrogate for Christianity as a
whole in its second great historic attempt to confront modernity. Can the Catholic Church succeed? Can the Catholic
Church actually update Christianity? Can it adapt to the
mentality of modernity Christian ideas and values, Christian
conceptions of God and man, Christian convictions of the
reality and seriousness of the religious life? Can it accomplish
this by giving to the challenging aspects of modernity the full
valence they demand and at the same time not lose its deeper
character and basic identity? Can Catholicism confront the
consequences, intellectual and spiritual, of modern developments in science and scholarship and in political, social, and
economic life and adapt to them and still preserve its own
lively sense of God's reality and presence?

Writing in 1933, Dr. F. L. Cross, an Anglican church-
man, identified himself with "those who look forward to a
world-wide Catholicism with its arms open to modern intellectual and cultural needs. . . ." The situation in 1933 did
not appear particularly auspicious, but Dr. Cross nevertheless
recognized the position of the Roman Church as historically
strategic. He said, "Upon the development and success of a
second Modernist Movement in the Roman Catholic Church,

the ultimate future of Christian culture in western Europe, humanly speaking, depends" [quoted in 97:268]. The term "a second Modernist Movement" may appear to some as unfortunate in view of the upsetting connotations it has for all parties and most observers. Yet it is time to emancipate ourselves from the psychological residues of the past. Dr. Cross's point is clear enough. The kind of updating of Christianity requisite for its survival as more than a marginal phenomenon in the West may depend upon the ability of the Catholics to confront modernity. They have the faith for it; only if they have the intelligence and courage as well can it be done.

The great historic task of relating Christianity and modernity reveals itself as full of promise and fraught with peril. The *Tablet* of London, a conservative and highly intelligent Catholic periodical, has pointed to some of the dangers. There is the danger of

taking the modern world too much at its own valuation . . . [of not allowing enough] . . . for the way the world we live in has been made for us, in such great measure, by the sin as well as by the virtues of our predecessors . . . [and that its] . . . cultural reality . . . has left their descendents with warps in their outlooks, blind spots and lost perceptions, so that contemporary society with its pre-occupations is not to be elevated into a norm to which the Church must learn to adapt herself, instead of bearing a witness precisely where it is least likely to be immediately understood or accepted [quoted in 61:315].

What thoughtful man, regardless of his own particular religious preferences and philosophical position, can doubt the general wisdom of the *Tablet* admonition? What thoughtful man can doubt the utter necessity of the kind of effort toward renewal and reform now being made within the Roman communion?

The Catholic attempt at *aggiornamento* does then represent a great and indeed probably final opportunity for Christianity. It represents the chance to confront modernity within the context of a unified religious community which possesses great creative energies and which, at the same time, has maintained genuine and currently operative ties with the past. Roman Catholicism alone has the basic characteristics without which success in this venture can hardly be deemed attainable: unity of various tendencies and the possibility of communication among them; a depth and reality of faith on both the popular and the elite levels; a worldwide communion reflecting, potentially at least, a great variety of cultures; a real rootedness in the past. Roman Catholicism has also the advantage of making a second attempt, of being able to learn from both the achievements and the failures of the first.

An additional advantage enjoyed by this second effort is the changed character of the secular world. The long process of the secularization of culture was in many significant respects an anti-Christian phenomenon—at times and in some ways openly and even militantly anti-Christian; at other times and in other ways indirectly and covertly so. Voltaire's "crush the infamy," Nietzsche's "absolute no," and Marx's emancipation from illusion exemplify many of the attitudes of the educated from the 18th century to our day.

It cannot be denied as well that the process of secularization, though it did empty out much substance from traditional Christian culture, was also a process of emancipation. In our day, religious thinkers have come to appreciate more and more the positive aspects of this emancipation, while many secular thinkers have become concerned with the genuine loss of substance that it entailed. The antireligious attitudes of the Enlightenment, the this-sided narrowness of the rationalism of the 18th and the scientism of the 19th century, and even the this-sided historicism of Marxism and related ideologies (Roger Garaudy presents an example of a new openness toward Christianity on the part of a Marxist [30]) tend no longer to be sufficient to satisfy modern men.

There is a growing inclination for men to transcend their own personal, and indeed the general cultural, adolescent rebellion against important values of traditional religion. Such rebellion may once have been necessary for emancipation, but a definite movement beyond it is now appearing. The world seeks for meaningful orientation as it faces the stupendous tasks of our century. The question arises, Can Christianity speak meaningfully to this quest? The final answer to that question will be fatefully affected by the success of Roman Catholicism in its current venture.

An analysis of this scope cannot escape the charge of resting upon a certain "impressionism." It lies beyond the powers and means at our disposal in the present endeavor to make anything like a study of the present Catholic situation that would be at once sufficiently thorough in detail and sufficiently general in analysis. The reader has the right to insist that the impressions be both accurate and genuinely diagnostic and to demand that the author recognize the incomplete and tentative nature of his conclusions. Within these limits, however, there is much to be gained from the attempt to delineate the crucial elements now characterizing the situation within Roman Catholicism and to estimate their significance for future developments. We shall divide our presentation into five parts.

In Chapter II, we shall make a preliminary examination of the *Dogmatic Constitution on the Church*, the so-called *Lumen Gentium*, perhaps the most basic document of the Council. We shall analyze this document in terms of looking for what has here been put together, for what has been taken from the encounter with modernity and brought into relation to the Church's definition of itself. The *Constitution on the Church* will be seen to reveal a series of such encounters which are at the same time both the points of strain and conflict and also the points of future growth and development in Catholic thought.

In Chapter III we shall look at what we consider the most diagnostic of the historical precedents which have led over time to the issues raised at the Council.

We shall follow this by a chapter summing up and defining the issues and problems shown both in the conciliar document and in the history of the last 150 years. We shall find that fundamentally the same issues appear in the conciliar document and in history, and we shall attempt to assess the character of the threat and promise they offer to the Church. By this point, our problems should be considerably clarified. We should in effect have presented an operational definition of "modernity" as it has impinged upon the Catholic Church and elicited responses from it. It will be possible to see those elements in modern thought and in modern society that called forth a dual reaction from Catholics—an attempt to accept these elements with qualifications and to understand the faith in the light of them, and the opposite response of a closed, hostile, defensive reaction against these elements and a positive Catholic response to them. It will also be possible to recognize that these constitute strategic characteristics of the consciousness of modern men that differentiate them from the men of earlier epochs or traditional societies. Moreover, it will be apparent that they involve, in some cases at least, what we cannot escape evaluating as constituting a vast expansion of awareness by history and science.

We shall then proceed to examine the problems we have disclosed in two settings of great significance for Catholic thought at the present time. It will be recalled that Aubert spoke of how the new trends in Catholic theology reveal a paradoxical concern simultaneously with the ancient sources of the faith and with the contemporary aspirations of the secular world.

In Chapters V, VI, and VII we shall consider the *Pastoral Constitution on the Church and the Modern World*. This is perhaps by far the most typically conciliar of the Council's documents. It developed out of discussions on the floor rather than out of the established commissions of the Council. Moreover, it came to embody in the clearest expression the newer currents of Catholic thinking that were expressed and legitimated in the Council and its decisions. In examining this document we shall try to probe in depth and with a measure of precision the character of the encounter of the Church with contemporary realities in science and in social, economic, and political life.

Finally, in Chapter VIII we shall look at the attitude of the Council toward biblical studies, as embodied in the declaration *De Revelatione*. The study of the Bible with the tools of modern social, historical, and linguistic science has long been a point of strain and an area of conflict. It is here that the most modern insights and perspectives of modernity come into intimate contact with the essentials of faith.

Our examination should reveal in several contexts the basic points of encounter between Catholicism and modernity, the basic structure of the confrontation out of which must come success or failure in *aggiornamento*. These points of encounter are also the lines of conflict, drawn by history and theology, that divide the parties involved. They are, moreover, the growing points—they are the loci where *aggiornamento* is to take place if it is to take place at all. Such an examination will enable us to achieve a deeper and more precise understanding of the present Catholic situation with its dangers and its hopes. It is that situation which we consider diagnostic for Christianity's future.

II

THE DOGMATIC CONSTITUTION
ON THE CHURCH (*De Ecclesia* OR *Lumen Gentium*)

THE *Dogmatic Constitution on the Church* is one of the great documents of the Council, and it represents the results of a long period of new theological thinking in the Church. The different theological tendencies among the assembled Fathers began to become apparent early in the Council. The differences could already be felt in the discussion of the schema proposed on Sacred Liturgy. They were clearly in the open in the debate on the schema on Revelation. They came out, as might indeed be expected, in the reception the first draft of this Constitution met on the Council floor. Of all the documents of the Council, this Constitution received perhaps the greatest amount of revision, so that the document passed by the Council on November 19, 1964, and again in the solemn session presided over by Pope Paul VI, on November 21, differs drastically from that originally presented for debate on December 1, 1962.

The earlier version resembled in its general treatment the typical theological manual of the interwar period. In the words of one Council Father, it presented the Church more as an institution than as a mystery, or, as another put it, the earlier version dealt too much with external characteristics of the ecclesiastical organization. Its "juridicism" and its great emphasis on hierarchy represented the typical conservative view as that view had developed in the centuries since the Reformation.

The proposed text was subjected to a thorough revision following the debates of the second session in 1963. More changes were introduced in the third session.

Although the document does not define any new dogmas, it is called a *Dogmatic Constitution*, which means that it is the most solemn form of conciliar document. It is unquestionably one of the most significant accomplishments of the Council. One Protestant commentator has observed that it "is the first full-orbed *conciliar* exposition of the doctrine of the Church in Christian history" [70:102], and another has commented that it is "by far the fullest dogmatic statement on the nature of the church that has ever been formulated by any Christian body" [47:219]. The document was formed in vigorous controversy. Yet, despite that fact, it received the approval of 2,134 Fathers out of 2,145 voting on the definitive text (10 voted no, and there was 1 null vote), and, in the solemn session two days later over which Paul VI presided, 2,156 Fathers voted *placet* as against 5 who voted *non placet*.

The Constitution is, of course, a compromise, as must be any such statement drawn up in a long process of argument and debate which receives the final approval of so large and varied a body. It is, moreover, a compromise that can be read to contrasting effect by men with different religious predispositions and different theological preferences. The conservative can find here much to reinforce traditional positions; the liberal can see a remarkable expression of the newer, more open tendencies in Catholic thinking. Placed in its setting, it will be recognized by the critical scholar as a compromise that brings forward with a new emphasis the progressive conceptions of the "newer" theologies and brings them forward in ways that ensure their having a genuine effect upon the future life of the Church and future development of theology.

The Constitution represents the fruits of ecclesiastical self-reflection; it is record and formulation of the Church's thinking upon and defining itself. As such a document, brought forth in discussion and debate, it reflects the two overall tendencies which came into contact and conflict in the Council. Thus we may expect to find in it the reflection and record of the basic encounters of modernity and the older theological positions as they pertain to the idea of the Church itself. Six of these encounters to be seen in the Constitution invite consideration as an introduction to our analysis. They are the following:

(1) The different and to some extent unharmonized conceptions of the Church found in the document;

(2) The contrasting conceptions of the world with their implications for the Church's mission;

(3) A new emphasis upon the dignity of the lay state and a new emphasis upon the priesthood of believers together with an older stress upon hierarchy and upon special clerical status as central to the Church's structure;

(4) The new idea that all callings, worldly as well as religious, share equally in God's plan, as against the older special recognition of the formally religious and quasimonastic religious roles as central and exemplary;

(5) The use of scriptural concepts in preference to the established scholastic vocabulary to describe the content of faith and the equally important reliance at certain junctures upon the scholastic conceptions; and

(6) The expression of a genuine and enthusiastic ecumenicity and the endeavor to reconcile it with a reformed version of the older exclusiveness of Catholic claims.

Let us examine each of these briefly.

1. *Conceptions of the Church*

The Catholic Church historically has seen itself as a sacramental entity mediating between God and man, a continuation of the incarnation of the Son of God, performing his high-priestly and mediating roles. (Journet gives a clear presentation of the Catholic theological understanding of the meaning of the Church [41]). Its sacraments embody this mediation, especially that of the Holy Eucharist and its propaedeutic, Penance (Confession). The Church gives priority of status to and invests authority in the clergy, who rule, teach, celebrate the Eucharist, and administer the sacraments. It holds up the religious life under formal rules in separated communities as the more complete realization of the counsels of the gospel.

This idea of the Church evolved in a long history that began when Christians realized that the second coming of the Lord was not imminent. It is the consequence of a shift from chiliastic expectation to a more ontological understanding of man's relation to God, a shift to be seen within the canonical scriptures themselves, especially in the Fourth Gospel and the Epistle to the Hebrews. It is a shift whose seeds are already present, in the writings of Paul, alongside expectation of the Lord's return. It is an understanding of the Church generally accepted from the 2d century on, one fundamental to the medieval Church and confirmed and reasserted at Trent. It reached its apotheosis of formulation at the First Vatican Council in the proclamation of Papal Infallibility.

In the background remained two other conceptions of the Church, both eminently scriptural but long allowed to lapse into secondary significance. It is these that the Constitution revived and gave both dogmatic and practical emphasis. Speaking of this Constitution, Julius Cardinal Doepfner, Archbishop of Munich, declared, "The Church is presented to us as the chosen people of God, with the men of every country and nation called to be her members; as the sign of salvation raised up in the world; as the Mystical Body of Christ, of which Our Lord, as Head, is the principle of life, working out salvation among men" [82:662].

The middle characterization of Cardinal Doepfner—the Church as the sign of salvation—refers to the classic conservative definition. The third—the Church as the Mystical Body, based upon the conceptions of St Paul—is capable of both a classic vertical interpretation to fit in with the definition presented above and a more historical understanding compatible with the revived synoptic conception. The Council put great emphasis upon the first definition—the Church as the Pilgrim

People of God—and, after discussion, placed it in Chapter II, before the treatment of the hierarchical structure and the episcopate. Moreover, it is to be noted that the Council document treats the doctrine of the Mystical Body rather differently from the way the encyclical of Pius XII had treated it.

None of these interpretations of the character of the Church is made primary over or fundamental to the other two in the Constitution. No doubt all three can be reconciled. Yet it is easier to reconcile the first and third and the second and third than to reconcile in depth the second and first. Between the older classic vertical conception of the Church as a mediating institution that continues the Incarnation and the revived biblical notion of the Pilgrim People there is an important difference of emphasis. The notion of the Mystical Body mediates between this contrast in emphasis, but this whole treatment of the Church opens up an important area of future conflict and discussion. There is here a great openness which calls for future theological development and will present ample occasion for dialogue and controversy.

2. *Conceptions of the World*

The traditional Catholic understanding of the world was ontological rather than historical. Although, for over a millennium and a half, the biblical ideas of salvation history remained latently present, the dominant emphasis has been upon a two-story, metaphysically conceived reality. It was a world structured vertically in terms of time—*the here below*, and eternity—*the eternal now of the divine life of the Holy Trinity*. The Church mediated between these levels, providing through its sacraments by divine gratuity the Christian equivalent of Plato's path from the Cave to the Sun. This notion of the world and the classic conception of the Church as the sacrament of salvation fitted together with satisfying intellectual and aesthetic elegance. The Constitution introduces a historical notion of the World as the setting for the historical Pilgrim Church. Concomitant with the first and second understandings of the Church discussed above are these two conceptions of the world, one ontological and one historical. Fitting the two together and exploring in depth the challenge of doing so offers a profound task for Catholic theology.

It is often overlooked by some critics of the Roman Church—often friendly Protestants, in fact—that a satisfying conception of the world, and not just a theological one, demands some putting together of history and ontology, as Professor Fackenheim has pointed out [25; 26]. (In fact, there are those who see scholasticism as an example of unbiblical conceptions that have been brought into Christianity unwarrantedly. At the same time they overlook the ambiguities of neoorthodoxy. These people are behaving in a thoroughly biblical manner: they strain at gnats and swallow camels!)

Related to these conceptions of the Church and the world are different emphases upon the nature of the Church's mission in the world. Is salvation to be seen as a group concern or as an individual matter? The vertical conception of the Church and the two-story metaphysical world gave individual religiosity and individual salvation precedence. The revived historical conceptions of both Church and world give the matter a more sociological tone and therefore more of a group emphasis. Here too, an important area of openness is left over from the Council.

3. The Problems of Hierarchy—Collegiality and the Papacy— Clergy and Laity

The new collegiality represents a drawing back from the long-term trend of papal centralization. The relationship of the episcopal college and the pope, however, is left most ambiguous. A direct quotation from the Constitution will indicate the basic ambiguity:

The order of bishops is the successor to the college of the apostles in teaching authority and pastoral rule, or, rather, in the episcopal order the apostolic body continues without a break. Together with its head, the Roman Pontiff, and never without this Head, the episcopal order is the subject of supreme and full power over the universal Church [art 22].

Here indeed the structural contradiction expressed in the 1917 Code of Canon Law is continued. That code recognizes the bishops as the successors of the apostles with genuine authority. That is, they are ordinaries having authority by virtue of their episcopal office and not by virtue of its being delegated to them by the pope. At the same time, the pope also possesses direct and immediate authority in every diocese of the Church. He is not simply an *episcopus episcoporum* but if need be can exercise direct rule and exert direct jurisdiction in the diocese of every bishop. Although this ambiguity remains, the very establishment of a collegial body is important and tends to tilt the balance away from the centralizing proclivities of the past. Only time will tell how this will work out, and it will no doubt be the occasion of inner conflict.

The Constitution also contains new conceptions of the dignity of the laity and a new insistence upon the priesthood of believers, as well as the older conceptions of the special character of the clerical status. The layman is seen as truly part of the Church, and the action in the world of the lay person as a matter of true vocation involving an "engaging in temporal affairs and ordering them according to the plan of God" (art 31). "The apostolate of the laity is not, therefore, their participation in the apostolate of the hierarchy. . . . This is why the exercise of a secular profession, of intellectual and manual labor, of administrative, industrial or commercial activities, which are carried out according to God's will are, properly speaking, the apostolate of the laity" [3:42].

Yet alongside the new emphasis upon the role of the layman and the legitimacy of the secular, the older segregation of clerical and lay status and function remains. The Constitution speaks in a conservative manner of "the distinction which the Lord made between sacred ministers and the rest of the People of God" (art 32). Within the Church itself the laity can participate in the work of the Church properly so-called. This work is seen in quite conservative terms as the "apostolate of the hierarchy" (art 33 et passim). A reading of the document as a whole, however, reveals a considerable change in conception from that characteristic of older papal documents, which saw the laity acting in the world under clerical guidance and leadership. Pius XI, for example, regarded Catholic Action groups as the agencies of the layman's Christian vocation and as organs for "the participation and collaboration of the laity with the Apostolic Hierarchy" [72:54]. Nevertheless, the position of the clergy within the Church remains basically unchanged as far as this document goes. Lay people do

... have a definite role to play in the life of the Church, in liturgy, missionary movements, etc. They may even be called to exercise some functions that properly belong to priests or deacons, such as distributing holy communion in crowded churches. In this context the participation of the laity in the teaching and sanctifying office of Christ assumes its fullest meaning. Laymen may be true Christian teachers, but as teachers of the Gospel they remain dependent on the hierarchy; laymen may exercise an active role in the liturgy but, again, their activity in this area remains dependent on the hierarchy [3:42–43].

However, the document also exhorts,

let sacred pastors recognize and promote the dignity as well as the responsibility of the layman in the Church. Let them willingly make use of his prudent advice. Let them confidently assign duties to him in the service of the Church, allowing him freedom and room for action. Further, let them encourage the layman so that he may undertake tasks on his own initiative. Attentively in Christ, let them consider with fatherly love the projects, suggestions, and desires proposed by the laity. Furthermore, let pastors respectfully acknowledge that just freedom which belongs to everyone in this earthly city [art 37].

The attempt to reconcile the traditional post-Tridentine position of the priest in the vertically conceived Church with the recognition of the priesthood of all believers in the Pilgrim People of God (art 10) reveals the dialectic between past and future characteristic of the Church's present position. Seen in the light of the general setting of the Council and the general overall thrust of its constitutions and declarations, clearly the document has here a most important growing point. Events since the Council have shown vigorous lay action, and the new reality of a public opinion in the Church in America is apparent everywhere. The fact is that relation of the episcopate and the papacy and of the clergy and the laity is undergoing change. The basic changes in modern society are having and will have their effect upon this ancient element of Church organization.

4. Inner-Worldly Vocation as Against the Older Special Calling of the Religious

From what we have said above concerning the recognition of the vocation of the layman in the world and the legitimacy of secular pursuits as the genuinely Christian activity of the layman, it is plain that the Council represents the fruition of an important trend in modern Catholic life. It is a far cry from the older position set down in the Middle Ages by the great canonist Gratian, which recognized, as it were, two species of Christians—clerics and monks as against the laity (seen as inferior in Christian substance and function) [16:41].

The Constitution recognizes as "evident to everyone that all the faithful of Christ of whatever rank or status are called to the fullness of the Christian life and to the perfection of charity" (art 40). Further, it is stated that "in the various types and duties of life, one and the same holiness is cultivated by all who are moved by the Spirit of God, and who obey the voice of the Father, worshipping God the Father in spirit and in truth" (art 41). Yet this does not immediately alter in principle the older position.

> The holiness of the Church is also fostered in a special way by the observance of the manifold counsels proposed in the gospel by our Lord to His disciples. Outstanding among them is that precious gift of divine grace which the Father gives to some men (cf. Mt. 19:11; 1 Cor. 7:7) so that by virginity, or celibacy, they can more easily devote their entire selves to God alone with undivided heart (cf. 1 Cor. 7:32-34). This total continence embraced on behalf of the kingdom of heaven has always been held in particular honor by the Church as a sign of charity and a stimulus toward it, as well as unique fountain of spiritual fertility in the world [art 42].

Moreover, the "evangelical counsels of chastity dedicated to God, poverty, and obedience are based upon the words and example of the Lord" (art 43). It is held that "the religious state by giving its members greater freedom from earthly cares more adequately manifests to all believers the presence of heavenly goods already possessed here below" (art 44). And through the religious, "the Church truly wishes to give an increasingly clearer revelation of Christ" (art 46).

5. *The Use of Scriptural in Preference to Scholastic Categories of Formulation*

The effects of renewed scriptural scholarship and the consequence of this scholarship upon the thinking of the more progressive theologians of the Roman Church is evident throughout the Constitution, as it is, indeed, in all the statements of the Council. The utilization of the categories of biblical thought—especially of what might be called "synoptic ideas"—is impressive; probably nothing superior to it is to be found in any Christian statement from any communion. The scholastic notions of "nature" and "supernature" are not explicitly used at all, either in this document or in any other conciliar document.

Yet in a very important sense the constitution still rests upon and derives from important aspects of scholastic theology. After all, behind this document stand the dogmatic definitions of the ages. Perhaps it is in dealing with the bishops and collegiality in the third chapter, and in the discussion of the Blessed Virgin Mary, that the scriptural scholar will feel least comfortable, whether he be Catholic or Protestant. Nevertheless, the issues of Mariology are subordinated to the conception of the Church to a great extent, and the general treatment is certainly less bothersome to Protestants than the policies of Mariological aggrandizement of the past. In reading this, the Protestant, as Dr. Lindbeck put it, "is happy that the maximalist surge in progress up until 1950 has not been pushed farther" [47:223].

This section suggests several future problems. There is first of all the problem of relating together the scholastic and the biblical conceptions which we have seen in the definitions of the Church, of the World, and of the various callings of Christians. If in the past ontology did not do away with the importance of history, so now, it should be frequently recalled, the recognition of history will not of itself solve ontological problems. A second level of difficulty concerns what biblical scholarship tends to regard as the likely interpretations of the scripture and the use made of the scripture by theologians in the defense of dogma and tradition. The latter are often seen in the light of a scholastic view of the world and understood in relation to scholastic categories. A third set of problems concerns the place of Mariology in the newly emphasized conception of salvation history and the relation of this to the older quasi-independent position the Blessed Virgin seemed to occupy in Catholic thought and popular piety.

6. *Ecumenicity as Against an Older Exclusiveness*

That the Council as a whole represents a great victory for ecumenism within the Roman communion is perfectly obvious. Specific documents on relations with other Christians, with Jews, with Muslims, with those outside the Western religious tradition, and even with those having no faith display a sophisticated good will and willingness for human dialogue. Yet the Catholic Church has not in principle surrendered its basic conception of itself. In this document the Church founded by Christ is not identified in any simple way with the Church of Rome but rather is said to "subsist" in it (art 8). Putting together ecumenicity with a liberally reinterpreted understanding of the older position will surely result in conflict and growth.

A brief examination of the *Dogmatic Constitution on the Church* reveals six areas where the encounter between past and future, between old and new, conceptions can be seen. Each case represents a compromise—a temporary equilibrium—of conceptions whose deeper relations of agreement and conflict will demand exploration and development. These six areas of encounter are aspects of a deeper confrontation—the confrontation of Catholicism with modernity. The conception of the Pilgrim Church and of the world as historical represents a revival of what might justly be called the theology of the synoptics and of the earliest Church, which lived in expectation of the *parousia*. (Werner has a good brief treatment of the development of dogma in its historical setting [102].) But it is a rediscovered as well as a primitive theology—rediscovered through the tools of modern scholarship. At the same time, the rediscovery entailed comprehension of the ancient ideas in relation to quite modern ones, such as the understanding of the world as process, itself the effect of developments in

27

philosophy, biology, and historical scholarship. Thus the notion put forth in this document, of the Church as the Pilgrim People of God to be seen in its world historical setting, is both a very ancient and a very modern one. Its emergence is the result of theological ferment, which Catholic authority tried to put an end to. It emphasizes process rather than substance, history rather than metaphysics. In the document this newer emphasis is presented alongside the older one.

The related issue of the bishops and the papacy, and that of the clergy and laity represent a relative victory for the newer ideas although the older structure has really not been altered. Important also is the new recognition of the seriousness of the lay state and of lay activity in the world. It must be recalled that the Church was older than and in a sense mother to Europe, that in Tillich's words it was until the 14th century Europe's schoolmistress. Furthermore, the lay civilization of the West came into existence in part nurtured by the Church and in part in secession from and revolt against it. To comprehend the genuine importance of the activity of laymen in the world and to relate itself to the institutions they created in the course of that activity presented severe problems to the Church from the Middle Ages on. In the Christian world view, religious values took precedence over secular values, although the worth of the latter was not necessarily denied. (For types of Christian theologies on this matter see H. Richard Niebuhr [63]). With the emergence of a vast objectified Church embodying the Christian world view and value emphasis, that institution necessarily found itself behaving as superior to the other institutions of society and therefore in conflict with them. The attempt in this document and in the Council as a whole to do justice to the significance and seriousness of lay life and to grant religious dignity to the laity and their vocation is a step toward countering the heritage of the clericalist past. The same may be said of the new openness and spirit of fraternity, evident throughout this document, with which the Church speaks to the world.

The document suggests much more than it actually announces or effects. It suggests the significant conceptual changes we have just considered; it suggests a kind of spiritual disestablishment, at least in the sense that the Church will now tend to rely upon the persuasive powers of its message and the call of its epiphany rather than upon alliance with other institutions or even reliance upon established tradition. It suggests great tasks of reworking and restating the faith in our day.

These suggestions conjured up two visions before our eyes. First there is the vertical Church in the two-story universe, mediating a transcendent God to man and conveying by special covenant his gratuitous gifts. This vision includes crystallized institutions of rule and worship; a self-enclosed, traditionally scholastic theology; and, in modern conditions, a posture of defense against a hostile world. Second there is the Pilgrim Church, a covenanted Christian people in history, a people with earthly as well as heavenly tasks and one evolving its social forms and its modes of thought as it goes along. These two visions are mixed together, but their reconciliation will entail a more profound understanding of transcendence and immanence and of their interrelations, of substance and process, of man as creator of culture and man conditioned by history.

These issues lurk beneath the compromises of the most important statement on the nature of the Church ever made by any Christian body. And they are the issues which, evolving with the modern consciousness, threatened or appeared to threaten the Catholic faith in the past. What is it that was threatened? What is the character of the encounter with modernity and what is its menace? The vitality and intensity of Catholic faith has been granted as fact by all serious observers of Catholic life. Whatever the criticisms of the Church of Rome, it is generally credited with preserving a deep and lively faith in God and Christ. This faith may be described as resting upon two significant psychological facts. One of the

great accomplishments of Catholicism is that it has succeeded
—by its liturgy, by its sacramental practice, by its teaching,
and by its discipline, within the context of a community of
tradition—in maintaining in its adherents a quick sense and
a deep conviction of the *reality* and the *immediacy* of God.
Closely related is the fact that it has kept unimpaired a *strik-
ingly realistic understanding of the Church as mediator between God
and man*, as the vessel or ark carrying through time the mediating function of Christ. The doctrine of the real presence of
Christ in the Holy Eucharist has been central to this understanding. It is upon these two elements that the Church ultimately rests.

The psychological basis of the Church's faith has long
been seen by Catholics implicitly and explicitly in terms of the
timeless vertical view of the Church we have discussed above.
It is infused with the thought and feeling of the Fourth Gospel
and the Epistle to the Hebrews rather than with the spirit of
the synoptics. It has been part of a religious conception that
emphasized substances with their proper accidents making up
a "natural order," created and sustained by the uncreated
supernatural Godhead, which also infuses human nature with
special supernatural gifts through the Church. The starting
point of this view is found in the scriptures, as we have suggested. It was developed by the ancient Fathers and the
Schoolmen of the Middle Ages. It replaced synoptic theology
because that form of the Christian faith became effectively
bankrupt with the failure of the *parousia* to come about.
Having at the time little of the modern taste for an eschatology
without an *eschaton*, the Fathers found a new way to recast the
implications they saw in the life and message of Jesus as
apprehended and interpreted by the ancient Church, and
thus to save the religious intensity and sense of reality of this
core deposit. It is that intensity and reality which Catholicism
has carefully preserved.

The problems here are often subtle. Modern process
theology can with justification call itself biblical because it

reinstates in a modern setting the horizontal, historical view of the Hebrews and the primitive Church. But scholastic theology too may make some claims to being a genuine continuation of the biblical tradition. There is, after all, the religious content as well as the form to be considered. Despite its Greek rationalist inclinations, scholastic theology does insist upon the reality of a personal God who can and does intervene in his creation like the God of the Bible, who like that God can intrude on the world of everyday experience. Such intrusions are not inaccurately conceived in terms of the unbiblical scholastic conception of the "supernatural." The Church saw the Bible as "supernatural" after it discovered the Greek concept of *Physis*, of nature. It was one way of bringing together the two conceptions of the world—Hebraic and Hellenic— with which it had to state its basic positions. Many of these designations of the older theology may be discarded, but in that case it will be necessary to develop the newer conceptions so as not to lose the important element of the faith which the older ones transmitted to the membership of the Church. Efforts to demythologize the understanding of the scripture— whether the radical attempt of Bultmann or the milder endeavors of his predecessors—resulted in a markedly changed idea of Christianity. Catholicism must relate itself to the modern conceptions. Can it do so without losing its basic psychological grounding? Can it modernize itself without emptying out its ancient substance?

The progressives would appear to be right, in the sense that Catholicism cannot continue to develop in a condition completely askew with respect to the important advances in human knowledge and the transformations of human outlook taking place in our day. Updating of both structure and idea is necessary. Yet the conservatives see real dangers. A recognition of man's historicity—of the horizontal dimension in human life and what it implies for the meaning of religion—is certainly required. Catholicism can no longer close itself to these new forms of experience and thought. But there is a serious danger of losing the sense of transcendence, of reducing God to the interpretation of a "natural experience" or to a psychological projection. Real possibilities of loss of the traditional bases of faith lurk in this pathway though the pathway must at last be taken.

Catholicism now is prepared to recognize the reality of history and the implications of man's embeddedness in the historical process. It is also ready to place the Church in its historical setting. But can it do so and maintain the idea of the uniqueness of Christianity, a peculiar notion of uniqueness that also involves universality? Without a transcendent which intervenes in the historical process, uniqueness becomes a characteristic of all events and all movements, and nothing distinctively important remains to Christianity. In such a case Christianity will be but one of the many forward surges of the immanent issuing in a temporary transcendence. It will be of interest as one example of a class, lacking universal significance as a unique rule or norm of religious life.

Catholicism has finally recognized that great insight of modern natural and social science: process is in some way fundamental. It sees that entities are not just closed and finished but are in certain respects the temporary equilibria of dynamisms. But this view, unqualified by the older insights into structure, undermines not only any ethic based upon a conception of natural law but also any ethic based upon a personalism. Hume, it is well to remember, extended nominalism to the self. To imagine that one can find permanent refuge from the corroding effects of these modern ideas in a scripturally based personalism is perhaps but to embrace an ethnocentric fideism.

It must be recalled what the Catholic Church was doing with the concept of the "supernatural." It was trying to eliminate magic and at the same time preserve in rational terms what it felt literally valid in the mythic view of God's relation to man. The concept indicated first of all real transcendence—radically other transcendence than the autonomous nature of the Greek cosmos. Second, the concept preserved the eminently biblical idea of the intervention of the transcendent personal God in human affairs, whether to heal the leper or to slay those who inadvertently desecrate the ark. It preserved ideas closely related to the psychological bases of Catholic faith—the reality and transcendence of God and the immediacy of man's relation to him through Christ and his Church.

One may object that such a conception of God is "magical." Perhaps. But if a God who can perform miracles is a magical God, then the God of the Bible is a magical God. The question really is, can God be abstracted from this kind of magic and remain real and immediate in the human consciousness?

Catholicism does indeed rest upon belief in the sacraments as the channels of God's divine aid to man. The idea is that the sacraments confer grace *ex opere operato*—that is, by the work worked—which means that they are an objective source of grace and give aid to men when the latter place no subjective obstacle in their way. We have here the bringing together of a sacramental objectivism with a deep psychological emphasis upon the proper subjective disposition of the recipient. Hence an elaborate objective structure of Church, doctrine, and sacrament is brought into intimate contact with individual subjective religious attitude. It is on this foundation that Catholic faith rests. Modernization of thinking in this area and the concomitant preservation of genuine faith will present great difficulties for Catholics and the Church.

This discussion at any rate indicates how deep and fundamental are the questions implied in the contemporary encounter of Catholicism and modernity. Certainly two things begin to become evident. The older traditional view cannot survive unchanged except among protected enclaves of the unlearned and among specially cloistered and somewhat precious intellectual groups. But the acceptance of the newer ideas must at the same time carry forward strategic elements of the older view. Without the preservation of certain elementary religious and ontological notions, there is grave danger of reducing Christianity to a set of historicoethical opinions and its God to a pale projection of what is best in man, ontologically and ethically.

To perceive difficulty, even grave difficulty, however, is not to discover impossibilities. Catholicism has faced the challenge; it has engaged itself in the encounter; it has already identified the basic points of conflict and growth. The question arises here, How does Catholicism grow? It grows and develops both through conflict between opposing tendencies and through a slower, long-term drift representing an extension of established positions. These characteristics it shares with all human institutions. But because of the great emphasis the Church has placed upon explicit definition and upon uniformity and authority, such development often takes place more subtly and more covertly than would be the case in more democratic and less ideationally oriented institutions. In consequence, significant conflicts may not always appear to the untrained observer what they are. Thus ideas which are at least in potential conflict are often presented together as though the possibilities of conflict did not exist.

This method of development of ideas may be called "context theology," or "setting theology." We see it used in the composition of the *Dogmatic Constitution on the Church*. Thus the document does not really change any traditional positions of the Church by redefining them or rejecting them or explicitly qualifying or "correcting" them. Rather, it presents them in a new context, in a changed setting. (Here, of course, context theology reflects with great accuracy what history actually does to traditional ideas.) The pope is still the supreme ruler of the Church, but that fact is now placed in the context of the collegial episcopate; the Church is still the sacrament and mystery of faith mediating between time and eternity, but that fact is placed in the context of historical process; God is still transcendent and related to man by the Incarnation, but that fact is placed in the setting of a more detailed historical specificity. It is a nice argument whether a change of meaning is effected or the older meanings are seen more profoundly. At any rate, dogmas of the Church can perhaps be perceived in a new way, a way more palatable to modern intellectual tastes, by placing them in the context of modern thought-ways. A dogma is defined and therefore irreformable. But put in a different total setting, it may be understood in a new way; it could have a rather different meaning for the believer. Consider, as an example, this statement by a contemporary Catholic theologian of note [43]:

> . . . perhaps the day will come when it will be fully recognized that although the term "infallibility" does indeed express the binding force of the formulations of faith, it does not indicate their fragmentary character. With this in mind perhaps a concept will then be found which, better than the term "infallibility," will present in an encompassing and balanced manner the strict binding force of decrees and at the same time their profoundly incomplete character [quoted in 47:230].

The suggestion is that context theology, in offering the possibility of changing contexts, offers thereby the possibility of seeing the defined element as a small part not necessarily implying the other aspects of its original context. What is defined is a fragment or anchorage point, since it is the core definition, not the setting, that is binding, and that core definition is of necessity minimized once it is removed from its context. (It is interesting to note in this respect that St Thomas' philosophical position is really a set of anchorage point conceptions rather than a system in the later, philosophical sense of the word.)

This evolving theology has also been called a "decision theory" of dogmatic development. George Lindbeck thus directs our attention to one of its important characteristics. He sees such a theory replacing both the "classical deductive"

35

theories of traditional Catholicism and the progressive "organic growth" theories deriving from Cardinal Newman [47:228]. That is, in certain historical situations in which matters of basic Christian concern are threatened with distortion, definitions must be made. In the press of a specific situation with a specific problem, a decision is called for. The decision must be understood both in its setting and in its limited and incomplete character in relation to other settings. Lindbeck states that "the modern historical awareness of the time-conditioned character of all human utterances, including ecclesiastical ones, has now become so pervasive that it will never again be possible to treat dogmatic pronouncements as if they were permanently adequate expressions of eternal truth" [47:228].

Leslie Dewart has proposed a radical removal of traditional context in his proposal for a "dehellenization" of dogma. By giving up the Greek philosophical language in which dogma has been defined, he would remove the ontological frame of reference of the old theology as the context of the anchorage points of faith. In this process, he concedes that it might even be necessary or helpful to give up using the term "God." Dewart, however, does not suggest changing the dogmas which the Church has defined. Here indeed many important problems are opened up. McLuhan may exaggerate in his pronunciamento that the medium is the message, but it is quite clear that medium (and setting is an important part of medium) affects the content of the message in ways hard to define and describe. Here theology comes up against the most advanced problems of language analysis as well as those involved in the social sciences [see 27 and 54].

A second characteristic of the Catholic milieu with respect to conflict and growth is the importance of nuance. In a highly defined ideational system, nuance becomes significant, and a change of nuance can have considerable practical consequence. In an authoritarian structure this characteristic is heightened. Statements of authority—themselves often compromises—must be interpreted and applied. When Rome has spoken they cannot be reopened, at least in dogmatic cases, and in others often not in the pontificate in which the original decision was made. Yet they need explication, interpretation, and clarification, during which process a position announced by authority can be severely curtailed. In this Council we see the resort to nuance in a case which will be the subject of much later commentary. The document states that "This Church [the 'one, holy, catholic and apostolic' Church, 'established and ceaselessly sustained' by Christ], constituted and organized in the world as a society, subsists in the Catholic Church, which is governed by the successor of Peter, and by the bishops in union with that successor, although many elements of sanctification and of truth can be found outside of her visible structure" (art 8). Great interpretive possibilities reside in the word "subsist." It does not say the Catholic Church is identical with the Church founded by Christ—nor does it say otherwise.

Our preliminary analysis has revealed important elements in the current Catholic encounter with modernity. Discussion of these elements has made apparent in what way they present a challenge and even a danger to the Church. Before further consideration of the Church's problems in the *aggiornamento* process, it will be helpful to look at the earlier attempts at updating made by Catholics in the last century and to view those efforts in the perspective of Catholic history.

III

EARLIER CATHOLIC
ATTEMPTS AT MODERNIZATION

ONE must realize explicitly and fully what an unusual organization we deal with when we consider the Roman Church. It is indeed, as Macaulay suggested, most worthy of scholarly attention. At any rate it is unique in human history. Rising in the Patristic period and becoming the sole major cultural institution to survive from antiquity in the Middle Ages, the Church developed in an unusual setting. Moreover, its conviction that it was God's covenanted community (and later a highly juridically and hierarchically organized one) gave it a vast overarching character. It was a great umbrella, and all human events took place in its shade. It organized man's relation to God and mediated God's relation to man. It developed a highly specific, detailed view of the meaning of man's existence and destiny and of the structure and fate of the world. As an intellectual, a cultic, and an organizational structure, the Catholic Church became the central institution in the society of the Middle Ages, so much a part of the order of things that it is hard in retrospect to say where the Church ended and the secular world began. But two rifts appeared in this overarching architectonic intellectual and social edifice. Humanism, from the Renaissance on, and the Reformation broke through the older structure of things. The Church was no longer the total institution it had been in the past; soon it was no longer the central one. Yet the post-Reformation Roman Church inherited and carried forward many characteristics of the medieval Church. Although it reformed itself in significant operational respects, it did not alter its basic structure or the basic theological conceptions with which it entered the modern period. As that period continued, it found itself more and more on the defensive and by the 17th century was increasingly alienated from significant modern developments.

In this perspective the Second Vatican Council may be viewed as the effort of the Roman Church to stand erect once again. The Council was a vast struggle to correct and complement the medieval heritage and the Tridentine reform, with their one-sidedness and defensiveness, to overcome the baneful consequences of that stand, and to liberate the Church from the cramping posture of its hostile attitude toward secularization. The Second Vatican Council ushers in a new age in Church history. It heralds the end of the "Counter Reformation," and the end of the "Counter Revolution"!

The Counter Reformation was indeed a counter movement—in van Bilsen's term "a *reactionary* reform." The Council of Trent "was very important and most beneficial to the Church; but it is impossible to deny that it was to a great extent characterized by a defensive attitude on account of the situation in which it was held" [94:23]. Trent emphasized points because they were denied by the Reformers, and left others unstressed because the Reformers attached importance to them. This may be seen in the strengthening of lay tutelage and the treatment of the hierarchy, the Church, and the sacraments [94:24–25]. While the Counter Reformation imparted vigor to Catholic life and elicited an authentic revival, it remains true to say that it was one-sidedly defensive, one-sidedly clerical, and one-sidedly hostile to new and creative facets of developing Western civilization. Even the "liberal" aspects of Trent were hemmed in and denied fruition in this defensive condition. For example, the Tridentine definition of original sin and its effects upon human nature is much more humanistic and liberal than the prevailing ideas of the contemporary Protestants, but it did not inspire or inform a liberal confrontation of the lay world in subsequent Catholic history.

As a consequence of the defensive character of the Council of Trent, the one-sided emphasis of the Middle Ages, though many abuses were done away with, has been prolonged and preserved even to our own day. This defensive attitude shaped the character of Catholic piety at the time of the Counter Reformation. Books dealing with the "spiritual life" developed this even further. Popular extracts of those books diffused this same spirit among all strata of society. Thus the onesidedness of the Counter Reformation became, not a new phenomenon, but a confirmation of an existing situation, at least to a great extent. And this trend was strengthened by the Counter Reformation, and given a better chance of success [94:24-25].

The Reformation had split the Church and had thereby deprived both sides of the great historic rift of the lessons to be learned from a total view of Church history. It had divided the Christian heritage in two. Moreover, the hostile attitude the two parties now took toward each other reinforced the incompleteness of their perspectives. The Church had lost part of its intellectual patrimony, and precisely the part which had been neglected in the Middle Ages. That loss would increase the one-sidedness of its overinstitutionalized medieval condition. The defensiveness involved in the new conflict situation and somewhat later to be engendered by the rise of secularization would increase the one-sidedness even more.

The character of the split in the Church and the character of the Church as a central institutional complex in the established order tended to put the Church on the side of conservative elements. The rise of secularized ideologies would increase the Church's defensiveness, while the Church's identification with or at least alignment with conservative establishments would make new ideologies anti-Catholic. The rigidity of the Church made it impossible for its thinkers to develop genuinely creative modes of meeting the new intellectual and political situations. Consequently what Marx called "our epoch, the epoch of the bourgeoisie" came into existence in a struggle against an *ancien régime* of which Christianity was a central part. What de Tocqueville has called a "great providential drift" toward democracy was looked upon by the Church with much suspicion. That it often involved un-Christian and anti-Christian ideologies (one need only recall such names as Rousseau, Mazzini, and Marx) indicates how wide was the separation. That the Church should have been defensive with respect to and alienated from the new world to which it stood as part progenitor is a great tragedy for Christianity.

Hilaire Belloc has written,

> It is impossible for the theologian, or even for the practical ecclesiastical teacher to put his finger upon a political doctrine essential to the Revolution, and to say: This doctrine is opposed to Catholic doctrine or Catholic morals. Conversely, it is impossible for the Republican to put his finger upon a matter of ecclesiastical discipline or religious dogma and to say: This Catholic point is at issue with my political theory of the State [5:223].

In this statement Belloc calls our attention to the tragedy that political ideas destined to become normative for the modern world, and to make important contributions to humane values, came into the world alienated from and in opposition to the Church. He suggests that despite all the complexities of the various historical settings—and they were intricately complex—ultimately there is no conflict between democracy and Catholicism.

De Tocqueville noted in the 1830s that a neutral and vaguely Christianized democracy such as that found in the United States actually provided a tremendously hospitable atmosphere for the Catholic Church. The fact that the Church was able to accept democracy in America, where it developed relatively free of the militant anti-Christian elements on the continent, is the proof of Belloc's position. As it happened, however, the Church was so embedded, structurally and ideationally, in the old order that revolt against that order was also revolt against the Church and her beliefs. Belloc was calling for two things: an emancipation of the Church from the old order and from the conflicts of early modern times, and its intelligent reappraisal of and creative readjustment to the political world of the postrevolutionary epoch. Vatican II is in fact the first major ecumenical event in this kind of creative undoing of the past and freely working for the future. It is significant that in the drawing up of Council statements the American Catholic experience of democracy proved crucial.

The Council document *Dignitatis Humanae* or *Declaration on Religious Freedom* was profoundly affected by American thinking, and John Courtney Murray was the strategic figure in its preparation.

Similar observations could be made with respect to the Church's historic opposition to the secular separation of church and state.

The doctrinal defense of the freedom of the Church and the inviolability of the sacred, which are essential to the concept of right order, carried over with greater or less emphasis to a defense of the institutions which had furnished an armature for those principles in the old historic order—an armature that was not perfect but was certainly more protective than the subsequent nakedness. In other words, upon the basic doctrinal conflict between two ideas . . . , there was built another conflict whose terms were not so pure. . . . These two conflicts—call them the doctrinal and the historical—were not readily distinguishable at the time of their turbulent raging, when the injuriousness of the "separation" served to cloud from view the ambiguousness of the prior "union," which had been brought into being as much, or more, by forces inherent in royal absolutism as by ideas inherent in the Catholic tradition. In any event, at our distance in time these two conflicts can and should be distinguished [57:22–23].

Here John Courtney Murray points to the same historical complex, from which the Church at the time could not disentangle itself. This kind of overinstitutionalization has often been condemned as "Constantinianism" and "triumphalism," but it is hard to see how any other kind of development could have taken place in the concrete historical circumstances. Moreover, once established in this manner, the Church found it difficult to change its policies for a multitude of reasons. For one thing, proposals for change threaten both the values and the interests of churchmen. Thus Murray, eventually the architect of the new Church policy at Vatican II, was in disfavor for a time in the previous period.

The Church, as Troeltsch put it, necessarily compromised with the world in order to penetrate the world with its message. As a consequence, it was seriously compromised by the world. When a new world arose in the context of the old and asserted itself against the old, it at the same time had to assert itself against the Church. This fact of the entanglement of institutions and their ideational and value systems in concrete historical complexes, and the attendant problem of their possible liberation from such contexts, presents great difficulties in theory and practice. (The present author gives a theoretical discussion of these problems [66, 67, 68], and Sister Marie Augusta Neal's empirical study of important effects of these problems in American Catholicism is excellent [58].)

A brief consideration of the early 19th century will reveal just how heavy was the price of overinstitutionalization. If we look at the Catholic Church at the point when it made a concordat with Napoleon, we shall see its weakness, but we shall also see the evidence of its hidden strength. The Revolution had conducted a militant campaign of dechristianization, and the Church in France was in a state of extreme disorganization. Yet even with the French Church in shambles, Napoleon felt that in order to rule he should come to some understanding with the Church.

It is important to remember how desperate was the position from which the Concordat with Napoleon saved the Catholic Church; it may be that it was one more ominous than any to which she had been driven throughout the centuries of her history, since the time of the persecutions under the Roman Empire. Harassed in the land of France, traditionally her "eldest daughter," it was the same story in Belgium (now annexed to France), in the Rhineland (also annexed), in Italy, controlled by anti-clericals dependent upon France, in England and Ireland, where the movement for Catholic emancipation had been rejected by King George III, in Poland, partitioned by non-Catholic powers. Even in Austria, where "Josephism" survived, the Church was far from free, while the governments in Portugal and Spain were anti-clerical [31:60–61].

This description of the Church as an institution suggests also the depth of the alienation of the ideologies of the Revolution from Christianity. In philosophy things were little better. "Kant had done in the sphere of thought what the French Revolution had done in the sphere of politics. He had brought down the long tottering edifice of the established order, and had made a new start possible by clearing the ground once for all" [100:210, quoted in 97:17; see also 99:424n]. Far from Constantine indeed.

Yet the Church remained strangely strong in her travail. What Napoleon saw was this strength, and he decided to capitalize upon it for his own purposes. As Hales points out,

... what matters to the historian of Catholicism is to notice that the tough resistance of the priesthood and the faithful in France, and in the territories the French armies occupied, during the ten years of the Revolution, had convinced the realistic man who, for the next fifteen years would be master of France and her dependencies, that he must base his power upon their alliance. ... There has seldom been a more convincing tribute to the underlying strength of the Church than that it was recog-

44

nized and accepted by this arch-realist, who could ill endure a rival authority [31:57].

This drama of the Revolution versus the Church was to be played again and again in Europe in the 19th century. It would be continued in a slightly different form with the rise of socialism and especially after the coming to power of communist movements in the 20th. Indeed we see the drama taking place even within the States of the Holy See itself. If in the pontificate of Pius IX we witness the alienation of the Catholic Church from the spirit of the age and the opposition between liberalism and Catholicism pushed to extreme, we must remind ourselves of the Church's earlier encounter with revolution. We must also call to mind the significant fact that Pius IX had at first sincerely tried to come to terms with liberalism in Italy, and that his failure in this regard appears even in retrospect as inevitable [32: chaps 2, 3]. At that point neither the Church nor the revolution could be extricated from its historically specific concrete embodiment. The Catholic faith, however, survived, deep, real, intense; but it survived embodied in a Church bruised in spirit, distorted in attitude, misshapen in structure as a consequence of the intrinsic over-institutionalization of its own ideational and organizational structure, and hence its more and more anachronistic character, and because of the context of increasingly bitter hostility from outside in which it existed. The Second Vatican Council represents a great effort to disentangle the Church from that inherited set of attitudes and postures. But it is itself the crowning of a series of genuine attempts that we shall find it interesting to consider.

In the second half of the 19th century there were shrewd observers who doubted that Catholicism would last. Many in the Anglo-Saxon world felt with Carlyle that, though "popery" might still be able to construct chapels, its future was confined to the backwaters of provincialism and ignorance. The tide of history had definitely and decisively turned against it. Some sober-minded devotees of an ideology of science felt that Catholicism as embodying an authoritarian obscurantism was a stubborn but passing obstacle to progress and enlightenment. Like Andrew Dickson White, they felt that the "warfare between theology and science" was in their own day being won at last by science. Yet Catholicism lived. It continued to exist in Europe in spite of loss of the Papal States, Bismarck's Kulturkampf, and continued anticlericalism of a militant sort in the Latin countries; it prospered in North America in the face of popular nativist reactions against Catholic immigrants, Protestant crusades, and the deep suspicions of the educated; it made gains in the mission fields of Asia and Africa; and it even survived in Latin America, where the unfortunate drama of Latin Europe was played over again complicated by the elements of Spanish colonialism.

The last quarter of the 19th century was generally, however, a time of serious decline for the Church. In Great Britain and the Empire, particularly in Australia, and in the United States (the faith in these places is sometimes called "oceanic," in contrast to "continental," Catholicism) she made great gains, but in the countries that had traditionally been Catholic she continued to lose ground. The inability of Catholicism to meet the development of the lay world had given rise in those countries to laicizing ideologies of a marked anticlerical type. Areas of living which the Church had long considered under her jurisdiction, such as marriage and education, were removed from her control. The public celebrations of the Church had long been part of the public festive life of these communities, but now processions were banned and the public veneration of the Blessed Sacrament was prohibited. Harassing of monastic orders and their expulsion from the country became commonplace. In old Catholic Europe and in South America this mood continued into the present century—indeed, in this hemisphere until quite recently. Yet Catholicism survived, and these regions remained in many ways Catholic in culture and outlook.

It was this difficult 19th century which saw several impressive attempts at Catholic renewal and revival. The beginning of such a renewal in France, stimulated by the romantic movement, is first evidenced by the publication in 1802 of Chateaubriand's *Le Génie du Christianisme*. Deriving remotely from Rousseau, whose ideas had inspired such militant anti-Catholicism, the romantic movement emphasized the importance of experience and emotion. Its effect upon Catholicism was to produce a species of Catholic thought which saw religion as having an attractive aura of mystery and as inviting men to an experience of adventure. It presented Catholicism as "ineffable in its mysteries, adorable in its sacraments, interesting in its history, heavenly in its morality, and rich and engaging in its ceremonies and circumstances" [97:18, my translation]. It had the effect of making Catholicism "intellectually respectable and emotionally attractive" [97:19]. Out of this romantic revival came liberal Catholicism.

Perhaps the first significant statement of liberal Catholicism is *Des Progrès de la Révolution et de la Guerre contre l'Église*. published by Lamennais in 1829. In this work belief in monarchy is abandoned, and in its place is a marked sympathy with liberalism and the principles of 1789. With the Revolution of 1830, Lamennais and his associates Lacordaire and Montalembert began to work for the reconciliation of the Church and the revolutionary currents in French society. In October of that year Lamennais founded his famous newspaper *L'Avenir*, which bore the motto "God and Liberty." This liberal group combined its attempts to reconcile the Church and the Revolution with efforts to utilize democracy in defense of the Church, trying to extend the rights of Catholics especially in the field of education.

The victories of the Belgian Catholics in defying the Dutch king and winning freedom for their religion, for the press, for education, were what inspired Lamennais; the similar victories of

O'Connell were the inspiration of Montalembert, who had been in Ireland. Rome, they said, must not accept favours at the hands of princes . . . she must demand and fight for what the Church needed [32:46].

The Church must, moreover, bless the cause of the people. "Lamennais had no doubt that the revolutionary cause in the years 1830–31 in Poland and in Belgium, in Ireland and in Italy, was the cause of truth and justice, and that the Church should lend her full support to democratic movements everywhere" [31:90]. The *Avenir* group were ultramontanist as well as liberal and looked to Rome for support against the Gallican French hierarchy, which was also often royalist in sympathy. The Church should rely on the "people," not on rulers and concordats. "Where the people were in arms against their rulers let the pope, Lamennais cried, support them instead of supporting their masters" [31:91]. In Lamennais's view, the Church should support complete freedom of speech, press, association, and education, as well as universal suffrage. It had everything to gain from the overthrowing of the traditional powers.

Neither in Paris nor in Rome was the Church in any way prepared for the role Lamennais advocated for her; nor, for that matter, was the bourgeois government of Louis Philippe "prepared for a thoroughgoing application of liberal principles" [97:22]. Cardinal Lambruschini, a conservative who was later the rival to Pius IX in the conclave of 1846, was at that time papal nuncio at Paris, and he denounced Lamennais to Rome as fomenting revolutionary disorder. The French hierarchy began to forbid the people to read *L'Avenir*, which was also suffering from government interference.

The liberals, feeling themselves pushed into a corner, at this point made a serious tactical error. Lamennais appealed to Rome. It was indeed wishful thinking of a most unrealistic kind to imagine that the Church, still so deeply involved with the ideas of the old order and so much at war with the forces of the new, fighting for her life against hostile movements, could at that time make the great leap Lamennais wanted. Indeed, "Gregory XVI was not at all disposed to play the part which these liberal ultramontanes had designed for him" [97:23]. Lamennais had shrewdly discerned the long-range trend of European development and saw what the Church would have to do eventually. But he had no sense for the tactical requirements of advocating such a course under the current circumstances. In fact, the moment of his arrival in Rome to push his cause coincided with the pope's calling in Austrian troops to put down a revolt of the Carbonari in the Romagna! This event indicated how highly dependent was the Church upon precisely the kind of conservative alliances which Lamennais sought to have repudiated.

The result was the precedent-setting papal encyclical *Mirari Vos*. Gregory's positions here laid out in general terms the line taken in 1864 by Pius IX when he issued the *Syllabus of Errors*. The encyclical did not mention Lamennais by name and in fact implicitly complimented his virtues. But his program—freedom of conscience, which Rome understood as religious indifferentism, freedom of the press, separation of church and state, and even alliances of men of varied religions for the common good—was explicitly condemned. Catholicism was still on the defensive, still embedded in the old way of thinking, still radically askew in relation to the spirit of the age. And it was, it seems, necessarily so, for the age itself was not ready for the kind of rapprochement Lamennais advocated. At first Lamennais accepted the decision in silence, but soon he began to write again. In a short time he published a book entitled *Paroles d'un Croyant*. In this work he saw truth as part of the evolutionary development of a people, a view condemned by Gregory XVI in June 1834 in *Singulari Nos*. This second condemnation anticipated the later censure of "immanentism" by Pius X in 1907 in his encyclical *Pascendi Gregis*. Thus Lamennais provided France with a recapitulation of much of the Catholic past and a dress rehearsal of much that was to come.

The 19th century also witnessed a Catholic revival in Germany and the development there of a liberal Catholicism. However, it was a more complex phenomenon than in France, and its main emphasis was intellectual rather than political. In France, facing the forces of rationalism and unbelief, the Church became conservative, defensive, and rigid. In Germany, the Catholic Church was juxtaposed to a powerful Protestant Church which offered it a constant challenge. The consequences were both stimulating and liberalizing for German Catholicism. Moreover, the proximity of Protestant and Catholic theological faculties in the state universities made it "impossible for Catholic teachers in Germany to disregard or to disdain, like their brethren in France, the development of modern philosophy and of historical and biblical criticism. Catholic apologetic, if it was to meet with any success, was compelled to take account of Kant and Hegel, of Lessing and Schleiermacher, of Strauss and Bauer" [97:32f].

The two centers of liberal intellectual Catholicism in Germany were Tübingen and Munich. The Catholic Tübingen School flourished from 1817 to 1840. After that date the center moved to Munich and the group about Döllinger. The Catholic Tübingen group, of which the outstanding figure was Johann Adam Möhler (1796–1838), developed a theological approach which was dynamic and organic rather than fixed and static. They stressed the importance of experience and of process. Influenced by Schleiermacher, like him they sought consciously to reconcile science and philosophy with Christianity. Though they felt he went too far in his emphasis upon emotion and thought his definition of religion as a feeling of absolute dependence was much oversimplified, they nevertheless considered his general position to contain important corrective elements with respect to the theology of the time.

Möhler and his associates confronted contemporary thought with understanding and sympathy. At the same time, they were critical where it "seemed to fail to do justice to the rich volume of spiritual truth which was embodied in the Catholic tradition" [97:35]. Nor were they afraid of biblical criticism; in their opinion, in fact, Catholics had less to fear from that quarter than had Protestants, since Catholic faith rested upon the living tradition of the Church. These men never became the cause of any marked controversy although they were denounced by conservatives and even at Rome, and although they anticipated ideas which would be independently introduced into Catholic thinking later to be condemned by the Holy See. They themselves were never condemned by ecclesiastical authority.

After 1840 a new and brilliant intellectual star appeared in the German Catholic firmament—Ignaz Döllinger. A man of vast learning, he was also of an aggressive and polemical temperament. This brilliant scholar organized a congress of scholars at Munich in 1863. Wilfrid Ward noted that in his presidential address to the gathering, Döllinger set forth a program for "treating dogmatic questions on lines more and more removed from the traditional scholastic philosophy." He declared that the traditional scholastic theologians were limited and one-sided in their Aristotelianism. "Their analytical processes could not construct a system corresponding to the harmony and wealth of revealed truth; and without the elements of Biblical criticism and dogmatic history they possessed only one of the eyes of theology" [97:37]. "Scholastic theology," he felt, "was to be considered a thing of the past. Catholic doctrine must be presented in its organic completeness, and in its connection with the religious life, 'rigidly separating that which is permanent and essential from whatever is accidental, transitory, and foreign.' " He stated that the genuine theologian "must reason boldly and thoroughly, and 'not take to flight if the process of his reasoning threatens to demolish some truth which he had deemed unassailable' " [98:562].

The congress concerned itself with the independent rights of scholarship in philosophy, science, and history—and the relation of these to theology. Döllinger and his group asserted that except in the case of a minimal number of dogmatically defined matters of faith there was to be no limitation on the conclusions of free intellectual inquiry. The ordinary teaching authority of the Church, the Roman congregations, or established theological opinions were not normative in this respect.

The congress was an impressive gathering, attended by theologians, philosophers, historians, and scientists from the universities of Germany. It had been called without seeking hierarchical permission from the Archbishop of Munich. It was hailed by enthusiastic liberal Catholics throughout Europe. In England, for example, Lord Acton and his associates on the *Home and Foreign Review* saw in Döllinger's address "the manifesto of a new Catholicism, designed to take the place of what they deemed to be a senile and out-of-date tradition" [11:344].

But the Church was no more prepared to make a creative readjustment in the intellectual sphere than in the political. Her defensive posture in intellectual as well as practical matters, and in matters of theology and scripture as well in social and political philosophy, kept her unable to meet this kind of challenge. Her authoritarian structure and her growing emphasis upon uniformity—greatly increased by defensiveness—made it impossible for her to ignore it. As might be expected, Pius IX, now embattled and under siege in his long-drawn-out conflict with modernity, condemned the findings of the congress. His brief declared that scholastic theology and the decisions of the Roman congregations on matters of doctrine must be regarded as binding on scientists and scholars. This brief was addressed to Archbishop Reisach, Metropolitan of Munich. It was soon followed by the encyclical *Quanta Cura* and the *Syllabus*.

In the meantime the political pot continued to boil in France. Earlier that same summer of 1863 another Catholic congress was held in Belgium, at Malines. That body too heard free intellectual inquiry defended, but its particular concerns were political—the great Latin problem of the Church and the Revolution. It was to this gathering that Montalembert, now highly respected by the leading political and religious thinkers of France and Belgium, was invited to speak. The aim of the congress was to "reconcile the Church with civilisation in north-western Europe" [32:278]. Montalembert, aware of the pressures under which Pius IX was laboring, hesitated to accept, knowing that what he had to say would further distress that unhappy man. Yet accept he did.

He made two notable appearances before the body. In his first speech he declared that the old regime of concordats was dead. It had its great virtues, but it was past and gone. He stood for freedom of education, of the press, of association. He ended on a dramatic note, quoting Dupanloup: "We accept, we invoke the principles and the liberties proclaimed in '89. . . . You made the revolution of 1789 without us and against us, but *for us*, God wishing it so in spite of you." The next day he gave a second address in which he favored religious toleration. This he claimed was a Catholic principle. He also treated of church reliance on the state as prejudicial to the interests of Catholicism and as rooted in false principles.

While Montalembert was making these stirring presentations of the creative attempts of a liberal Catholicism to reconcile itself with the Revolution, Pius IX was engaged in a difficult struggle with the liberal Italian government at Turin. In fact, Montalembert explicitly condemned the Turin government in his Malines remarks. "Montalembert's speeches at Malines were greeted with immense enthusiasm; but the shrewder spirits who heard them, and especially the papal nuncio, knew they could never be approved at Rome." Pius IX's current encounter with liberalism and revolution summed up the worst aspects of the modern history of the Church and induced in him an attitude toward modern liberties anything but hospitable to the ideas of the liberals. "Though Dupanloup tried hard at Rome to prevent it, a condemnation of Montalembert was really inevitable, and it duly arrived, courteous, confidential, and friendly, in February, 1864, pointing out that in 1791 Pius VI had condemned the Edict of Nantes, and reminding the orator of Gregory XVI's *Mirari Vos* [32:279f; 31:129]. (Lord Acton's *Home and Foreign Review* was also indirectly condemned at this time.) At the end of "the fateful year" of 1864 came the *Syllabus of Errors*, which led to the total eclipse of liberal Catholicism.

The *Syllabus of Errors* and the encyclical *Quanta Cura* which accompanied it present a general condemnation of modern ideas and modern social and political practices as these were confronted in specific instances challenging, contradicting, opposing, or otherwise in conflict with the Catholic Church or the Roman See. These documents "plunged— though not with dogmatic force—into the most controversial problems of thought and politics" [32:266]. The condemnations they make are sweeping. The animosity that had come to prevail in the relations between the Church and the liberal spirit of the time is plain to be seen.

It has been suggested that the *Syllabus* afforded "most satisfaction to the more authoritarian party within and to the more ardently hostile without" the Catholic Church. To the former, it seemed to give firm official blessing and to put its liberal opponents under a permanent cloud. To the latter, it "seemed so completely unreasonable and absurd as to spell the doom of the Papacy" [32:266].

The *Syllabus* contained 80 propositions condemned as erroneous by Pius IX during his pontificate and here gathered together with references to their original sources and occasions. They are divided into 10 sections, dealing with: Pantheism, Naturalism and Absolute Rationalism (7 propositions); Moderate Rationalism (7 propositions); Indifferentism and Latitudinarianism (4 propositions); followed by a paragraph condemning Socialism, Communism, Secret Societies, Bible Societies, and Clerical-Liberal Societies; Errors Concerning the Church and the Rights of the Church (20 propositions); Errors about the Civil Society and Its Relation to the Church (17 propositions); Errors about Ethics (9 propositions); Errors about Christian Marriage (10 propositions); Errors Concerning the Pope's Temporal Power (2 propositions); and Errors Concerning Liberalism (4 propositions).

Although a proposition is condemned only in the sense understood by the people who had currently maintained its truth in the original context in which the pope's condemnation was made, the document read like a sweeping and summary condemnation of the age. The *Syllabus* was in fact an unfortunate document, badly drawn and clumsily conceived. Pio Nono himself is supposed to have called it raw meat needing to be cooked. A couple of examples must suffice.

Proposition 77 calls it an error to say "that it is no longer expedient that the Catholic religion should be established to the exclusion of all others." Actually, the statement, as the reference shows, is drawn from a papal allocution given by Piux IX concerning Spain in which he dealt not with universal principles but with specific Spanish conditions; he expressed his "wonder and distress" that a Catholic country should be considering giving other religions an equal position with Catholicism. If we recall that disestablishment was not yet a general practice, the pope's position is not especially noteworthy. But it comes through in the *Syllabus* as a general statement. To be understood, it must be read with the Catholic sense of nuance to which we made reference earlier. It is then seen to declare that the pope "is only saying that he refuses to recognize it as a rule of *universal* validity that in *all* countries *every* sort of religion should forthwith be *openly* tolerated, and the Catholic Church should be disestablished" [31:125].

The proposition that caused the strongest reaction was the final one. To see how alienated was the Roman Church from the evolving spirit of the age one needs only imagine how such a statement sounded to the ears of a Lincoln or a Gladstone! Proposition 80 read as follows: "The Roman

Pontiff can and should reconcile and harmonize himself with progress, with liberalism, and with recent civilization." Its condemnation in the *Syllabus* certainly seemed a blanket condemnation of the 19th century. Checking the original context of this statement, one finds that it was part of an allocution, *Jamdudum Cernimus*, issued March 18, 1861, denouncing anticlerical laws which were being extended from Piedmont to the newly acquired provinces of the Turin government. The latter was acting upon its policy of holding that monasteries, convents, the Catholic conception of marriage as a sacrament, and Catholic religious education were all obsolete in the present age. Pius IX was here using the terminology of his opponents. In putting together the *Syllabus*, Cardinal Antonelli was giving such specific usage a questionable universality.

Yet the situation was even worse than that. Cardinal Newman stated in one of his discussions of the document that this proposition is indeed not condemned in the original declaration. According to Newman, what the pope said was that people who championed these things used them "so seriously to the injury of the Faith and the Church, that it was both out of the power, and contrary to the duty, of the Pope to come to terms with them" [12:7].

Nevertheless, it was as condemned that the *Syllabus* sent forth this proposition to western Europe. It is hardly surprising that such a collection gained a poor press for the Church. In France and Italy, to make matters worse, the press published the *Syllabus* and commented upon it, but the Catholic bishops were not allowed to discuss it publicly. The chasm separating the Church from "recent civilization" was never wider!

What was the effect of this statement upon 19th century Catholicism, already so strained and so subject to disability in that age? Roger Aubert has said that on receiving this papal document "the majority of Catholics were stupefied" [31:125]. Many bishops did not know how to deal with it. Dupanloup, Bishop of Orléans, who had earlier tried to save Montalembert from condemnation in Rome, came to the rescue in a pamphlet. What was condemned, he said, was the notion that these liberal propositions described an ideal and universally desirable state of affairs. The Catholic Church could not consider a society of many faiths all equally tolerated an ideal to be universally desired. Such a belief would contradict her own conviction of her unique truth. The condemnation was a condemnation of the "thesis." In fact, however, the Church accepted the actual situation described as it existed in England, America, and elsewhere and had no intention of doing otherwise. These conditions were accepted as "hypothesis."

Dupanloup's solution was accepted at Rome with an extremely guarded approval. His "explication" and the pope's "acceptance" show, again, the great significance of nuance in this kind of internal struggle over how to interpret a decision of authority. Also evident is the way an uneasy *modus vivendi* within the Church could be allowed to settle in on the basis of not simply subtle but ambiguous use of nuance. The "solution" was not too satisfactory and it was to cause misunderstanding in the United States for decades.

Consequences of this "thesis–hypothesis" notion invented to place limitations on reactionary positions were often utilized in the United States by Americans suspicious of Catholicism to suggest Catholic enmity to democracy and separation of church and state. This use seemed particularly appropriate to some when such "evidence" could be found in the writing of liberal Catholics. A prime example was Monsignor John A. Ryan, the important Catholic social thinker and a liberal influence in the American Church. "In the election of 1928, Ryan figured as a combatant and also as an authority. A statement in his *The State and the Church* (1923) [78] encouraged critics to think that once in power Catholics would deny religious freedom to non-Catholics. Ryan rejected this idea" [59:767]. A statement in the textbook *Catholic Principles of Politics* [79] which repeated the thesis–hypothesis idea became the *pièce de résistance* of much of this intolerant American dialogue.

It was said in Paris that when the Church condemns the Jews, that is thesis, but when the nuncio has dinner with Baron Rothschild, that is hypothesis. The *Syllabus* and the Dupanloup solution testify to the severity of the conflict between the Church and those aspects of the 19th century which we may call secular liberalism.

In an attempt to consolidate its post-Tridentine "integrity," the Church in this period did two other things which "shocked" its opponents. In 1854, in the bull *Ineffabilis Deus*, Pius IX declared the Immaculate Conception (not to be confused with the Virgin Birth) to be "a doctrine revealed by God" and stated that it "must be believed firmly and constantly by all the faithful." There was no scriptural basis for the declaration except the Catholic understanding of the words "full of grace" in the salutation of the angel Gabriel [Lk 1:28]. In 1870 the Vatican Council proclaimed the dogma of Papal Infallibility. Interestingly—and most significantly—authoritarianism and defensiveness in the Church are definitely found correlated with a strong emphasis upon Mariology. It is as if the masculine behavior of decision and combat, and the dominance of the male authority structure of clergy and hierarchy, required some fantasy compensations of a feminine character. It is also interesting how much anti-Catholic and antipapal imagery utilizes feminine symbolism (e.g., "whore of Babylon"). This is an area deserving much sociological and psychological study but it cannot be pursued here.

To suggest balance in this complicated picture we should note four other phenomena. First, in the next pontificate—that of Leo XIII (1878–1903)—the Church began to improve its relation to modernity. The bitterness of the war with liberalism lessened as a somewhat more satisfactory general condition came to prevail. In terms of social problems the Church began to face up to the implication of industrialism.

Second, there is the long career of Cardinal Newman. Newman cannot be called a liberal Catholic in the sense that

Montalembert was, but he was a force for scholarly reconsideration of important intellectual matters and represented a fresh current of creative theological thought. Although he was devout and orthodox, he came under suspicion at Rome. Leo XIII's decision to make him a cardinal was a kind of victory for reasonableness after the highly emotional conflicts of the preceding decades. It has been suggested that Leo was attempting to "encourage the development and presentation of Catholic ideas" [11:382].

Third, one must note the policy of *Ralliement* pursued by Leo. The word refers to that pontiff's effort to get the French Church to come to terms with and accept the Republic, which, he recognized, had won the support of the majority of Frenchmen. Leo stated that the form of government was not a matter of Christian principles and that a republic was as legitimate a form of government as any other.

Finally, there was the Catholic situation in the United States, so full of promise for the future. The Catholics were destined to become an important minority in America, and America was destined to become a superpower in the 20th century. Friendliness with the North American republic would be more important to the Church than the older concordats in the 20th century, despite the absence of formal diplomatic ties with the tiny restored Vatican state.

The story of the American Catholic experience is a varied and indeed an exciting one. It combines a host of paradoxes: great possibilities for free and unfettered Church life combined with extreme hostility from non-Catholics; a high degree of lay practice combined with clericalist monopoly of decision and policy making after the defeat of earlier lay aspirations; unprecedented development of Catholic educational institutions combined with poor performance in the intellectual, scientific, and cultural spheres; a definite alienation from important liberal core elements in popular American values combined with a high and possibly compensating identification with American nationalism; a subtle acceptance in practice of ideas and values officially condemned—pragmatism, separation of church and state, preference for action over contemplation, etc. American Catholic history was also marked both by the intolerance of the Protestant majority, which met Catholic immigration with nativist movements and "Protestant crusades" [8; 42], and by internal conflicts within the Church between ethnic groups, between clergy and laymen, and between hierarchs supporting contradictory ways of adjusting the Church to American society. In addition, the American Church witnessed a struggle between liberals and conservatives with respect to political life, cultural assimilation, the Bible, and science, and 19th century American Catholicism produced impressive and outspoken liberal figures. Yet the Church was basically conservative—conservative, that is, in relation to the quite novel American milieu.

This development of an Americanized Church has been called the "emergence of a liberal Catholicism," a term that is really ambiguously descriptive of what actually happened. The Catholic Church in America came to combine a kind of liberal spirit about politics and community with a kind of integralist conception with respect to its own inner life, its own ideas, and its own place in the society. The result was a marked aloofness from and askewness to American culture.

Was the Church in America liberal in the sense of the liberalism fought by Pius IX? Yes and no. There were genuinely liberal Catholic voices, clerical and lay, raised eloquently in America. But what emerged was a Church which came to accept, as a matter of fact and unideologically, principles that in their European guise and setting threatened the Church, however easy they were to live with and even to live by in America. Before the Second World War the Church in America was substantially Americanized in its practice. It acknowledged the political ground rules; it got along with government and its non-Catholic neighbors—not without conflict in the latter case, but well enough. It became part of the American scene despite the phenomenon of "Blanshardism" among non-Catholics and the use of the kind of pressure tactics by the Church itself which strengthened such anti-Catholic reactions. Yet it could hardly be seen as a liberal force in American life. It was liberal, let us say, in the sense that Cardinal Spellman was liberal compared to Cardinal Lambruschini—that is, in the same sense that Dirksen is liberal compared to Metternich! The main result, then, was the Americanization of the Church and its sincere acceptance of the American system.

The Church in America long remained a symbolic issue. Americans of non-Catholic background often continued to be influenced by earlier conceptions of Catholics and Catholicism, conceptions that were the inherited residues of the post-Reformation struggles. There were public arguments concerning a diplomatic representative at the Vatican—seen by many as subversive to the American system—and whether or not a Catholic could be elected President of the United States. To the latter question the American people gave one answer in 1928 and another in 1960. The matter of having an ambassador at the Vatican, while it excited some Protestant and even liberal circles, never seemed to have much impact upon the American Catholic imagination.

Yet despite these symbolic hangovers, relations between Catholics and their non-Catholic fellow citizens improved decade by decade. The long-term trend was toward an American Catholicism accepting the basic liberal principles of the American Constitution and the Bill of Rights, and accepted as one of the religions to which Americans legitimately belong. What is notable about this American Catholic experience is that it brought to fulfillment tendencies found generally in "oceanic" Catholicism—in the British Isles, Australia, and New Zealand, as well as in this country. Most important of all, the experience became of strategic significance in the Church's rethinking of its positions in the 20th century. It found its theoretical spokesman in John Courtney Murray, SJ, and it was a major basis for the Vatican Council's

Declaration on Human Freedom. The Church was ready by 1963 to look at the lessons of America: There was a large and obviously prospering American Church; the Church itself in most places was no longer part of an old, traditional, established order; Europe was diminished in importance in an expanding world; and America was the world's strongest power. Metternich was long since dead, and with him Montalembert and Pio Nono! From America's nonideological liberalism, her pragmatic laicism, and her nontheoretical Catholicism came the basic solution for one of the bitterly contested problems of the 19th century.

We have made this summary examination of the various attempts to reorient the Catholic Church in its relation to evolving modernity in order to discover the points of strain. Obviously, no single phenomenon can be designated as "liberal Catholicism." Rather, a series of efforts have been made around specific issues to change the direction of Catholic policy and the tenor of Catholic thought and feeling. We must now ask what tendencies expressed themselves again and again, to be generally rejected and condemned by the authorities in the Church. What were the issues involved in the attempts at "proto *aggiornamento*"?

First of all, the thrust of the whole undertaking was to break out of the condition of overinstitutionalization which was characteristic of the Church in that period. This condition involved two different but related aspects. One was an overdevelopment and overrigidity of forms of thought and organization: detailed definitions carried down from previous ages and half-forgotten cultural settings; rigid social forms such as exaggerated differential clerical and lay status; and a high degree of verbalism. The other was an inherited burden of forms of relationship with the world—intellectual and political—evolved in the past and fast losing their suitability. These may be called fundamental ossifying consequences of overinstitutionalization such as are likely to plague any old human organization.

There is a second side of the matter in the Catholic case. The askewness characteristic of the relation of the Church to the world from the late Middle Ages on, an askewness increased greatly by the Reformation and exacerbated into an open warfare on basic principles by the Revolution, introduced a more and more rigid defensiveness into the picture and made creative rethinking extremely difficult—and liable to authoritative rebuke when it did come about. Yet we have seen, in these most unlikely circumstances, significant attempts at creative innovation in Catholic thought and action. They were struggles to escape from the overinstitutionalized condition of such long standing and to confront the new world with a renewed freshness and vigor. They were efforts to emancipate the Catholic faith from the defensive hostility and encumbering bureaucracy of the spirit in which it had become encased.

We may summarize in a series of dichotomies these attempts at breaking out of the awry cage which history had jerry-built for the Church. It must be stressed that we describe here tendencies, not fully developed religious attitudes or theological positions. It must also be recalled that there were not two parties in any simple sense, and that many who would appear liberal on one issue might indeed show up as conservative on others. Yet what becomes visible is a series of new emphases and perspectives which amount to the emergence of an open and liberal view of the implications of modernity for religion.

The *innovators* placed their emphasis upon *experience*, while *those who held the established positions* gave priority to *codified definitions* derived from past experience.

The *innovators* recognized the significance of *emotion* and *feeling*, while *those who maintained the established positions* rested their faith on *assent to intellectual formulas*.

The *innovators* recognized that life was in some basic way a *process*, while *those who held the established positions* saw it as an interaction of *fixed intellectual, cultural, and social forms*.

The *innovators* saw the coming victory of *democracy* and

faced the implications that social forms came into being and passed away, while *those who maintained the established positions*, though they might cite Aristotle on generation and corruption, saw the world as a substantial *hierarchical order*, within which particular social and political forms were sacral.

The *innovators* suspected the vast implications of *historical specificity* and the problems they raised for the transmission of lasting truths, while *those who maintained the established positions* appeared to be satisfied with their own earlier *general statements* made in medieval Latin as adequately embodying older ideas and immediately comprehensible to men of "right reason."

The *innovators*, with a new understanding of experience, of emotion, of the historical process, and of the inevitability of change, saw the importance of coming to understand the forces and tendencies that are *immanent* in social life, how they achieve expression, and their relation to what is already evolved and established, while *those who maintained the older positions* saw in their old codified formulas an adequate and timeless embodiment of the *transcendent*, and seemed often to understand transcendence in a manner closer to the rationalism they condemned than to their own admitted philosophical sources.

The *innovators* saw, to one extent or another, that life was *open ended*, while *those who maintained the established positions* seemed to think there really was *nothing new* under the sun.

The *innovators* saw that the Church could not base its propaedeutic to faith upon reason and history and then make its own rules to curtail reason and enclose history, while *those who maintained the established positions* pretended to see no problem in this circularity.

The *innovators* saw the approach of a greater *equality* and a *coming of age* for modern man, while *those who maintained the established positions* saw *submission* of inferior to superior as part of the divinely ordained nature of things and emphasized the religious importance of *obedience*.

The work of the *innovators* suggested that no historically evolved conceptions of being or value could be final and definitive, while *those who maintained the established positions* tended to see both being and value and their human formulations as fixed and complete.

The *innovators* began to appreciate that men act out, in their lives and generations in history, complex and subtle dramas, whose script is original and whose source and consummation are obscure, while *those who maintain the established positions* were prone to see the activity of the layman as having meaning only in its moral aspects, and to see in their own highly conventionalized presentation of the religious experience the only noble human end.

Once again, at the end of the 19th century and the beginning of the 20th, before the fateful assassination at Sarajevo put an end to the 19th century world, this drama of innovation and its repression was to be reenacted within the Church of Rome. The history we have briefly surveyed suggests three areas of conflict and of growth: the philosophical, the historical, and the practical—the social and political. And in these three fields, a new attempt was to be made to bring the encounter between Christianity and modernity to a happy issue for the Catholic Church. This attempt, though the work of a small number of scholars and thinkers, was—at least in proportion to its numbers, and indeed perhaps absolutely—to shake the Roman Church more thoroughly than any of its predecessors. The reaction it called forth would remain intense for half a century, and its effects are still very much with us.

The pontificate of Leo XIII had, as we have seen, witnessed essays to come to terms with the modern world and to normalize the relations between it and the Church. Leo was no liberal, and the significance of his efforts is still a matter of dispute. He did recognize the legitimacy of republican government, though he certainly understood little concerning the spirit and the function of a democractic polity. He addressed himself to the social ills of industrialism but showed scant grasp of the kind of transformation industrial technology was bringing into the world.

In all this process of attempted rapprochement, Leo was conservative. He condemned the so-called "Americanist heresy," which tended to give a higher value to action than to contemplation. This issue was complicated by its involvement in the intricate liberal-conservative conflict in the Church in France. In *Aeterni Patris* (1879) he revived Thomism as the philosophy of the Church and made it a compulsory part of seminary education and central to the statement of Catholic doctrine. In *Providentissimus Deus* (1893) he dealt with the study of the Bible, gave a doctrinal exposition of what is meant by inspiration, and fixed the limits he considered proper to biblical criticism.

The new encounter with modernity was to involve the areas with which Leo was concerned, but the most important of the three would perhaps be that of a critical study of the Bible and its consequences. Here abrupt change was about to take place in the context of a remarkable backwardness. The state of Catholic biblical studies as the 19th century drew to a close could hardly have been less prepared for the confrontation. Said one practitioner, Alfred Loisy, writing in 1903,

> . . . it must be said that the position of a priest occupied with the scientific study and teaching of Biblical exegesis fifteen or twenty years ago was a terrible one, if he were open-minded and truthful. He beheld an enormous field of study which had not been hinted at in his previous instruction, namely, the unfinished but extensive work accomplished by Protestant and Rationalist exegesis . . . [48:xv, as translated in 71:42].

As another commentator put it,

> Eyes accustomed to narrow and rigid limits had suddenly to focus themselves on the boundless perspectives of the new sciences, where established fact jostled with arbitrary hypothesis [15:17].

For the greater part of the nineteenth century the leaders of Catholic thought had held aloof from this movement of new ideas which was changing world opinion. They took up a defensive attitude. Never in all its long history was the Church's biblical exegesis so wilfully conservative and at times even retrogressive. Nothing at all was known of the work done in Germany except that it was extremist. Renan's Life of Christ [sic], which wrecked the faith of a whole generation, only made this work more suspect, and it was rejected wholesale in the name of a tradition which was blinded by fixed and narrow ideas. It was for Leo XIII to broaden this narrow outlook. His encyclical *Providentissimus* (1893) encouraged many to get to grips with independent criticism [15:18].

In any case there was a burst of activity in biblical studies in the last decade of the 19th century. Catholics began to move away from apologetically "disproving" the Wellhausen hypothesis to be seen in the works of Cornely and Vigoureux, and toward more creative kinds of work. This newer work can be seen in the Pentateuchal studies of M. J. Lagrange, OP, and also in the work of such men as Prat, Durand, and von Hummelauer. Cautiously Catholic scholars were making a first serious confrontation of the great Protestant biblical work of the 19th century.

In October 1902, Leo XIII issued the encyclical *Vigilantiae* and established the so-called Biblical Commission. This body, as part of the Roman Curia, was empowered to ensure that "Holy Writ should everywhere among us receive that more elaborate treatment which the times require and be preserved intact not only from any breath of error but also from all rash opinions."

It is ironical to note that a French Catholic scholar, a priest of the Oratory, Richard Simon (1638–1712), was in fact the father of all biblical criticism. "He saw and formulated the major problems that have occupied criticism since his day, and boldly applied scientific methods to their solution. As a pioneer, it was inevitable that some of his solutions should be weak, and others too radical (his works were put on the Index); yet the 'orthodox' exegetes (notably Bossuet) who so vigorously condemned, not his errors alone, but his whole critical approach, had no idea of the importance of the work he was trying to do. In any event he founded no school, and further Catholic work on these lines was discouraged. The result was that critical analysis of the Bible, when it came, was entirely non-Catholic—indeed anti-Catholic—and vastly more irresponsible and destructive than it need have been" [22:61].

Yet such a cautious and tardy beginning was soon to become bolder, and in consequence the commencement of modern Bible study among Catholics would be harshly interrupted. It was to lead Catholic thought to a profound encounter with modern ideas and to cause a reaction which would stifle Catholic intellectuality for decades. The *fin-de-siècle* revival was to issue in the modernist crisis.

The modernist crisis eminently deserves to be studied by Catholic scholars if they are to understand the social psychology of their own milieu, but so far the psychological atmosphere of their own milieu, deeply affected by that crisis, has prevented any such venture. All we can do here is offer a brief and suggestive summary.

Perhaps the most significant figure was Abbé Alfred Loisy. Loisy introduced into biblical studies a radical and uncompromising historicism. He insisted that both the Scriptures and the Church be seen in their full historical setting. He then proceeded to treat them as one would treat any religious, theological, or social phenomena, utilizing the most advanced methodology of his time. In this effort Loisy came to feel that a thorough and scientifically sound historicism would offer the Catholic Church its best apologetic. The Church had nothing to fear from history. Loisy's book *L'Évangile et l'Église* showed convincingly how Harnack had violated a true contextual historicism when he found in the New Testament a Jesus who was a 19th century Protestant.

Loisy insisted in seeing Jesus as an eschatological figure believing in his own messiahship, and the Church as the community which was founded on the religious experience he provided for his disciples. Loisy viewed the Church, throughout its history, as continuing this community of faith and hope developing its ideas to maintain the deeper continuity of its core religious meaning. Harnack's "historical Jesus" and "Christianity" were the consequences of sheer arbitrariness; they represented Harnack's own preferences, not the historic Jesus of the historic Church [49].

The official reaction was negative, and the book was banned by the Archbishop of Paris. Though Loisy had thought he showed by solid history that the Catholic Church was the proper and legitimate continuation of the mission of Jesus, and the Catholic cult was founded "in the most indisputable reality of the Gospel, and in the most intimate necessities of religion" [48:258f, as translated in 71:53], he departed from the current Catholic understanding of these matters.

> The conceptions that the Church presents as revealed dogmas are not truths fallen from Heaven, and preserved by religious tradition in the exact form in which they first appeared. The historian sees in them an interpretation of religious facts, acquired by a laborious effort of religious thought. If they are divine in origin and substance, they are human in structure and composition. It is inconceivable that their future should not correspond to their past [49:158f, as translated in 71:53].

Similarly, his view of the Old Testament reveals his view of ecclesiology: "The impartial critic will find that the history of the Israelite nation consists in a series of events ordinary in the life of nations, and in the action of religious men of character much more than ordinary; the whole, events and men, converging in a work greater than themselves, that is to say, in the monotheistic religion" [48:43, as translated in 71:52].

Perhaps we can focus more directly upon the crucial

issues by looking at Loisy's Christology. He declares, "Jesus himself lived on earth in the consciousness of His humanity, and He spoke according to that consciousness; He lived in the consciousness of His Messianic vocation, and He spoke according to the consciousness He had of that vocation." Further,

> The Divinity of Christ is a dogma which has grown in the Christian consciousness, but which was not expressly formulated in the Gospel; it existed only in germ in the notion of the Messias, son of God. No principle of theology, no definition of the Church oblige us to admit that Jesus made any formal declaration of it to His disciples before His death. It is, on the contrary, very conformable to the spirit of Catholic tradition to suppose that this revelation was gradually affirmed.

Again,

> The revelation of the Messianic secret was really made by the Spirit who acted on the community of the first faithful. . . . The many heresies on this subject could not have existed without some cause. If the belief had been clear from the first it would not have made its way with so much difficulty. For the historian the work of Christian tradition is a continuation of that of the writers of the New Testament. The whole represents the continued effort of faith to lay firmer hold of an object that surpasses it. This effort moves gropingly; it does not at once attain its term; one may say that, in a sense, it has not attained it yet, but it follows ever the same line, placing Jesus ever higher, and giving a more comprehensive idea of His mission in proportion as a larger aspect of the world and of humanity opens itself out to the eyes of a more intelligent faith [48:116ff, as translated in 71:87f].

Moreover, the resurrection of our Lord is not a simple event like any other, to be proved by the indirect physical evidence of the "empty tomb." Indeed, it cannot be proved historically by "the historian who approaches the question without preliminary faith" [49:74ff, as translated in 71:86].

The Church, at this time completely out of touch with modern ideas and seeing them whenever they appeared as possibly dangerous, was quite incapable of understanding what was said here. The teachings of the current Church were as follows. "First of all, the historical fact of the Resurrection was not only an article of our Creed, but was also a main proof and support of it." "Secondly, we were taught that Christ definitely affirmed His own Divinity." "Thirdly, in virtue of the Hypostatic Union [Christ's uniting in his person the divine and human natures as defined as Nicea and Chalcedon], He possessed, even as man, a certain omniscience." "Fourthly, the Church was His direct foundation; her hierarchy and her sacraments were His direct institution; every one of her definitions was, explicitly or implicitly, included in His teaching" [71:84f].

> The existence of many schools and countless volumes of theology is a proof that, even without the work of criticism, there were many possible points of view in regard to these as to other doctrines, and it is not to be supposed that the work of theology had been brought to a close. But as criticism made, at last, its way within the Catholic Church, such was the position which it encountered [71:85].

What the Church taught was a highly defined, highly specific, highly fixed view of itself and its origins and development. It saw itself a fixed entity, established in all essentials, full blown from the words of its divine founder. Such an entity might have a career, but it had no genuine history. More conservative people than Loisy—Newman, for example —had seen the necessity of introducing a Catholic theory of dogmatic development, but such ideas were not well received in Rome [62]. The Church insisted on seeing the increasing accumulation of dogmatic definitions as something other than dogmatic growth. It was simply making explicit what was implicit in the scripture and the tradition—the latter a concept bristling with difficulties.

The Church now paid the price of its high-handed repression of every intelligent attempt to bring it into the 19th century in being completely unprepared to see what was really at issue here. The official Church no more grasped what Loisy was trying to do than Bossuet had understood what Richard Simon was doing. It has been said that people like Loisy "abandoned tradition" and risked losing the fundamentals of Catholicism, that a "work of adaptation had been transformed into a work of demolition" [18:301]. But would this have been the case had not authority for so long sought protection in the prolongation of archaic intellectual attitudes by repression and thereby inhibited the normal historical processes of thought within the Catholic body?

A conservative historian summarizes what the Church officialdom and its conservative supporters saw in these developments:

> All teaching and dogmatic formulation, Loisy insists, is conditioned by its times, and this rule applies to the times of the Gospel as well to any other. So he does not treat of the New Testament as of a *depositum fidei*, to be explained and developed but never *changed* by the Church, he treats it rather as something in itself subject to change, and it was in treating *development* as though it were *change* that the essence of his heresy consisted [31:181].

This set of problems gave rise to "a widespread intellectual agitation." The Church saw in all this a demolition of that bureaucracy of the spirit which it had all too frequently confused with spiritual health and the peace that passeth understanding. Frightened by the basic issue of how to put together transcendence and immanence, and unsure of itself in a new intellectual milieu, it tended to see here "haste, lack of wisdom, and rashness . . . and . . . the work of destruction for which many modernists finally became responsible . . ." [18:305] and to respond with panic. Galileo was being told this time that, though the earth move, the Church does not.

What does it mean to speak of *development* and to say that it is not *change?* Does development involve discontinuity as well as continuity? What indeed is it that impinged so traumatically upon the Catholic mentality? Something central to Catholic faith is involved here: What is it that from a Catholic point of view may be said to change and what not to change in the course of the Church's life; what is it that may properly be viewed as *in history* and involved in the historical process, and what is it that must be considered as *transcending history?*

The question is obviously a subtle one laden with its own intrinsic difficulties. It was, in the circumstances, made more difficult by two facts. First of all, there was a tendency toward hysteria in conservative Catholic circles when they perceived that the faith was endangered, a tendency prepared and exaggerated by the defensive posture and self-inflicted provincialism of the preceding decades. Secondly, there existed at the time no language in which careful distinctions might be made and areas of confusion sorted out. Such a language would at least have provided the technical instrument for calm intellectual discussion if the hysteria did not rule out the possibility in any case. The modernists used the current language of science and history, which had picked up objectionable connotations from the Protestant and rationalist milieus in which they had been developed. They also made use of traditional language, which they understood in a more historical and more psychological manner. The conservative churchmen used the old language—that is, they used the scholastic categories as they understood them after the long period of scholastic decline and the latent distortions of their own crypto-rationalism. The verbal fundamentalism of the conservatives and the scientific and critical language of the modern scholars and thinkers lacked any common medium for discussion. We must recall that we today have become much more aware of the extent to which scientific and philosophical problems may be complicated by linguistic factors than was even the scientific milieu of that period.

Consequently there was, to put it mildly, considerable misunderstanding! The Church saw Loisy as leaving nothing outside of history and thereby destroying transcendence; Loisy saw the Church as confusing what is genuinely permanent and transcendent with its own temperally conditioned attempts to grasp and formulate it. To Loisy this behavior seemed to destroy transcendence since it made what was transcendent coincidental with historically conditioned expressions. And the latter could only appear dated and even obsolete to later generations and render it absurd to minds trained in the newer social sciences and aware of the genuine expansion of modern consciousness. What Loisy was striving to formulate in his own historically conditioned way was that the core of faith is not easily defined or permanently defined adequately in any language, but it is genuinely transcendent and the Church is its guardian.

If Loisy did not meet the Catholic requirements by not possessing a language for talking about what is timeless—by remaining a man of his period and too "historical"—the Church, by insisting upon a fundamentalist position in seeing itself and its verbal conceptions untouched in any profound way by ambience and history, failed completely to meet the question. It countered it with a sheer verbal fundamentalism within the context of an authoritarian and indeed autocratic organization. The problem posed by Loisy could not be made to disappear by exorcism, and the Church could not be made into an ahistorical magical phenomenon by Latin logomachy; on the other hand, the core problem bothering the conservatives was no less real for their inability to state it intelligently. Could an ineffable transcendent be made the object of a human attitude and relation in any but the most fleeting and effervescent way unless it could somehow be reduced satisfactorily to verbal formulation? Some verbalization was certainly necessary to keep a grip on it in the midst of flux. And could the reality and immediacy of God and the sense of the genuinely real function of the Church as a mediating agency be kept a central element in the Catholic religious consciousness if all verbal statement was completely historically relative?

Here the problem of substance versus process, of ontology versus history, which we found lurking beneath the formulations of the Second Vatican Council's *Dogmatic Constitution on the Church* arose in a most threatening form in an ecclesiastical milieu not at all prepared to face it. If all was flux, then all sense of direction was gone; if all was historically specific and culturally relative, then all secure relation to the transcendent had vanished. It is this open abyss that we see beneath all the Aesopian language of the ultramontane apologists. They seek the sense of direction and the transcendent element in a strengthened central authority. Some said that it was necessary to protect the little ones from scandal. But here all were little ones; all were unprepared to face the intellectual, historical, and psychological implications of the new advances in human knowledge. These advances were not simply a matter of quantitative accumulation; they wrought a change of perspective and consequently a change in the structure of mentality. The shock of the encounter derived from the fearful anticipation of a loss of all structure for faith.

In Father George Tyrrell, a Dubliner converted from Anglicanism to Roman Catholicism, modernism found its religious thinker and its proto psychologist. (The same may be said for Maurice Blondel in France. Blondel, however, missed being condemned by a hairbreadth. His ideas found little favor among Catholic thinkers for some time after the modernist crisis.) Tyrrell, like Blondel, saw that the facile verbalism which had come to characterize the current Catholic apologetic was both unsound and unconvincing. It was unsound because it had lost vitalizing contact with the inner realities of men and their real motivations and orientations in their situations of life. It was unconvincing because it spoke a language which fell on deaf ears when addressed to men of that time.

Tyrrell emphasized the importance of the interior energic character of man; he saw man as composed, in a centrally significant way, of his will. Religion, he felt, was based in "the impulse of the spirit—of the religious sense—that drives us to action and experiment, and enables us thereby to build up a system of religious doctrine for our practical guidance" [91:43]. Deep forces in men pushed them to action; the deepest pushed them to religious action. Experience and relationship were fundamental; their definitions were secondary. The purpose of theology was not to erect an intellectual edifice for its own sake but to clarify experience and choice in the service of the life of prayer. Revelation itself was a matter of experience—experience that transcended its verbal description or statement. It was not the imparting of dogmatic definitions. "Thus the Creeds of the Church are directly the creation of her collective human mind, but guided by her collective religious experience—by the spirit of Christ that is immanent in all her members. This, no doubt, modifies the truth-value of our Creeds. They are not divine statements, but human statements inspired by divine experience" [93, quoted in 71:60]. Tyrrell's opponents called this view immanentism, but it must be recalled that they themselves embraced a specious verbal transcendentism. It must also be recalled that Tyrrell based his view upon a lively sense and an authentic conviction of the reality of the transcendent and the reality and genuineness of man's relationship to it in the Church.

What may be seen emerging in both Loisy and Tyrrell is an idea of a religion that is not simply transcendent in some respects and historical in others. And that in ways easily distinguishable by the conventional theologian of the diocesan seminary.

This subtle and difficult problem area, still very real and very much with the Church, is handled in practical matters by a kind of Aesopian language of nuance. There is a complicated graded set of distinctions and qualifications to be applied in a sophisticated interpretation of the Church's teaching. The distinctions go from ordinary magisterium through extraordinary magisterium to papal infallibility. The last notion is hedged about by a host of qualifying conceptions. Moreover, all statements of ecclesiastical authority are to be understood in reference to their historical context. No area ever needed a careful, thorough study—neither apologetic nor polemic—more than this one. For example, it is said that the ban on artificial contraception was taught by extraordinary magisterium but not papal infallibility. But who will do such a study!

Rather, they regard Christianity as in its deepest reality simultaneously transcendent and historical. They see human experience as complex and not unilinearly verbal. (Larger, in McLuhan's terms, than what the man of print can level out in his medium!) They consider the experience of religion similarly complex and many-sided. Father Tyrrell added to Loisy's historicism psychological insights that anticipated the later psychology of our day—both the Gestalt and the dynamic schools. Loisy and Tyrrell taken together suggest a view of history as a process which involves the evolution of the forms of human consciousness. Man is making himself and his thought forms as well as his forms of feeling and emotion in his historical experience. Both held that men evolved these forms in relation to a "Beyond" (the word is Tyrrell's), to a transcendental realm. They saw the Church as the special community for the continuation of the experience of the original revelation. They saw also that other religions were not simply error but shared to some degree in this process. But the special character of the Church was important to them. "In regarding the 'institutionising' of Christianity as a corruption; in vainly hoping to perpetuate and generalize the 'inspirational' phase, Protestantism seems to me to ignore universal and natural laws" [91:60].

Maurice Blondel in his work *L'Action* [9] also tried to recognize the reality of immanence and to reconcile it with the reality of transcendence. His analysis of human action was both profound and useful to Christian apologetic. It represented an effort to find life and reality and to escape from verbalism and desiccated "intellectualism." It stressed the ideas of "becoming" and "experience." "Action, as he understood it, was the complete spiritual life, made up of the interplay of all the faculties—intelligence, emotions, and will—and was found fully only in God." Blondel was, of course, "accused of implying solipsism and fideism" [18:299].

Another important phenomenon classified by ecclesiastical writers with modernism was the attempt to develop a Christian democracy. Men like Romolo Murri, Luigi Sturzo, Marc Sangnier, and others tried to foster a popular Christian democratic movement. They are the real founders of the Catholic Christian democracy that played so strategic a role in Europe after World War II and remains important in Europe and Latin America. The objective was a rapprochement with the left-wing working class and to some extent with socialism. Here too the Church was unprepared. Its transcendent ideas were again quite unhistorical! In a *motu proprio* given on December 18, 1903, Piux X told the left-wing Catholics that it was "in conformity with the order established by God that there should be in human society, princes and subjects, patrons and proletariat, rich and poor, learned and ignorant, nobles and plebeians." In a letter to the French bishops dated August 25, 1910, condemning the left Catholic movement "Sillon," which had been extremely successful in France, Pius X quoted Leo XIII, pointing out that "a Christian democracy 'should maintain that distinction of classes which is proper to a well-constituted city, and should seek, for human society, the character that God, its author, has given it." Pius and his advisers really believed in—were taken in by, would be more accurate—their verbal realism. They seemed undaunted in probing and formulating God's intention for human history. While this is not infallible papal teaching but simply—and how simply!—extraordinary magisterium, it is not an impressive example of the capacity of the Church to formulate timeless truths free of the conditioning effects of historical situations.

On July 4, 1907, Pope Pius X issued a second syllabus, the *Lamentabili Sane Exitu*. This decree stated that, because of the "fervor for novelties" which characterized the times, errors were being taught "under the color of science and progress." These the pope divided into two main groups, one concerned with the scriptures and the other with faith and dogma. In the first category he listed 38 erroneous propositions; in the second, 27. They all expressed "dangerous errors concerning the natural sciences, the interpretation of Holy Scripture, and the principal mysteries of the faith." Dansette remarks, "In fact, most of them were taken from Loisy. One came from Le Roy and one from Father Tyrrell" [18:305].

In so far as these interpretations were repetitions of previous censures and definitions, pronounced by Pius IX and Leo XIII, they had as their object to reaffirm the fundamental idea of an objective revelation, disclosed in Scripture, and safeguarded by the Church. In so far as they were new, they were concerned to insist upon the integral truth and historical authenticity of the Gospels, (especially that of Saint John), of the sacraments of the Church, and of the primacy of the Holy See. These historic dogmas were the skeleton of the Faith; they might be capable of development, in Newman's sense of the word, but they could not be *changed*, since they owed their principle and origin to the teaching of Jesus Himself [31:186].

The decree was the work of one of the Roman congregations and, "according to Monsignor Mignot, did not involve either the personal or incommunicable infallibility, nor the infallibility of the Church itself. But he added that the judgments thus expressed had particular authority because they were written with the agreement and confirmation of the Holy Father" [18:306]. This sociological device makes them binding now when they are deemed useful and capable of abandonment later, should that prove necessary. (This is not Machiavellianism but a development in a very old legal system which has had time to work out various ways of handling practical problems.)

Two months later, on September 8, came the encyclical *Pascendi Gregis*. Many have complained of the injustice of this document. Vidler pointed out that it caricatured the movement [97:1ff]. The encyclical drew upon the writings of modernists, putting together various points of view and integrating them into a single ideal typical "modernist" position. It then attributed this position to the modernists and condemned it and them. "The Holy Father," explained Monsignor Dadolle, Bishop of Dijon, "has given what I might call an encyclopedist description of the modernist, describing a person who, it must be admitted, does not exist. We know of no one writer covering a field as vast as the one described by Pius X and whose work shows all the aspects of the picture presented" [18:306]. Two thirds of the encyclical was taken up with this presentation. Pius found the two basic errors of the modernists to be "agnosticism" and "immanentism." "Taken together they represented a playing down of the rational element in religion and a playing up of the intuitional, subjective, and romantic element." The encyclical points out that its ideal typical modernists leave science and historical criticism free of religious supervision and control even when treating the gospels or the sacraments. *Lamentabili Sane Exitu* had declared the following proposition erroneous: "As it is only revealed truths that are contained in the deposit of faith it appertains in no respect to the Church to pass judgment on the assertions of human science." In *Pascendi Gregis* Piux X declares, "Complete freedom of science in relation to faith; rather, indeed, enslavement of faith to science."

A French Catholic historian offers a summary:

> The errors mentioned included agnosticism with regard to rational proofs; the doctrine of vital immanence, which derived religious truth from the individual need for faith and gave it no more than symbolic importance, attributing the origin of dogmas to the perception of God by the intelligence in man's innermost consciousness; attributing the origin of the sacraments to the need to give religion a tangible aspect and to make it

known; and denying the place of the supernatural in history [18:306].

Obviously the problems involved in and caused by the need of a new language to discuss the issue continue to plague the treatment of Catholic historians.

The last part of the encyclical presents a series of demands attributed to the modernists calling for reform of the Church, intellectual reforms, reforms in seminary education, reduction of multiplying popular devotions, reform of Church government, and reform of moral theology. These are all repudiated. Says Pius X, "Note here, Venerable Brethren, the appearance already of that most pernicious doctrine which would make the laity a factor of progress in the Church."

Pascendi Gregis reinstates and reasserts the one-sidedness of the Council of Trent and of the First Vatican Council. It reaffirms a literalist notion of revelation and sacred community not unlike that of the most anachronistic position of fundamentalist Protestantism and the Torah Min Sinai of orthodox Judaism. It asserts a substantive and unhistorical view of man repeated parrot-like from earlier ages with no recognition of the real import of contemporary learning, and does the same with respect to the history of the Church. It amounts to a rejection of the basic insights that today have become premises of psychology and the social sciences.

The encyclical suggests the condition of desperation to which this encounter with modernity, coming after four centuries of retreat, had reduced the Catholic Church. Its tone and diction in condemning the "compendium of all heresies" reveal the state of mind. The modernist view is called "a delirium," "insanity," and "audacious sacrilege." It is a "monstrosity," and Modernists are characterized as guilty of "pride and obstinacy," as having lost all "sense of modesty," and as being the most "pernicious of all adversaries of the Church" because they "are within her" and because they "lay the axe to the root not the branches." The encyclical "called for a weeding out among the staffs of faculties and seminaries, the nomination of a censor for each Catholic publication, the institution of a watch committee in each diocese." Modernist literature was not to be read in seminaries (M. J. Lagrange's works were forbidden as seminary textbooks although they were not put on the Index), and bishops were to report to Rome every three years on the doctrinal condition of their clergy.

> To soften the rigour of these articles, and to meet the "ancient calumny which portrays the Church as the enemy of science and progress," the Pope announced the foundation of an International Catholic Institute of learned men who, "with Catholic truth as light and guide," shall "foster the progress of all that could rightly be called science and erudition." Little as yet has come of this project; but the precautionary measures outlined in the seven articles were undertaken with some industry [31: 188f].

Between 1908 and 1913 there followed a series of disciplinary measures. Books and other publications were placed on the Index. On September 8, 1910 (by this time Loisy had left the Church and Father Tyrrell was dead), Pius X published a *motu proprio* entitled *Sacorum Antistitum*, in which he recalled *Pascendi Gregis* and stated that modernism was still strong and further measures were necessary. Said one Catholic historian, "In this group of repressive and preventative measures were some that seemed excessive and even unjustified. There have always been cases like that of Galileo and there always will be" [18:307].

These measures included the "anti-modernist oath," which was prescribed for the clergy with few exceptions. (A heretical Protestant government would not allow it to be taken by priests on the faculty of German universities, and Rome, always respectful in those days of a political order which is ordained of God, agreed.) The oath well illustrates what we have called fundamentalist verbalism. It says, for example, "I admit of external proofs of revelation, and acknowledge certain divine facts, in particular miracles and prophecies, to be most convincing signs of the divine origin of the Christian religion; and I hold them to be perfectly pro-portioned to the intelligence of men of all ages, and also in our own day." One wonders what young priests, the products of the protected conditions of the monitored seminary education, thought such a paragraph was about! More knowledgeable men had to turn to the strategy of nuance to take this seri-ously, to resort to a kind of do-it-yourself Dupanloup: per-fectly proportioned for all ages in "thesis," but not in "hy-pothesis" for ourselves or our contemporaries! No wonder George Tyrrell could have written, "Is this what Catholicism has come to—so grand a name for so mean a thing?" [92:185].

Thus the reaction to the frightening challenge of modern-ism stiffened the emotion-laden intellectual rigidity charac-terizing what was then the official Catholic position. Thus was stopped short all the efforts to bring the Church into anything resembling a creative encounter with modern thought and society. A creative upsurge was cut off, a promis-ing awakening destroyed.

> Through the encouragement of Monsignor d'Hulst, the first international scientific congress of Catholics was held in 1888. Four others followed, the last taking place in 1900. The object was to bring Catholic scientists together and to provide theolo-gians with the means of countering the scorn of the intellectual world toward the faith and the slothful mistrust of the religious world for science. The congresses ceased when Monsignor d'Hulst was no longer there to inspire them, and when the development of modernism made such gatherings temerarious [18:300].

For some time Catholic biblical studies "came to a standstill." Indeed, "stringent measures of defense were adopted by the Church authorities, and for some years anything that savored of 'novelty' in exegesis became suspect." More than that, "the very term 'higher criticism' became synonymous with 'ration-alistic criticism' " [22:63].

The encyclical *Pascendi* enjoined bishops to keep a watchful eye on men and ideas and to treat with severity priests imbued with modernism. This made an exaggerated reaction all the more likely, following the condemnation of modernism. As Monsignor Mignot remarked, "The disciplinary part is extremely serious because it leaves an open door to delations." It was also serious because it required plenty of discernment and a calm sense of justice from those responsible for applying it. It became deadly when the seal of the authorities was excited by the intervention of men who held no mandate except from themselves, whose chief means of action were spying and denunciation and who, taking advantage of the confusion to which the idea of modernism gave rise, treated as heresiarchs Catholics anxious to reconcile modern liberties with ecclesiastical discipline [18:310f].

There arose at that time the phenomenon known as "integrism" (or "integralism"), a strident right-wing Catholic reaction against modernity. Through the activities of the German occupation police in Belgium during the First World War, the world became aware of a secret federation of right-wing groups known as the *Sapinière* [18:311]. "The *Sapinière* co-ordinated resistance to modernism and 'demochristianity,' and to inter-confessionalism, behind all of which it saw an international judeo-masonic plot against the Church" [18:311]. During this period, in part because of the influence of the organized rightists—prelates with integrist sympathies were important in the Roman congregations— Catholics suspected of liberalism and modernism were severely treated, while the integrists carried on their activities and attacked important Catholic men, institutions, and publications. One historian has said that in America churchmen "became so antimodernist that the infant intellectual life of the Church was retarded" [17:215]. Indeed it may be asked whether it was not the results of this antimodernism that gave the American Church the same integralist character it had until after World War II, which kept so many hopeful prospects of 19th century American Catholic history from fruition. Until 1914 none of the integrist publications were placed on the Index save two attacking Pope Leo XIII and his policies. Not until the accession of Benedict XV was an end put to the integrist excesses. Said Benedict in his first encyclical, *Ad Beatissimi*, "It is above all necessary to end conflicts and disputes between Catholics, of whatever kind they may be." What Monsignor Mignot had called a real sense of terror in the Catholic world would soon be over. The many ideas raised by the modernists could now slowly and cautiously be reconsidered.

The Catholic Church had experienced a most thorough crisis—a confrontation that rocked its faith in a fundamental way. It had come upon the abyss that modern knowledge reveals in the flux of process. Almost losing hold of its ancient beliefs, now encased in the hardened chrysalis of outdated verbalism, it had reacted in ways typical of all severely threatened communities. Being based upon shared ideas rather than upon the bonds of ethnic or family solidarity, the Church was particularly vulnerable to threats of an ideational character.

> Gerhart Lenski found in the Detroit Survey that of all religious groups Catholics were predominantly integrated into the Church by "associational" ties rather than "communal" ties. The Jews were integrated predominantly by the "communal" [46:17ff, 32ff]. These categorizations—associational and communal—derive from Toennies' concepts *Gesellschaft* and *Gemeinschaft*. The findings emphasize once again the importance of ties based upon formal assent in Catholicism and hence the vulnerability of Catholics to ideas affecting their religious life.

It met this frightening challenge with what was basically a fundamentalist response—with its own functional equivalent of a "nativist reaction." Throughout the century, centralized authoritarianism in the Church had been increasing as part of the defense against the threats of modernity. Now centralized authority had responded with all the vigor at its command to limit the ideational field of Catholic activity and thought. Moreover, there was loosed within the ranks of the clergy a kind of hysteria, a clerical equivalent of witch hunting. The result was an ecclesiastical "Stalinism" combined with a sacerdotal "McCarthyism." The *Sapinière*, with its quasi-paranoid visions of a "judeo-masonic plot," brought once more into the picture the antisemitism long associated with nativist reactions in Europe (and to continue to be so associated in the 20th century!) and prominently indulged in by Catholics at the time of the Dreyfus affair.

What had happened, in brief, was this: One side stated its case in terms of the new historical and scientific insights, using the languages of science and history and attempting at times to use also older theological terms in a new sense. The other side, recognizing the genuine threat which such new knowledge and perspective might offer to the ancient faith, and feeling especially its undermining effects upon that faith conceived in the static concepts of an outdated philosophy, reacted strongly. The reality and immediacy of God and the realistic understanding of the Church as mediator were threatened. Were these modernists saying that Catholic faith was merely "symbolic"? Were they denying it genuine reality? To those who could understand genuine reality in no other sense than verbal realism, such seemed to be the case. Consequently everything started to give, to dissolve, to become lost in historical process. The conservative clergy reacted with their defense mechanisms rather than their heads. They tried to make verbal definitions simply and simplistically an Archimedean island in the whirlpool of the Heraclitean flux — and to insist upon it with all the power at their disposal. Becoming frightened, they sought the recourse to power.

The Church insisted that the human intellect could know God from his effects, that the historical proofs of Christ's divinity were perfectly proportioned to the minds of men of all times, that there was an objective supernatural order adequately defined by the Church's doctrine. It called its critics insane, delirious, and audaciously sacrilegious. It did not occur to men brought up with such an essentialist and verbalist education and so ignorant of psychology and history to wonder why, if all the things they insisted on were actually true and not simply symbols of loyalty among frightened men, it was necessary so punitively to enforce belief in them! And if the opponents were insane, why did an insanity which consisted simply in discussing ideas call forth such fear and recrimination? Pius X and his supporters acted out the terrible irony of their situation—a situation that recapitulated the history of four hundred years—which concentrated in one intense point the overwhelming threat so little understood but so thoroughly felt, the living proof of the "immanentism" they were denying! Yet from this extreme, too, Catholicism was to recover. Beneath it all, it had preserved in devout minds the core of faith. Even this unseemly fanaticism would not destroy its genuine religious riches.

Two world wars would break out, and the traditional order, on the retreat throughout the 19th century, would vanish before new revolutions and the rapid development of technology. The "liberal" world, against which Pius IX fought such a bitter rearguard action, would become the conservative world. Change and the "regrettable fervor for novelties" decried by the 19th century popes spread across the entire globe, now more disorganized yet simultaneously more united than ever before. But the questions raised by the 19th century and restated in such challenging form by the modernists would remain the concern of thoughtful Catholics. The latter slowly began to express themselves as the antimodernist rigidity slowly began to "thaw." The strategy hit upon seemed to be an admission that modernism had been a short-circuited attempt and that its dangers must be avoided. And on this basis the new thinkers started to raise the central issues once again. In the process the use of caution and qualification in raising questions and of nuance in interpreting old decisions and disciplines became important. Earlier men who were far less extreme than Loisy had been struck down. Monsignor Battifol tried hard to dissociate himself from the condemned modernists, even to the extent of claiming that he had anticipated the *Pascendi Gregis*, but it availed him little. His book *L'Eucharistie* was placed on the Index, and he was himself removed from the rectorship of the Institut Catholique in Toulouse, a position he had held for a decade. Père M. J. Lagrange also found himself in considerable difficulty. Now a new beginning had to be made slowly.

Yet made it was. In the early years after World War I evidences of this new beginning were apparent. Karl Adam brought out two books, *The Spirit of Catholicism* in 1929 and *Christ Our Brother* in 1931, neither of which could have been published by a theologian one or two decades before. The posthumously published work of Léonce de Grandmaison, *Jesus Christ: His Person, His Message, His Credentials*, while adhering to the conservative positions, does so in a spirit which takes account of the findings of modern scholarship. In his *Spirit of Catholicism*, Karl Adam in fact attempts to reinterpret by the use of nuance the meaning and import of *Pascendi Gregis* and the antimodernist oath. They do not rule out the historical method, he says, but simply forbid "that men should make the affirmation of supernatural faith dependent exclusively on the results of this method, thereby subjecting it wholly to philologers and historians, and to profane science" [97:231]. At any rate by 1922 Miss Petre noted in the *Hibbert Journal* (April) that theological writings not entirely traditionalist were being tolerated in Catholic circles, and Giorgio la Piana suggested in the *Harvard Theological Review* (July) that some revision of traditionally understood orthodoxy was being put forward even by conservative Catholic thinkers. Alec R. Vidler, who felt in 1934 that in the course of time the antimodernist condemnations and the practical measures adopted to enforce them would "be emptied of their worst meaning," nevertheless thought acclimatization of "new knowledge about the Bible and Christian origins" in the Vatican not likely very soon. "The process of neutralizing the anti-modernist excesses will be a long and delicate one," he said [97:228f].

Yet always suspect by the conservatives and always in danger of calling down upon themselves the censures of authority, the Catholic theological intelligentsia continued the work of proto *aggiornamento*. The years following the Second World War saw a veritable Catholic renaissance. In this period there developed the men who were to become the strategically influential *periti* of the Second Vatican Council. Despite their skirmishes and clashes with traditional authority, they carried on. In the early 1950s their work brought from Pius XII the encyclical *Humani Generis*, but, though slowed down, it did continue.

How could Catholic defensive segregation any longer be artificially maintained in the dynamic, disorganized, and rapidly changing world of the third quarter of the 20th century? It was becoming more and more clear that some major change was due. Then came Pope John XXIII and the Second Vatican Council. To the progressive groups in Catholic life it seemed that the words of the Fourth Gospel took on new meaning: *"Fuit homo missus a Deo cui nomen erat Johannes."* Now the problems of the last century and a half would receive an airing under favorable conditions, the like of which was never seen before.

IV

VATICAN II
AND SOME OF ITS PROBLEMS

WE began our analysis originally with a brief consideration of the *Lumen Gentium*, the *Dogmatic Constitution on the Church*. That declaration constitutes the basis for the other 15 documents issued by the Council. It is a fundamental theological statement re-presenting the established and traditional definition of the Church and its mission held by the Roman Catholic Church. Moreover, it is a re-presentation that exhibits two novel characteristics.

First of all, what has been called a "pastoral tone" and "an ecumenical spirit" take the place of the earlier partisan, polemical, immobilist, and formalist presentations of Trent and Vatican I. The original text of this Constitution submitted to the Fathers in 1962 has been characterized by a Protestant observer at the Council as an "ominous sample" of the "siege mentality of pre-conciliar Rome" [70:102f]. The final document was described by the same observer as having "reopened the way to serious and fruitful discussion of Christian unity after four centuries of cloture," and as calling to mind "the spirit of those great Catholic reformers of the sixteenth century (Contarini, Sadoleto, Gropper, Morone) whose efforts on behalf of unity were thwarted then by both the 'Papalists' and the 'Protestants' " [70:103].

Second, we have here a traditional presentation of the Church's self-definition which is open to history and to the concerns of modern men. At the same time, it reemphasizes an earlier eschatology. Its perspective upon the Church is in the words of Henri de Lubac, "at once collective and dynamic" [50:161]. It shows a Church aware of its human frailties and open to self-criticism, a Church recognizing that it "is at the same time holy and always in need of being purified" (art 8), a Church capable of conversation with the world and of changing itself in response to history, while remaining in some mysterious way the paradoxical meeting ground of man and God. In his allocution to the opening of the second session of the Council, Pope Paul VI declared, "The Church is a mystery. It is a reality imbued with the hidden presence of God. It lies, therefore, within the very nature of the Church to be always open to new and greater exploration." This idea of the Church as "mystery" is explored in the first chapter of *Lumen Gentium*. To use the term "mystery" is of course to use the vocabulary of the theologian, not the social scientist. Yet the social scientist must recognize the empirical referents of that word. It means to see the many-sidedness of the Church, which renders it nonreducible to any set of neat theological formulas; to see the possibility for development and change in its structure and the methods of its vocation—the possibility of emergence of new forms; to understand that the relationship to the transcendent is never fully understood and never fully captured in human language. By this kind of recognition the *Lumen Gentium* offers a potentially dynamic and open definition of the Church while preserving its traditionally essential characteristics.

In considering that important document, we identified several points of possible conflict and potential growth. These we saw as bringing together older and newer perspectives, emphases, and interpretations with respect to an understanding of the Church, its role and competence. All of these points, it was suggested, represented different aspects of the great and fundamental encounter between the Church and the modern world. Our examination of the relationships that came into being between the Church and the world of evolving modernity disclosed the increased hostility and profound alienation marking that history. By the end of the 19th century, the world to which the Church stood as remote progenitor and to which it had for centuries been schoolmistress regarded that Church as alien and even, in strategic respects, as enemy. The Second Vatican Council became the dramatic and largely unforeseen occasion for reversing this historic condition.

We saw also that the sociological structure and the specific historical experience of the Church tended to increase its alienation from the world of secular modernity and to maintain it in a posture of aloofness, suspicion, and indeed outright hostility. Viewed now from the postconciliar vantage point, the efforts of the recent popes before John XXIII seem partial, superficial, even petty in the face of the great problems involved in the Church's encounter with the modern world. The basic ideas of the Church in its approach to the world remained static, moralistic, and, in the pejorative sense of the word, condescending.

The *Lumen Gentium* represents a great change, one that found further development in other Council documents. Taken together, they provide guidelines for a renewal of the inner life of the Church and a revamping of the ways the Church will handle its encounter with secularity. The Church

> ... in the middle of the twentieth century ... seemed to be trembling from the shock of the Protestant Reformation, and following her reaction against the new theology of the sixteenth century she had reacted also against the whole general stream of progress in that area of the world's surface where she was, geographically but no longer spiritually, at home. The tremendous dynamic movement that had flung her upon the Graeco-Roman world of the early Christian centuries seemed to have taken shape in a parabolic curve, carrying her now ever farther from the living, moving center of human affairs [12:7f].

The shock of the Reformation was followed by that of the Revolution and of science. The *Lumen Gentium* begins what Butler called an "aggiornamento in depth," the radical undoing of this rigid, long-standing, defensive attitude.

To sociologists since Durkheim, the central problem of all religion is involved in the paradox of simultaneously relating together and segregating the *sacred* and the *profane* [21; 23; 69; 95]. These problems have been variously conceptualized and explored in their different facets by a number of investigators. It has been pointed out that religion, when viewed from a sociological perspective, presents a great dilemma. Religious men and religious institutions are seen to be engaged in trying to live in two basically different dimensions, simultaneously attempting to reconcile two radically heterogeneous spheres of experience: on the one side, the religious, the sacred, the ultimate, the charismatic; on the other, the secular, the profane, the less than ultimate, the everyday [68:98ff]. Many aspects of this complex set of problems, though not without significance for our present analysis, must remain outside it. Suffice it to say that the great historic problem of the Church and the world represents the specific form of expression of the sociological dilemma of religion in Christian history.

A number of critics, some sociologists, some theologians, have pointed out that *religion* and the *sacred* themselves can represent a "worldly" form of thought, organization, and practice. They can lose the sense of ultimacy and of transcendence and hence become corruptions of Christianity. Consequently a conflict between organized religion and secularization, between the sacred and the profane, may indeed embody not only a conflict between ultimacy and less-than-ultimate interests and values of men, not simply a tension between spiritual and transcendent values and the material interests of men in the world, not just the antinomy of "God" and "Mammon." Institutionalized religion, like all institutionalized human activity, comes to express a variety of aspirations and to satisfy a variety of needs. Vested interests come into existence disguised and concealed by the symbols of transcendence and ultimacy. Secularization can often, then, purify institutional religion of the accretions it has collected in its history. Such considerations point out how complex and many-sided is the history of the Christian Church. All these problems dogged the Church's course in the modern period, exaggerated by the defensiveness and rigidity made necessary and inevitable by concern for survival.

The most profound as well as the most embracing view of this historic predicament of the Church and the world is still the one provided us by Ernst Troeltsch in his work *The Social Teaching of the Christian Churches*, and in the continuation of that effort in H. Richard Niebuhr's *Christ and Culture* [63]. Troeltsch saw the underlying tension in Christian life to be the dilemma of how the Christian as a person and the Church as a community responded to the transcendental call of the New Testament and at the same time participated in the life of the general society and in the human enterprises of the age. Obviously this basic tension and the problems derived from it took on different forms according to the different conditions under which Christians and the Church lived. In the ancient world, when the Church was a withdrawn community in the Empire, such problems were of one kind; in the medieval world, over whose formation the Church presided and within which it constituted a central institutional structure, they were of another; in the period following the Renaissance and the Reformation, when a marked secularization of culture became the most fundamental characteristic of the age, they were of still another; and today they assume yet a different form. Solutions in one period, however, become the precedents for later activity, and with the increasing age of the Church, spontaneity and creative response become more difficult. Vatican II represents the beginning of a highly significant "molting process" in this respect.

Troeltsch saw the challenge of the Church and the world finding its expression in three forms of living in the world while attempting to adhere to the transcendent call of Christianity. These three he called "church," "sect," and "mysticism." The Church was the form of the institutionalization of Christianity which compromised with the world; it entered the world in order to affect it but was in the same process greatly affected by the world. The Church represented the conversion of the inner world of Christian values into an objective architectonic value universe; it tended to become an internally differentiated hierarchical community, objectifying in itself and its structure the mediation of God's relation to men. In contradistinction to this view he regarded the sect as the small fellowship of those especially converted, inclined to emphasize subjective religion and rejecting both the world and the Church's compromise with it. Mysticism, to Troeltsch, was an individual response in which men sought their own personal communion and even union with God.

Troeltsch defined the *world* in terms of four areas of human activity—family, politics, economic life, and learning. The early Church met the challenge in these areas in a variety of ways. It accepted the family despite its suspicion of the flesh, and it recognized marriage as a sacrament. At the same time it gave virginity and celibacy a higher value. It recognized the legitimacy of the political and social institutions of the Empire, although in cases such as slavery it tried to reform them to protect individual morality. The Roman institutions of law and government were acknowledged as legitimate and, in ordinary matters which did not touch his religious life or demand idolatry of him, binding upon the Christian. Despite intermittent and at times severe persecution in the first two and a half centuries, the Church never questioned the legitimacy of the state; it never became revolutionary. In relation to economic activity, the Church saw labor as necessary and good, but it was suspicious of commerce and saw in finance a dire danger to the Christian soul. Money making was always viewed with a certain suspicion, and as the occasion of serious temptations. Avarice and greed were considered grave sins, and the Church was always prone to view economic life as consisting of individual efforts to supply needs and a matter for individual morality. In intellectual life the Church accepted the philosophical heritage of pagan an-

tiquity and made use of it in the development and presentation of its own teachings. But this receptivity was selective.
The Christian Fathers tended, in harmony with the specific
intellectual preferences of late antiquity, to reject the more
historical, critical, and natural science aspects of classical
culture. In all these areas the Church worked out a *modus
vivendi*, an accommodation—in Troeltsch's term, a "compromise."

Whether one interprets the message of the New Testament as an "interim ethic" of an eschatological community or
as the invitation to a life in relation to transcendence in the
midst of the present world of the here and now, some kind of
adjustment with life in these four areas had to be made. It
was in the area of the family and of intellectual life, Troeltsch
felt, that the Church made the adjustment most easily. Yet
significantly enough, precisely these two areas are the ones
that have remained principal sources of tension and conflict in
Christian life. Christianity never succeeded in putting together sex and spirituality without marked uneasiness at best.
The early Church remained true to its Hebrew antecedents
and resisted the intrusions of Gnosticism; it accepted the
God of the Old Testament as the Father of the Lord Jesus
Christ. Its rejection of Marcion represented the search for
creative compromise. As a result, being in the world, and the
body as its specific created modality, was defined as good. Yet
the exaltation of chastity denigrated sexuality, and sex was
seen increasingly in practice as evil and dangerous. The
reaction against sexuality to be seen in the late Empire—and
not only in the Church—seems a reaction against the moral
and physical conditions of the time. It provided receptive soil
for Manichean ideas, which in turn strengthened the earlier
revulsion. These attitudes had a profound effect upon the
attitudes of the early Christians.

The problem, indeed, has a deeper root. We can only
suggest it here, but we would do well to keep it in our awareness as we consider the modern problems with which the

Council is concerned. Christianity is based upon the idea of a relationship to a transcendent God through Christ as Mediator. It is a call to transcendence in relation to the Transcendent. As such, it is closely related to the emergence of the ego — the conscious center of self-awareness and self-direction. In the young child, ego is slowly developed in interaction with parents and peers; it requires the holding back and inhibiting of drives and needs which, by demanding immediate expression and satisfaction, would inundate the newly emerging "I." In adulthood, ego remains in a condition of tension with the various elements of human interiority and between interiority and the conditions and demands of the outside world. The ego represents the evolution of a person, although it is not the whole person. Its protection is part of the defense of individuality — of man's refusal to be merely the plaything of fate or the helpless element in cosmic process. In the development of the ego and in its preservation and defense, sex is certainly the strongest drive which can threaten ego dominance. This is attested to by the fact that all societies surround sexual relations and sexual activities with prescriptions and proscriptions. These have in part the function of preventing disruptive social conflict; but in part they serve as protection for the ego.

Early Christianity, concerned with a relation to Transcendence, of necessity concerned itself with a kind of ego development and took up ascetic techniques as aids to it. The ascetic attitude was affected also by the semi-Manichean elements to which we have referred. One consequence was to make sexuality seem the prime foe of the spirit. In this fashion was the tension of spirit and flesh understood. The model of Christian personality became the monastic model, of which celibacy and ascetic discipline were central features. It is significant in this respect to note that liberal and revolutionary ideas and movements in modern times tended to embrace — sometimes timidly and sometimes with extreme enthusiasm — the advocacy of sexual liberation [37].

(Hobsbawn points out that aristocratic mid 17th century free-thinkers were "libertine" in both thought and behavior [37:260]. Such tendencies existed side by side with secularized "puritan" attitudes in the liberal and socialist movements and in opposition to them.)

Christianity had a profound encounter with Greek thought and came out of the experience incorporating into itself important insights of antique intellectual culture. Yet utilization of what was offered by that intellectual world was for the purposes of Christianity. Knowledge for its own sake — other than the knowledge of God — was not seen as an autonomous value. As the Church's teachings hardened into formal doctrine and as its truly religious aspects became part of an overall philosophical view of the world, any radically new hypothesis about the fundamental nature of things was increasingly likely to be experienced as a threat to the already formulated view of man and his world. The tension between faith and reason and that between philosophy and theology, so characteristic of the Christian Middle Ages, bear witness to the continued existence of this problem. The spiritual life was based not only upon the inhibition and control of the passions and drives but also upon the focusing of the mind upon otherworldly realities. It was based upon a discipline of mind and will.

Economic life and political life were seen by the early Church as the performance of necessary functions. Yet they were not organically central to the true vocation of man. No one had yet conceived of the idea, prevalent in our age, that economic capacity can be "developed" and human welfare drastically improved. And in the Empire politics was the domain of elites to which the early Church had little relation, except through the conversion of wealthy Roman matrons who sought escape from their imperial and aristocratic world. The Church considered it a higher calling to accept the challenge refused by the rich young man in the gospel (Mk 10:17–

22; Mt 19:16–22; Lk 18:18–25), and felt it only fitting that those who exercise command recognize the unworthiness of their calling, like the centurion (Mt 8:5–13; Lk 7:1–10). Yet the Church came to bless productive activity, as in the Benedictine monasteries and later the guilds with their patron saints, and to ratify rulership, as in the development of the idea of Christian kingship. It saw its own mission, however, as central to man's vocation—as dominating it. Man was in transit to a beyond; his true fulfillment lay in another world. To the early Church, man's role in the economy was a matter of lot. A lot had fallen to a person, and it was his duty to perform the tasks it involved. Existing as a community of the withdrawn in the older and vaster structure of the Roman Empire, the young Church could hardly have been expected to feel otherwise. But during the Middle Ages and with the rise of the medieval city, a change took place. The Church was older and larger than the society which now developed. The new institutions were affected by the Church's teachings and values. One result was that man's job in the world was seen not simply as one's "lot" but rather as a "calling," a vocation in which he responds to God and does his will. The medieval idea of the calling was mainly passive; it did not become dynamic until much later. Yet the notion of the world's work as a structure of callings was an important development. It represented a more positive putting together of man's job here below and his final end as Christianity conceived it. Specifically, however, religious callings were thought much superior in worth and dignity. The lay life remained religiously inferior, ancillary to the real purpose of man's sojourn upon the earth.

These developments in the history of the Church took place as men sought to live in relation to the call of the gospel under different and changing social and historical circumstances. We must not forget that Christianity began as an eschatological community living in expectation of the *parousia*. Many converts were made in the empire during the time of the Pax Romana. It was a period characterized by a degree of stability and prosperity, a decline of the slave markets, and a comeback for the artisans and the lower middle classes. In this same period, however, the hardening of political and social structures led to a lessened participation and interest in public life. The monarchy—the emperor and the imperial officialdom—came to monopolize the ruling functions. Politics, properly speaking, as a sphere for the expression of human aspirations and an arena for satisfying self-expression, was a thing of the past. The earlier period of the *polis* and *civitas* was over. Men looked inward to find freedom and fulfillment; they turned to spiritual realities—to philosophy as spiritual contemplation, and to religion, even to such a religion of radical alienation from the world as was found in Gnosticism. The inward turning was typical of the age and had its effect upon the lower middle classes. Moderately well off by the modest standards of the time, these people were cut off from rewarding activity. They resorted to religion. Indeed, the modal class of the new converts is found in this group, although converts were made in all strata.

In this situation the Church became the community of the withdrawn—in the world but not of it. It compromised with the world but it was not really a part of it. It was its own community of the inwardly oriented. In time its eschatological expectations were replaced by a sacramental emphasis. Men were related to God through Christ in the worship and sacraments of the Church. Thus was the original transcendent relation continued in the mediatorship of Christ and on earth in the institutional Church. Thus was the original call to transcendence made more otherworldly by the specific cultural temper of the period and by the sectarian situation of the earliest churches. The historical conditioning of the first five centuries increased the otherworldly emphasis potential in Christian values. The challenge of Gnosticism and the need to defend Christian beliefs against Gnostic intrusions led to much rigidifying of thought, organization, and behavior. The

Church emerged as a hierarchically structured community, otherworldly directed, and with its great majority of members in a state of tutelage to the clergy, who had emerged as the official teachers, rulers, and celebrants of the cult.

The fall of the empire brought widespread disorder and led to a general deterioration of life. The harshness of the physical conditions and the decline of the old culture, the precariousness in terms of political irregularity, and the dangers of illness and death, over which man had little preventive control, all conspired to narrow tremendously the opportunities open to men for a satisfying life in the world. To this situation the Church brought its transcendent message, understood and reinterpreted in terms of the inward turning and otherworldly emphases of late antiquity. In the new conditions the indifference to the world characteristic of the Gospels was transformed into a contempt for the world. Monasticism had arisen, and it became the exemplar of the full Christian life—celibate, withdrawn from the world, practicing ascetic exercises, and explicitly concentrated on liturgical behavior.

Thus developed an exaggerated otherworldliness conditioned by the first millennium of Christian history. It found its embodiment in a highly institutionalized hierarchical Church, ruling men's religious and moral lives, teaching them what to believe, and ministering to their spiritual needs according to its established disciplines and sacraments. The marked orientation to otherworldliness and the vested interests of ecclesiastics often combined to produce a disguised but quite real "worldliness." Since the clergy were the only educated members of society for centuries, they were early drawn into the ruling function, a development which in fact tended to secularize them. Yet the world of the layman received little official recognition or legitimation. The sphere of lay activity—in the words of Teilhard de Chardin to Maurice Blondel, what nine tenths of mankind are doing nine tenths of the time: coping with the environment, building up commercial or political structures, creating new communities, pursuing knowledge for its own sake or for its usefulness, making love, getting married and raising children—remained secondary. The Church was concerned with it chiefly as the arena for moral action, over which it saw itself standing as guardian and indeed as policeman.

Although the Church compromised with the world and became a "church" in Troeltsch's sense, nevertheless its original indifference to the world was transformed into contempt of the world, in part as a reaction against the compromise. As Christianity came—as it definitely did with St Thomas—not only to accept the ancient idea of the goodness of God's creation but to grant the legitimate autonomy of a realm of nature, its teaching more and more proposed to the laity a model for Christian living and the development of a Christian personality based upon monasticism. Thus even in the period when it gave birth to a new culture in Europe and infused it with its own values, Christianity was not able genuinely to recognize, in practice or in theory, the values of the lay life. It was incapable of evolving a model of lay Christianity; it could not understand how lay activity in the world might have any considerable spiritual nobility in itself. To use the language of Bishop McGrath, the Church was unable to understand "the proper values of the things and structures and situations of which the life of man is made" [51:410].

The secular values of politics, commercial development and economic affluence; learning for its own sake; the relationship of the sexes—these important human values might be exploited by the church for its own ecclesiastical ends, but they were never given full recognition in their own right. In all these realms of life, the lay classes of the medieval and early modern world asserted the autonomy of secular values against the recalcitrance, and often the open opposition of churchmen. Consequently, from the fourteenth century on, the society of Europe (what had once been Christendom) seceded from the Church and proclaimed the independence and autonomous worth of this-worldly values [68:78].

The Church itself and the dominant elements of Christian thought were not able to affirm the life of man in the earthly city. The Church had provided the value basis upon which Christian man would build the worldly community, yet that community would be built outside the Church to a considerable degree. It may be justly said that the laity seceded. In now open, now subtle, now partial, now complete, revolt, the laity built its own world. Said one of the important new theologians who was also an important *peritus* at the Council,

> During the middle ages the ecclesiastical institution included and formed human society; but from the beginning of the fourteenth century society began slowly to assert its independence. First to cut loose were rulers and their politics, then various activities of urban life and welfare, then thought and the sciences, then morality and spirituality itself, finally, and much more radically, the common consciousness of the people in their daily life of sorrows, joys, hope. . . . Now there was a kind of divorce between . . . community of men who were hardly the faithful anymore and a community of clerics whose problems, activities, interests, language were no longer those of the living human community [16:41].

It is significant that the *Pastoral Constitution on the Church in the Modern World* begins by identifying the Church with the "joys and the hopes, the griefs and the anxieties of the men of this age" (art 1) and that it takes its name from the first Latin words, *Gaudium et spes*.

It was against this revolt—this long process of secession which did not begin with the Reformation and continued long after it—that the Church gradually assumed its defensive posture, its siege mentality. The Reformation was an important part of the secession, which was in many respects a lay revolt, but one in reaction, ironically enough, against the secularization of the Church as well as against its rigid clericalism and ecclesiasticism.

Actually, the presentation we have sketched needs some qualification. It is necessarily oversimplified. From the 12th century on, there did develop a secular world, establishing — at times in alliance with the Church, at times in opposition to it—legitimate spheres of lay activity. A Christian humanism did begin to evolve. The works of Chaucer, of Dante, and of More testify to its depth and vitality. The art of the Middle Ages and the Renaissance, in tempera, in oil, and in stone, speaks the same message. At this time, also, churchmen became worldly in the pejorative sense. It was a period in which an old Church rendered highly complex by a long and varied history struggled in vain —as in the conciliar movement —to reform itself. For a century and a half before 1521, such efforts failed. Protestantism involved all these varied elements, from the pure religious motivation of the devout to the scheming of kings and rulers. Yet the early Reformation was in important ways a reaction against the secularization already achieved, a reaction which, in Troeltsch's words, "swept away such beginnings of a free and secular civilization as had already been toilsomely established"; the reaction's contributions to the rise of modernity were both "against its will" and "indirect and unconsciously produced" [89:138]. What might have developed had not schism and religious conflict intervened is a matter for speculation. One basic fact remains of significance to us here. When the religious conflict broke out in the 1520s, western Christians had not evolved, as a result of their accomplishments in building a lay civilization, a viable model of the Christian layman in the world. The monastic model, adapted to the "compromises" and "inferior" conditions of lay life, remained the basic operative model.

It is significant in this respect that the only Reformation group to develop a new model for life in the world did so on the basis of the older monastic model. Calvinism was successful in offering to new classes a ground for activity in the world and for an identity built upon it. It did this, to use Weber's words, by carrying asceticism "out of monastic cells into everyday life" [101:181]. While favoring the specifically religious calling with its asceticism, Catholicism permitted a laxer behavior of the lukewarm. Calvinism, however, attempted to "remodel the world" along monkish lines [101:181]. Catholicism in general did not pay attention to the content of the calling as long as it was not specifically and formally unethical. But the Calvinist calling was also secularized and lost all reference to its religious origins. In the end, the worldly asceticism which derived from it led to a state in which "material goods have gained an increasing and finally inexorable power over the lives of men as at no previous period in history" [101:181].

The Church had begun as something very like a sect, as Troeltsch defined a sect. However, the Church related itself to the world, compromised with the world, and became a church in Troeltsch's sense. Yet this great development, which created Christendom and left so profound a mark upon European men and European culture, led to an ironic combination: The Church became more worldly but at the same time was rendered incapable of recognizing and doing justice to genuinely secular values. Eventually it emerged as a hierarchically structured institution, its ideals and values spelled out in terms of its own philosophical system, and its chief function defined by itself as the mediation between God and man in preparation for the life to come. It was the vertically structured Church in the two-level universe to which we have earlier made reference, viewing itself as the dispenser of God's grace, a grace already purchased for men by the suffering and death of Christ. Within this community of grace, shared through the sacraments and hence through participation in the merits of Christ, men were for practical purposes free to choose between good and evil. Despite the subtleties of the doctrine of grace and the deep conflicts concerning it among Catholic theologians, in fact the average Catholic felt free to choose good or evil, and felt that he would finally be judged for all eternity on the nature of his choices.

Thus the world, which early Christianity had seen as the cosmic setting for the great drama of human salvation, now, with salvation really accomplished, became instead the arena for the performance of the moral act. Here is the root of that combination of institutionalism and moralism so characteristic of much of modern Catholicism. It was this view which became corrupted by semimagical practices in the distribution of the "treasury of merits" dispensed by the institutional Church, such as the indulgences sold by Chaucer's pardoner and by Luther's Tetzel.

Against this Church, protest and revolt took place. In the north, Protestantism revolted because the Church was too worldly, too secularized, too rigidly overinstitutionalized, too compromised. In the south, humanists revolted because the Church was incapable of affirming wholeheartedly the values of culture and of man's earthly activity.

A significant consequence of the "institutional – moral" view of the Church and its relation to life in the world is that it tended to make the moral aspect of human action the salient and significant one so far as the Church was concerned. The Church saw action, not with its intrinsic aims, expressions, and methods as its defining characteristics, but rather in terms simply of its moral dimension. The clergy considered themselves "sacramental technicians," involved in preparing man for "the last things." To them, the content of other roles as related to man's essential vocation existed only in terms of ethics. The result was a conception of the world in which all lay activity, if it was licit, was of equal worth. Man did these things in support of a higher destiny, and of that destiny the Church stood as custodian. Lay activity was essentially neutral, of little ultimate worth in ontological or religious terms.

Since Christianity was thus incapable of giving secular

values the recognition they demanded, lay classes, with their own needs, aspirations, and potential for creativity, revolted. There developed an autonomous secular civilization which simply pushed Christianity aside. By the 18th century, many countries that remained Catholic developed a militant opposition which would try in the Revolution to bring about the complete demolition of the Church and to erect the secular fraternity of nationhood in its place.

In this situation the Church was driven to an extreme defensiveness. Post-Tridentine Catholicism became in important respects a sect once again. But it became a complex sect—a sect which had been a church and which continued to try to remain a church while events forced it into an increasingly sectarian posture. It was a church in structure but became a sect in spirit. It combined overinstitutionalization, overspecification of doctrine and morals, and overrigid authoritarianism with a more and more militantly withdrawn condition in relation to the world of autonomous civilization which flourished without its gates. The earlier ambiguities of its relation to the world were compounded and made more difficult to comprehend and to handle.

Our consideration of the history of the Church reveals how an institution which provided western civilization with its central values could be rendered peripheral to that civilization as it developed. The institutionalization of its otherworldly orientation under the circumstances of late antiquity and the early Middle Ages did not prepare the Church to be able to grasp the true worth of the unfolding aspirations and actions of lay classes in European history. The growth of religious thought within this historical setting made the combination of the otherworldly view and the institutional – moral view of the human condition appear to possess a certain plausibility. Man was pointed beyond this world; the conditions of this world were in a basic sense either obstacles or helps to his greater destiny.

The only metaphysical language available to the Church

for understanding the structure of existence in the world came from Plato, Aristotle, and the Stoics. From the last it borrowed the idea of law to put together Old Testament morality with Greek rationalism. Plato had indeed anticipated and therefore aided this development of the Church's understanding of itself and its function. In the *Republic*, he had essayed an ontological map of the proper relationship among the elements making up the human constitution, and, by projection, a general outline—in a nonliteral, metaphorical form at least—of what a just human society involved. In Plato's view, existing societies represented concrete forms of deviation from the Idea of the Good. The Church also came to see the world in this manner—in terms, that is, of a static model based upon a permanent and timeless archetype. Catholic thinking regarded the development of modernity as generally a deviation from the right order of this implicit model.

Aristotle, who combined a sense of the rationality of nature with an empiricist epistemology, made this archetypal universal an 'essence realized differently in different settings. In place of Plato's religious conception of the world—demythologized, yet religious—Aristotle set an autonomous nature. In place of Plato's religious conception of man's self-realization in relation to the Form of the Good, Aristotle had men working out the innate potential of a specific natural entelechy. Man was a structured being whose life was the process of realizing his entelechy by the reduction of potency to act. After Thomas Aquinas this notion became part of Catholic thinking. An autonomous nature was seen operating according to its own laws, its own "secondary causes."

Aristotle's empiricist theory of knowledge did not, however, persuade theologians of that age to a more observational and historical view of man, although in the sphere of physics it did lead to experiment and observation in the medieval university, as in the work of Jean Buridan and Nicholas Oresme at the University of Paris. Aristotle's philosophy did direct attention to an autonomous nature and to the central significance of process in nature. Yet it perceived this nature as a closed sphere and this process as the repetitive course of a nature that was basically finished.

In one sense this was a dynamic view—it saw motion as part of nature. In another it was static since it conceived of nature as endlessly following already established paths. All organisms worked out a previously set entelechy. So did man. St Thomas accepted this notion and in the *Summa Contra Gentiles* showed how man could not find final satisfaction in those earthly goods to which his entelechy was ordained. Man pointed beyond to a relationship with God. Man was endowed with a capacity for which he had no corresponding capability. He could reach his fulfillment only beyond nature through grace.

Certainly this doctrine contained dynamic possibilities of interpretation. Yet in the context of the vertical Church, which provided the established and structured paths to that beyond, it became a static doctrine. While it retained a certain personal force and pointed to personal development, it lacked all historicity. Ontology replaced history, and man's activity in the world received no philosophical justification. This was an essential element of the Thomistic view, which Leo XIII reestablished as the official philosophical mode of the modern Church.

Thus we see, not only that Catholicism was outside the dynamic lay currents of modern history which were constructing an unprecedented lay civilization, that historical circumstances had placed it in opposition to new forms of social life and new intellectual perspectives as they developed, but that to reinforce its historically structured position of aloofness and askewness toward modernity the Church was burdened with a static conception of society and of man. What man was doing here below was really significant only with respect to whether or not it deviated from an archetype conceived almost entirely in abstract ethical terms. The chief fulfillment of the human entelechy was to be found not through life in the world but by participation in another world made available through the sacraments of the Church. Morality defined the path to this heavenly Jerusalem proclaimed by the Church, and the sacraments were God's gratuitous aids for man along the path of the earthly pilgrimage. For men as strangers and sojourners the other activities and interests along the way were secondary, though they might be functionally necessary for the journey—government, economic activity, and technology, for example. Building empires, constructing national communities, discovering galaxies and exploring continents, producing the David of the Accademia and the Moses of St Pietro in Vinculi, developing Newtonian physics or non-Euclidean geometries, or the myriad other efforts so laden with meaning for men active in the world—all these in themselves were of only peripheral interest to the Church. The Church was concerned with how they affected its mission (which might lead to quite worldly kinds of involvement under the guise of otherworldliness) and with the moral problems they posed. Plato, Aristotle, institutionalism and moralism, and the historical conditions surrounding the Church all conspired to produce this most serious astigmatism in the Christian vision.

The problem of putting together man's otherworldly destiny as Christianity saw it and man's activity in the world as possessing serious dignity and worth in terms of self-fulfillment persisted. Calvinism came closest to solving it, by introducing the revolutionary alteration of seeing the calling in the world and acknowledging that it had to be rationalized. Spontaneity had to be repressed. All the powers and energies of the human person had to be directed into the methodical performance of the earthly task, no matter what it might be. In a formal sense Calvinism too continued the indifference to specific content characteristic of the older view since any occupation could be a suitable calling. However, it must be noted that once the activity of the calling is placed in the world and becomes a matter to be rationalized—once a worldly calling is given close methodological attention—its content, though left open and unspecified, is no longer irrelevant. The earthly occupation is given dignity by the very fact that the locus of the ascetic practice is now in the world, is now the occupation. Its content becomes worthwhile because individual identity and value are found in its careful and rational performance. Catholicism had never found a way to give earthly callings genuinely religious significance and hence was not able to present a basis for a deeper secular identity that was at the same time religious—at the same time essentially Christian and Catholic. It remained always plagued by the segregation of sacred and profane. A chasm separated supernatural destiny and earthly fulfillment.

We have seen that Catholic culture did in fact find a larger place for lay action and worldly values than did Calvinism. It remained aware of the importance of spontaneity and emotional expression, of art, and of what Sombart called in the larger sense the "erotic." It also retained the loyalty of the two classes which possessed a sense of the worth of nature beyond utility and manipulation: the aristocracy and the peasantry. Catholicism had refused to rationalize life on the basis of total repression in the service of total utility. Consequently, despite its failure to handle the developing lay world, it remained in touch with a broad spectrum of the human potential. This was one of its great hidden assets as it moved into the Second Vatican Council. But never, in the period of pre-conciliar modernity, was it able to harmonize its sensitivity and receptivity to this potential, as seen in artistic and musical accomplishments, with its narrow moralistic concern with the ethical aspects of the lay world. Catholicism's acceptance of a genuine vocation of lay activity, sympathetic understanding of what laymen act out in their varied earthly dramas, and intuitive comprehension of the kinds of aspirations for fulfillment men evolve in different societies and cultures were only partial and pragmatic. To all these it remained theoretically obtuse.

The Calvinist model for lay vocation in the world soon

became secularized, as Max Weber noted. It tended to remain as an unconscious psychological element in many modern mentalities. It was retained as a sense of validation through ascetic discipline now mostly seen as work on the job, but it lost the sense of the religious meaning it had once had. In its secularized version, action might be disciplined and formally ethical, but activity in the world as the center of Christian self-realization in dimensions which do some justice to the human potential was not realized in the bourgeois secularization of the Calvinist calling. Only perhaps in some of the professions, where the intrinsic worth of the activity provided ontological dignity, has this become the case.

The vertical conception of the Church, the ultimate religious insignificance of the lay world, the moralistic concern with human action, and the static model of human realization and of human society—all these characterized the view of churchmen as they confronted the development of the modern world. Deeply involved in the old social order and securely a part of the older political system, the Church was conservative. The conservatism was the result of its "successful" compromise with the world, of the conditioning of its peculiar historical odyssey, which we have considered here, of the reaction to the threats to which change exposed it and which those who advocated change leveled against it, finally of its own ideational history as it developed over time.

It would be unjust to minimize the concern of Leo XIII for the workingman under capitalism or to overlook the quiet heroism of that small group of priests who for decades tried to implement his pronouncements. Yet the famous labor encyclical *Rerum Novarum* and the commentary upon it by Pius XI, *Quadragesimo Anno*, represent a demand for social justice seen in a remarkably conservative and static context. Papal social policy until the pontificate of John XXIII showed little grasp of historicity, little understanding of process, little sense of the genuinely dynamic as ontological attributes of the human condition.

Christianity was the source of the culture of modern Europe. Moreover, as Troeltsch pointed out, despite "all the hostility to the Churches and to Christianity" in the modern world, western culture and values had Christian foundations. To Troeltsch, "individual autonomy," "belief in progress," "confidence in life," and indeed the "impulse to work" were derived from and supported by the Christian heritage [89: 38f]. But Christianity had provided the basis for a great autonomous civilization unintentionally; its world view was a by-product of its deliberate performance of the religious function of the vertical Church. As we have noted before, this otherworldly overarching Church presents a unique socio-religious phenomenon in human history. The Church saw itself as God's agent among men and understood historical reality in terms of its own position and function—its own otherworldly orientation and institutional and moralistic concerns. The new lay classes were Christian and perceived their own places, problems, and aspirations most often in Christian terms, at least until late in the 18th century. Yet they tended to assert the worth of their own activities, the dignity of their own functions, to see human fulfillment according to their own specific needs and longings. Their own functions, they felt, constituted a mission or vocation and suggested a destiny in this world.

Nevertheless, other functions seemed, even to the lay mind, more worthy than work. When the first cities replaced the village and kinship structures of the earlier societies, men assigned a greater merit to the activities of politics and religion. Imperial and sacerdotal bureaucracies monopolized scarce values, material and psychological. Work was seen as servile, illiberal, banal, the appropriate activity for slaves and lower classes. Upper classes were concerned with power over their fellow men. Power over nature through work was not so highly valued. In classical antiquity there existed a strict divorce between learning and work, a social segregation of the strata pursuing each. In the Middle Ages this gap began to close, as the record of useful inventions in that period shows. In the Renaissance the final coming together of the men of thought and the men engaged in practical work gave rise to modern science.

We must recall, however, that only in our own day has the idea of planned economic growth and directed social development become recognized as a centrally significant activity genuinely deserving of the investment of human energies. The ruling classes throughout the ages have acted out dramas of power and domination which, while they became increasingly secularized, never emerged as self-conscious attempts to change man and his world. The new awareness of our day owes much to Marx and the socialist movement, which fought the Church and was fought by it.

It is against this complex background that the work of the Second Vatican Council must be understood, most significantly in the *Pastoral Constitution on the Church in the Modern World*. This document addresses itself to all the problems we have been discussing in the present chapter. To be sure, the Constitution is concerned—and rightfully concerned—with ethics. To be sure, the Constitution still asserts the primacy of man's eternal destiny. To be sure, the Constitution maintains the special character of the specifically religious calling. But these traditional concerns are expressed in a totally new setting and in a completely new spirit. The document is deeply committed to eschewing a narrow moralism and an ahistorical ontologism, and to seeking to comprehend the significance of "man's total vocation" as it is to be observed in our day. To a consideration of this document we must now turn.

V

THE PASTORAL CONSTITUTION
ON THE CHURCH IN THE MODERN WORLD

WRITING in 1922, shortly before his death, Ernst Troeltsch felt that the position of Christianity was a precarious one, that its future was unpredictable. Christianity was, he thought, "at a critical moment of its further development." Moreover, if Christianity was to have any future, "very bold and far-reaching changes were necessary, transcending anything that had yet been achieved by any denomination" [88:60].

The nearly half century that separates Vatican II from Troeltsch's observation saw two important developments in Protestant theology. Again to oversimplify, we may suggest the substance and significance of these developments with the names of Karl Barth and Rudolf Bultmann.

Barth called for a return to the basic meaning of the Bible as the Word of God, for the abandonment of the *Kulturprotestantismus*, whose sociological and cultural bases had been demolished by the First World War. In contrast to the complacent liberalism of the dominant prewar theology, Barth called European man back to transcendence—to an accounting. The uneasy peace ended in 1939 with a second catastrophe, greater even than the first, and the old world, with Europe as its crown and liberal Protestantism its fairest jewel, vanished forever.

In this situation Bultmann came forward in an attempt to free the New Testament message from those archaic and mythical elements that made it incomprehensible to the men of our day. Several centuries of secularization, of scientific development, of technological revolution, and a half century of total war, had deprived western civilization of its older institutional and cultural substance and had removed it from world dominance. The world itself was being "demythologized": its consensually validated convictions were disappearing. Bultmann tried to demythologize the scripture so it could speak once again to the men of this age.

Was Barth's emphasis upon transcendence and Bultmann's attempts to shear off the culturally specific elements in Christian understanding the beginnings of the "very bold and far-reaching changes" which Troeltsch thought necessary? And does the Second Vatican Council represent the "beginnings of these beginnings" within the historic Church of Rome?

To ask these questions is to suggest the magnitude of what needs must be involved in an *"aggiornamento* in depth." We must not think of the Roman Catholic Church as an unchanging monolith, standing recalcitrant and intransigent across the path of history, which has suddenly as by some intervention from on high become an engine of progress and a force for liberation. The preconciliar Roman Church was not unchanging. Indeed, in many of the matters dealt with by the Council—liturgy, the Bible, attitude toward democratic civil government, and others—alterations of considerable scope had been introduced, often on curial initiative and with curial approval. The preconciliar Church was rather the locus of a struggle in which a new spirit attempted to bring about the renewal of the Church, and in which the forces and structures of that ancient organization were, almost of historical necessity, "rigged" or "loaded" against such renewal. Yet whatever historical accidents attended the decision to call a council, the fact is that the time was fast approaching when Rome had to consider what Troeltsch called "very bold and far-reaching changes."

We have already seen that in the century and a half preceding this Council attempts to advocate *aggiornamento* had been put forward by thoughtful Catholics. Although most of them were suppressed, they did have some degree of influence and did create a kind of officially disavowed sub-rosa tradition. Such semirejected traditions, however, are hard to transmit. They do not have at their disposal the resources of the general ecclesiastical community. Consequently there is an element of reinvention in their continual reappearance. What keeps such a tradition alive is much more the continuing need for what it suggests and prescribes than the transmission of its own ideas from one generation to another. Authority could condemn and proscribe, but it could not conjure away the dilemmas to which the proto *aggiornamentists* addressed themselves. Whatever astigmatisms of time and cultural setting—and they were many, of course—may characterize the list we have suggested, from Lamennais and Möhler to Loisy, Tyrrell, and Murri, it becomes more and more clear that they were responding to real existing dimensions of modern civilization, real elements of the human situation as it was experienced by men in the new society which revolution and technology were bringing into the world. The tradition they inaugurated and supplemented never achieved genuine legitimacy. Their ideas had to be either consciously sought or met with by fortuitous accident. Yet from the end of the French Revolution to the close of the Second World War, Catholics invented modernization over and over again. They made repeated attempts at *aggiornamento*. They did not do so because of the institutionalization within the Church of a legitimate opposition party to authoritarian episcopal and ultramontane conservatism. They did so because the meaning of the Catholic faith and the realities of modern life stood in a state of reciprocal challenge in the minds of the educated and intelligently devout. The modern conditions could not be dismissed. They continued to issue their challenge. In fact those elements of modernity which the Church saw as particularly threatening to its traditional institutional and intellectual positions became ever more salient aspects of modern society.

This century and a half came after many previous centuries of change and saw an intensification of it. It was a time of political revolution, of unprecedented technological advance, of social transformation, of scientific development, and of intellectual metamorphosis. It was the time of the German historians—of Ranke, of Harnack, of Troeltsch; of Wellhausen, of Bauer, of Schweitzer. It was the time of the sociologists, from Auguste Comte and Saint-Simon to Emile Durkheim; from Fredinand Toennies and Max Weber to Karl Mannheim. It watched the development of cultural anthropology from Tylor to Boas. It was the era of Marx, Darwin, Freud, and Einstein. It was a time in which both Whig and Liberal England and Revolutionary and bourgeois France passed away, together with Catholic Austria and Spain. Pitt and Gladstone, Robespierre and Bonaparte, Metternich and Thiers—all were gone. The time had witnessed the decline of Europe, torn by two bitter world wars, and the rise of America; the end of czarist Russia and the rise of a new Marxist orthodoxy. It saw the end of empire and the development of the third world.

The third quarter of the twentieth century found a less structured, more insecure, less stable, more open world than man had perhaps ever been in before. It was a world shedding the institutions within whose context it had lived for decades, for centuries, and in some cases for millennia. It was a world being denuded of its illusions and its assurances. It was a world being demythologized. It could be a world come of age, or it could become the scene of frightened and frantic attempts to escape the freedom into which man was emerging. It was a world full of chaos and suffering, and under the threat of nuclear destruction. But it was at the same time a world in which man began to realize that, together with the dissolution of the older contexts of his vanished security and the enormous dangers surrounding him, he was also offered greater promise than at any previous time in his history. Science put within his grasp the instruments for making life truly humane, the tools, material and intellectual, not only for subduing the earth to human designs but also for transforming himself.

To the evolution of this world the Church, officially and in terms of its ordinary teaching, had juxtaposed Gregory XVI, Pius IX, Leo XIII, Pius X, and Pius XII. To this world the Church responded by proclaiming the dogmas of the Immaculate Conception, Papal Infallibility, and the Assumption. To this world the Church had presented the two syllabuses—that of 1864 and that of 1907.

The Church had made a palpably inadequate set of responses, yet to human observation they appear almost inevitable under the circumstances. Small wonder that within its ranks the semioutlawed forces of modernization began to gather momentum once again. The defensive position assumed by the Church, though seemingly inevitable and the predictable consequence of historical conditioning and sociological situation, was becoming obviously less and less tenable. The Church was reaching that point in its development when to remain in its own self-enforced isolation was to lose its catholicity. As Abbot Butler said, "Aggiornamento in depth" became "a pastoral necessity." He wrote,

> A species, when no longer adapted to its actual environment, can evolve, or it can perish. The Church cannot perish. But there is a third possibility. Sometimes a species succeeds in taking refuge in a backwater of existence, where—in diminished numbers and with no further relevance except to historians of past evolution—it prolongs an insignificant story. As we look back on the Church before 1962, do we not sometimes seem to be catching a glimpse of what might have become a monumental irrelevance? [12:7]

It is not easy to understand the multitude of factors that influence such a major restructuring of outlook. The Church's defensive behavior of the previous 150 years is precisely what a sociologist would have predicted had he known all the conditions and been able to look at them with some objectivity.

But the interesting question is, Why did that defensiveness give way to a radical shift of attitude at this point in the Church's history? We have argued that the time was fast approaching when the choice was between change and irrelevance. But that it was recognized was a surprise to all. An Anglican historian had written in 1961,

> If the full measure be taken of the revolutionary changes that have taken place in the worlds of thought and invention, in political and social structures, and in the conditions of living and working, and if the rootedness of the Churches in the pre-revolutionary order or the *ancien regime* be borne in mind, then their survival with so many of their ancient characteristics and appurtenances intact is remarkable, to say the least. They have not survived because they were well-prepared for the turmoil in which they were to be ineluctably involved, nor because, when it came upon them, they showed ready powers of adaptation to new circumstances and of taking time by the forelock. On the contrary, we have seen how recalcitrant they were to change, how blind or short-sighted in the days of visitation, how disposed to stone or silence or jettison the would-be prophets in their midst, and how lacking in the imaginative compassion and sensitive humanity that might have given them a secure standing in the hearts of peoples when they were deprived of earthly privileges and the active support of governments [96:270].

But recognized it somehow was. There were many influences, many changes of conditions. There was, of course, the older liberal Catholic position, quite in the background. There were the slow thaw in theology and biblical studies and the new developments of the postwar years. There were the continuing external conditions, the continuing challenge, the brute facts of reality that could be conjured away neither by the prayers of the pious nor by the regulations of the authoritarians.

Most important was the fact that the "defeats" suffered by the institutional Church did have the end effect of uprooting it. The Church was no longer a part of the traditional culture, no longer integrated into a conservative institutional complex central to civil society. It was now "freed" from that earlier outmoded "incarnation"—freed against its majority will, no doubt, but not less free for that. The greater part of its "vested interests" had been taken away from it by history. It was now free to seek new ways to embody itself in the life of 20th century man. In Europe the Church was no longer part of the old order. In the mission regions of the world, the breakup of imperialism put churchmen in touch with the most advanced and at times the most chaotic realities; in America and throughout the entire "oceanic" Church, the Church was functionally a denomination in a pluralist society.

Shortly before his death in 1878, Pope Pius IX, who had fought so valiantly to preserve the Church in the only way he knew how—by defending its concrete form of organization and doctrine—is reported to have said the following: "I hope my successor will be as much attached to the Church as I have been and will have as keen a desire to do good: beyond that, I can see that everything has changed; my system and my policies have had their day, but I am too old to change my course; that will be the task of my successor" [96:153]. Pius IX did not find his true successor until John XXIII, who called the Council in which the great change came to fruition.

A council offered a new kind of arena for the activity of the forces of modernization, at that time working under difficulties and official disapproval. The first significant fact to note in this respect is an obvious but a structurally strategic one. A council is a place of discussion, and discussion means that problems are faced in the discursive mode—not in action but in discourse. They are talked about. Talking about them requires that they be defined in general terms and thought about. By its very structure a council gives genuine leverage to those who are skillful in the intellectual sphere. It gives an advantage to the intellectuals.

From the 19th century on, bishops assumed the role of functionaries—of bureaucrats. They held an office in a hierarchical structure. Catholic theology considered them "successors to the Apostles," and canon law defined the episcopal office as possessing "ordinary authority," that is, authority in its own right, not authority delegated by the pope. Yet this older version of the bishop's office was embedded in a later developed bureaucratic one. The bishops were line functionaries of a centralized organization with authority coming from the top down. However, after a brief period of being disoriented by their unwonted collegiality, the bishops at Rome came to feel themselves a college once again. The establishment of a context in which problems were to be handled discursively and intellectual problem solving was consequently to become the mode of conduct, and the discovery of their own collegial discursive role by the bishops set the stage for the changes that were to come.

One of the revolutions that had brought about the world so long resisted by the Church was the revolution in communications. The consequences of that transformation of human relationships placed the Second Vatican Council in the closest contact with the outside world. The eyes of the world were literally upon it; the ears of the world heard its discussions. *Urbi et orbi* took on a new literalness.

Furthermore, the outside world was not simply nearer; it had changed too. The great changes we have pointed out before had dissipated much of the old Reformation attitude of antipope and anti-Rome—so much so that John XXIII became a transconfessional and interconfessional symbol. Protestants looked to the Council John had called with vague but real, and indeed often enthusiastic, hopes. Men of no formal faith, aware of the danger and promise of our age, hoped that the oldest and largest Christian body might say something useful to men. Especially in America, perhaps, where a liberal Democrat and a Roman Catholic had just been elected President, and where a successful pluralist society enjoying unprecedented prosperity emphasized good will among its diverse confessions, the Council was greeted with anticipation.

The Second Vatican Council thus became responsible to the world in a quite genuine and immediate sense. In considering the *Pastoral Constitution on the Church in the Modern World* the Council discussed the problem of whether to direct the document to Catholics or to all men. It decided to address itself "without hesitation, not only to the sons of the Church, but to the whole of humanity" (art 1). Thus it followed the precedent set by John XXIII, whose encyclical *Pacem in Terris* was for "all men of good will." Paul VI adopted the same mode of address in his inaugural encyclical *Ecclesiam Suam.* In this the Council and the popes reflect the new position of the Church.

In this Council the Fathers gathered to *discuss*, a fact that was to increase the influence of intellectuals—both among the episcopate and among their advisers—on policy making. In this Council the Fathers soon came to feel their own collegial status and responsibility. As we have indicated, reflection might well suggest to the more thoughtful the bankruptcy which threatened the defensive policies and rigid postures of the past. In this Council the Fathers met within view and within earshot of a world favorably disposed to expect something worthwhile from them, a world which would hold them responsible in a new way. They were, in a sense, on trial.

In this situation the modernizers, who had come into existence with the slow thaw of the antimodernist mentality, came into their own. The context threw the balance in favor of the intellectuals, but conservative theologians were prepared to do scarcely more than repeat the older positions. They had little to offer except further condemnations of the well known sources of threat: communism, atheism, etc. Yet John XXIII had called the Council in the spirit of dialogue, of pastoral concern, of updating the Church, and not of polemic and anathema. The conditions within the Church and the position of the Church in the world—the total context —cried out for something new. In this situation the new theologians—those who, under official discouragement and disapproval, explored the theology of the secular world, of the Church, of history and the Bible—had something to offer. Not surprisingly, they were more and more called upon. It was a great moment of fulfillment for a century and a half of unsuccessful efforts at *aggiornamento* when the progressive theologians emerged as the most influential *periti* at the Council. It meant that the Church would meet the trial it faced, that it would begin the massive task of reorienting itself by rational discussion and fraternal dialogue. The molting of the old Church would begin.

Thus the Council was called and thus it became occupied with *aggiornamento* in depth. Its results record the beginning of such an *aggiornamento*, genuine though in a sense—in relation to the magnitude of the tasks—modest. "The Council marked the decisive beginning of the aggiornamento, it established the renewal, it called us to the ever necessary repentance and return; in other words, it was only the beginning of the beginning" [77:19f]. Yet in view of the condition of the Roman Catholic Church in the late 18th and 19th centuries, in view of the historical burdens with which it entered the modern period, a decisive beginning of the beginning represents a tremendous accomplishment. In braving the "terrifying, threatening, unknown future facing the Church" [77:39], the Fathers considered the two most fundamental questions concerning ecclesiology. The first, as Pope Paul VI put it, was "What is the Church? This has been the great question of the Council." And the second was "the other theme, which inquires as to how the Church, in its turn, views the world" [quoted in 82:745]. Paul observes that the conciliar answers to this second "immense question" are marked by "optimism." A "beginning" begun with "optimism" of a genuine "aggiornamento in depth" could indeed point to the "very bold and far-reaching changes" necessary if Christianity in our day is to survive with relevance. It is against the background of these considerations that one should attempt to evaluate the *Pastoral Constitution on the Church in the Modern World*.

Judged according to a variety of criteria, this Constitution is without question the most typical Council document. It is the only major document to arise out of a suggestion made by a bishop speaking on the floor of the aula of St Peter's Basilica. It expresses more directly than any other conciliar document the new spirit of dialogue between the Church and the world which all observers agree is the distinguishing characteristic of the Council.

It is the product of a long process of preparation in which commissions, mixed commissions, subcommittees, and general floor debate made a series of drastic and fundamental alterations in it. Many of the concerns it takes up can be found in the more than 70 schemata drawn up by preconciliar commissions but scattered throughout the various documents. Curiously enough, the Council called to effect *aggiornamento* had no one prepared statement on the Church in the world. After the first session, Pope John appointed a Coordinating Commission to reduce the number of prepared documents to a manageable number. The result was 17 schemata, the last bearing the title *De Presentia Activa Ecclesiae in Mundo* (*On the Active Presence of the Church in the World*). Under the guidance of Leon-Joseph Cardinal Suenens, whose original remarks in the first session had set the project of such a Constitution afoot, the document started its long evolution. Its number, its contents, and even its name changed in the course of its preparation. With a further reduction of the number of documents it became schema 13. Reworked, reformulated, restated many times in committee and on the floor, it finally emerged, as Archbishop Garrone said in presenting it to the Fathers for their approval, as a genuine endeavor "to place the Church in dialogue with the world, truthfully and realistically" [51:398]. It represented, he said, "the very heart of the Council." It had come through its long preparatory and revisory history as a statement which recognized the condition of the modern world and strove to speak to its problems in a language that world could understand.

Its preface stresses the intimate ties binding the Church

to mankind, stating that the Church shares the "joys and the hopes, the griefs and the anxieties of the men of this age" (art 1). Its basic approach is empirical and it attempts to understand the modern situation before all else. Only then does it try to relate Christian values to the contemporary scene. Its empirical realism and its spirit of dialogue are most striking. It eschews altogether the old attitude of ecclesiastical eminence—what is sometimes called "Constantinianism." Says Donald Campion, SJ, "The most distinctive note sounded in the text, many already agree, is that of the Church putting itself consciously at the service of the family of man" [13:185].

At long last the Roman Catholic Church was putting together a document which reflected the true condition of the Church in the world in our time. As Bishop McGrath put it, "Here, at last . . . for the first time in a Conciliar document, a biblical Catholic synthesis of the meaning of Christian man and Christian society on earth and in time striving toward eternity" was presented [51:408]. In this longest conciliar document in the entire history of the Christian Church there evolved a most striking attempt to take the world of secular man seriously and to relate it in depth to the concerns and teachings of the Church. Here, to quote Bishop McGrath again, we find "a frank pursuit of the proper values of the things and structures and situations of which the life of man is made, values which are theirs of themselves, and which must be understood to be lived and to be offered to God through the men who live them together in their striving for him" [51:410].

In this document the Church lays aside an older defensiveness for open confrontation; an older ecclesiasticism for service to man; an earlier pessimism about what Cardinal Antonelli called "the chief errors and false doctrines of our most unhappy age" [32:267] for a marked tendency, despite qualifications and cautions, "to accentuate the positive in a realistic appraisal of trends and movements at work today in the City of Man" [13:185]. In this document also the Church faces up to experience instead of repeating its own stock formulas, and adheres with scrupulous care to a marked respect for the autonomy of the social science disciplines in observing and interpreting their data. It would appear to the thoughtful reader that Lamennais, Montalembert, Döllinger, and even perhaps Loisy and Tyrrell had not lived in vain. And this first impression is strengthened rather than dissipated by a more careful reading of the Constitution.

The Constitution begins with the preface we have quoted above and then moves to an introductory statement dealing with "The Situation of Men in the Modern World," which recognizes that today "the human race is passing through a new stage in its history" and characterizes this new stage as "a crisis of growth" (art 4). Then follows the Constitution proper, divided into two parts. The first part consists of four chapters dealing with the Church and man's calling in the world; the second, of five chapters concerning "Some Problems of Special Urgency" dealing with contemporary problems, from those affecting the family to those concerning the dangers of total war. The first section represents the more general teaching of the Church; the second applies it to specific current problems. While this is a pastoral constitution attempting to develop and set forth the Church's relation to the world, the first part may be considered, not without some justification, a more dogmatic statement—a presentation of basic ideas on the Church in the modern world. We shall here summarize, analyze, and comment upon this important first section. In Chapter 6 we shall assess the significance of the Council in the light of this statement and in Chapter 7 summarize and comment upon the more specific second part.

The text of the Constitution rests upon two fundamental insights concerning man in our age. It recognizes that men have now achieved the capacity to control and direct the external conditions of their lives; they have, in fact, unprecedented power over the environment. Science, as Descartes predicted, is about to render man "master and possessor" of nature. Toward this development the Church was long caught in an odd ambiguity. Its positive Old Testament evaluation of the creation as good, and its acceptance of human rationality, tended to line up the Church on the side of human progress. As Alfred North Whitehead pointed out, science developed out of the mentality that the Church had formed in the Middle Ages. But the defensiveness of the Church against secularization and the need to defend the closed formulations of its faith against new ideas placed it in opposition. Humanism was in some respects the revolt of Prometheanism against this effort to contain man's endeavors. Now the Church recognizes the nobility of and justification for human efforts. It recognizes also, however, that the process of external mastery, the achievement of rational control, has at the same time dissolved the older cultural contexts and disrupted the older social structures within which men found security, meaning, and identity itself. The development of the modern world, with its urbanized society based upon scientific technology, is the simultaneous development of scientific mastery and social anomie. Man has subdued the earth, but he is not as a consequence the master of his fate or the captain of his soul.

Man's outward triumphs have placed him in a position to remake the world. "Technology is now transforming the face of the earth, and is already trying to master outer space" (art 5). Man's technical accomplishments have set off "profound and rapid changes," which are now "spreading by degrees around the whole world. Triggered by the intelligence and creative energies of man, these changes recoil upon him, upon his decisions and desires, both individual and collective, and upon his manner of thinking and feeling with respect to things and people" (art 4). The impact of his mastery has torn up the established traditional context of life, annihilated the older provincialism so protective of his traditional beliefs and values, and brought a new interdependence and a new cosmopolitanism. The "traditional local communities . . . experience more thorough changes every day. The industrial type of society is gradually being spread, leading some nations to economic affluence, and radically transforming ideas and social conditions established for centuries" (art 4). Urbanization brings a "multiplication of cities and their inhabitants" and "a transplantation of city life to rural settings" (art 6). The modern revolution in the means of communication not only spreads a "knowledge of events" but gives "the swiftest and widest circulation to styles of thought and feeling" (art 6). Moreover, the "destiny of the human community has become all of a piece, where once the various groups of men had a kind of private history of their own" (art 5).

Yet the modern Prometheus remains at war with himself. Despite a great increase in power for both construction and destruction, the rivalries, competitions, and animosities characteristic of earlier stages of human history remain with us. "Although the world of today has a very vivid sense of its unity and of how one man depends on another in needful solidarity, it is most grievously torn into opposing camps by conflicting forces. For political, social, economic, racial, and ideological disputes still continue bitterly, and with them the peril of a war which would reduce everything to ashes" (art 4). His genuine progress has denuded man of traditional values to a considerable degree. "As happens in any crisis of growth, this transformation has brought serious difficulties in its wake. Thus while man extends his power in every direction, he does not always succeed in subjecting it to his own welfare. Striving to penetrate farther into the deeper recesses of his own mind, he frequently lays bare the laws of society, only to be paralyzed by uncertainty about the direction to give it" (art 4). External victories are purchased at the price of unsureness and indecision, precisely at the time when both the avoidance of tremendous dangers and the accomplishment of great good make a sure sense of orientation more important han ever. Moreover, even the fruits of the external victories remain spottily distributed, thereby contributing to a greater instability and danger for man at large. "Never has the human race enjoyed such an abundance of wealth, resources, and economic power. Yet a huge proportion of the world's citizens is still tormented by hunger and poverty, while countless numbers suffer from total illiteracy" (art 4).

Man is thus not only changing the earth, his dwelling; he is changing himself. Aspects once considered part of an unchanging human nature are now seen altered by the historic experience of external mastery, which produces at the same time a profound modification of the modes of thought and feeling. "The institutions, laws, and modes of thinking and feeling as handed down from previous generations do not always seem well adapted to the contemporary state of affairs. Hence arises an upheaval in the manner and even in the norms of behavior" (art 7). The mind and outlook of modern man are "increasingly based on the mathematical and natural sciences and on those dealing with man himself, while in the practical order the technology which stems from these sciences takes on mounting importance" (art 5). Further, "biology, psychology, and the social sciences not only bring men improved self-knowledge. In conjunction with technical methods, they are also helping men to exert direct influence on the life of social groups" (art 5).

"Finally, these new conditions have their impact upon religion. On the one hand a more critical ability to distinguish religion from a magical view of the world and from the superstitions which still circulate purifies religion and exacts day-by-day a more personal and explicit adherence to faith. As a result many persons are achieving a more vivid sense of God" (art 7). The desacralization of the world is regarded as having a positive religious significance, and man's critical abilities, so highly perfected in modern times, are thought of as providing the basis for a purer faith.

Here the Council sees the maturation function of modern developments. Old contexts—social and cultural—are dissolved, and the individual emerges in a new freedom. Knowledge advances, and the individual emerges with a new understanding. This at least is the case with some, and such is the promise, although it is accompanied by a new insecurity and too often by a lack of orientation. Yet the positive possibilities of emancipation in this molting process are acknowledged.

The Council is also quite aware, however, that desacralization, criticism, external mastery, and the evolving social and cultural disorganization of which they are a part have affected religion in a negative way.

On the other hand, growing numbers of people are abandoning religion in practice. Unlike former days, the denial of God or religion, or the abandonment of them, are no longer unusual or individual occurrences. For today it is not rare for such decisions to be presented as requirements of scientific progress or of a certain humanism. In numerous places these views are voiced not only in the teachings of philosophers, but on every side they influence literature, the arts, the interpretations of the humanities and of history, and civil laws themselves. As a consequence, many people are shaken [art 7].

Thus does the Council perceive the "true social and cultural transformation" (art 4), which like all great changes "calls accepted values into question." It is also aware of the self-transforming aspects of the modern experience. "To a certain extent, the human intellect is broadening its dominion over time: over the past by means of historical knowledge; over the future by the art of projecting and planning" (art 5). Men are learning "to exert direct influence on the life of social groups. At the same time, the human race is giving ever-increasing thought to forecasting and regulating its own population growth" (art 5).

Commenting on all this, the Council most significantly recognizes that "the human race has passed from a rather static concept of reality, to a more dynamic, evolutionary one" (art 5). It notes that the rapidity of the changes and the "disorderly fashion" in which they often occur "beget contradictions and imbalances, or intensify them" (art 8). Men are "more conscious than ever of the inequalities in the world," and this has an upsetting effect (art 8). There are imbalances within the person and within society, between practical achievement and "the demands of the moral conscience," between the demands of theory and of practice, between the individual and the group—"the conditions of collective existence and the requisites of personal thought"—between the demands of specialization and the need for "a comprehensive view of reality" (art 8). Quite apparent are "the mutual distrust, enmities, conflicts, and hardships" so characteristic of human life as phenomena of which man is "at once cause and victim."

In this difficult, distraught, but developing world, the Council sees mankind seeking "to consolidate its control over creation" and identifies itself with the human aspiration to "establish a political, social, and economic order which will to an even better extent serve man and help individuals as well as groups to affirm and develop dignity proper to them." The Council is aware of the growing demand of all men for the material conditions of a decent life and their equally significant need for human dignity. It is also cognizant of aspirations for freedom and selfhood. "Now, for the first time in human history, all people are convinced that the benefits of culture ought to be and actually can be extended to everyone" (art 9).

Thus "the modern world" is "at once powerful and weak, capable of the noblest deeds or the foulest. Before it lies the path to freedom or to slavery, to progress or retreat, to brotherhood or hatred" (art 9). But beneath all of these phenomena "lies a deeper and more widespread longing. Persons and societies thirst for a full and free life worthy of man—one in which they can subject to their own welfare all that the modern world can offer them so abundantly" (art 9). In this state "man is becoming aware that it is his responsibility to guide aright the forces which he has unleashed and which can enslave him or minister to him" (art 9).

Thus has the Second Vatican Council recognized all those trends in the modern world which in the past were the bane of the Church's existence—those it tried to resist, those to which it reluctantly attempted to adapt itself, changing itself as little as possible in the process, and those it chose to ignore. The development of modernity involved both secularization and emancipation, the improvement of the means of life and the destruction of traditional culture and social structure, an increasing individuation and an increasing interdependence—in short, liberation and genuine opportunity together with the threat and real possibility of chaos. It is admitted that old modes of thought and feeling and old forms of social relations are passing away and being replaced by emerging new forms, even "new social relations between men and women" (art 8). And all this is suffused by men's aspirations for and efforts to achieve "a full and free life worthy of man" (art 9).

To subdue the earth and make its forces minister to human welfare, to build a genuine human community, and to realize full and free development the Council recognizes as central to man's purposeful activity on the earth. Such recognition modifies much in the earlier formulations of man's destiny in the practical teaching of the Church. It brings a new specificity and a new historical character to the Catholic view. It replaces the older static view with a dynamic one in which men not only change their circumstances but continually transform themselves. The importance of experience in shaping man, of immanent forces in man seeking expression and fulfillment, of the involvement of life in a historical process, of the situational conditioning of human consciousness is made plain in this characterization of the situation of men in the modern world with which the Constitution begins.

Every one of these elements was argued for by the liberal Catholic movements which in the last 150 years advocated *aggiornamento.* The Church now knows that in some way man is in fact a historical being. In some profound sense he is emerging or evolving. That realization supplies the context for the perennial questions of meaning for man, arising anew, and with renewed poignancy, in our age. "For in man himself many elements wrestle with one another. Thus on the one hand, as a creature he experiences his limitations in a multitude of ways. On the other, he feels himself to be boundless in his desires and summoned to a higher life" (art 10). Many expect a "total emancipation of humanity wrought solely by human effort," while others "despair of any meaning to life and praise the boldness of those who think that human existence is devoid of any inherent significance and who strive to confer a total meaning on it by their own ingenuity alone" (art 10). "Nevertheless, in the face of the modern development of the world, an ever-increasing number of people are raising the most basic questions or recognizing them with a new sharpness: What is man? What is this sense of sorrow, of evil, of death, which continues to exist despite so much progress? What is the purpose of these victories, purchased at so high a cost? What can man offer to society, what can he expect from it? What follows this earthly life?" (art 10) It is to these questions in particular that the Constitution addresses its message in its first section. The introductory statement of the document closes with the wish "in the light of Christ . . . to speak to all men in order to illuminate the mystery of man and to cooperate in finding the solution to the outstanding problems of our time" (art 10).

Part One of the *Pastoral Constitution on the Church in the Modern World* looks at the present situation in the light of faith, to "decipher authentic signs of God's presence and purpose in the happenings, needs, and desires" with which the Church today and all men are involved. "For faith throws a new light on everything, manifests God's design for man's total vocation, and thus directs the mind to solutions which are fully human" (art 11). Next are presented the three basic

questions which the Fathers will seek to answer in this document. "What does the Church think of man? What recom-
mendations seem needful for the upbuilding of contemporary
society? What is the ultimate significance of human activity
throughout the world?" (art 11).

"What does the Church think of man?" The Fathers
assert the dignity of the human person made in God's image
in a brief section (art 12) studded with references to and
quotations from Genesis (1:26, 27, 31), Wisdom (2:23),
Ecclesiasticus (17:3–10), and Psalms (8:5–6). They see him
appointed "as master of all earthly creatures that he might
subdue them and use them to God's glory." They then
restate the doctrine of original sin in that "made by God in a
state of holiness, from the very dawn of history man abused his
liberty, at the urging of personified Evil. Man set himself
against God and sought to find fulfillment apart from God."
The result has been "man split within himself," his relation
"to his own ultimate goal" disrupted, and "all of human life,
whether individual or collective," showing itself "to be a
dramatic struggle between good and evil, between light and
darkness" (art 13).

Yet, "obliged to regard his body as good and honorable
since God created it and will raise it up again on the last
day," man "is not wrong when he regards himself superior to
bodily concerns." For though "wounded by sin," by "his
interior qualities he outstrips the whole sum of mere things"
(art 14). His mind "shares in the light of the divine mind,"
and through it he "has won superlative victories, especially
in his probing of the material world and in subjecting it to
himself." His mind can know "reality itself" though "in consequence of sin" his certitude "is partly obscured and weak-
ened." He can rise "through visible realities to those which
are unseen" (art 15). In particular is man's dignity related to
his conscience—"the most secret core and sanctuary"—in
the depths of which he "detects a law which he does not
impose on himself . . . summoning him to love good and

avoid evil" (art 16). The dignity of man's mind and conscience requires freedom; it demands the right to act "according to a knowing and free choice" (art 17).

But man is the creature who must die and who knows
that he must die. Despite his dignity and worth he faces
death, and "it is in the face of death that the riddle of human
existence becomes most acute." The problem is constitutive
to man's very being. "Tormented by pain" and "by a dread
of personal extinction," man "rebels against death because he
bears in himself an eternal seed which cannot be reduced to
sheer matter" (art 18). To this knowing and choosing being,
this being of "grandeur" and "misery" (art 13), this man who
feels "that desire for a higher life which is inescapably lodged
in his breast" (art 18) — to him the Church brings its message
of salvation from sin. It announces that "the Lord Himself
came to free and strengthen man, renewing him inwardly"
(art 13) and expresses its hope "of a divine life beyond all
corruption," for "Christ won this victory when He rose to
life, since by His death He freed man from death."

There follows a consideration of atheism, "accounted
among the most serious problems of this age." This treatment
has been often remarked upon because it attempts to understand an aspect of the modern mentality as found in large
numbers of our contemporaries, not simply present prepared
counterarguments. It points out that the Church "cannot
cease repudiating" atheism as a human option but sees the
answer as being given "chiefly by the witness of a living and
mature faith" (art 21). The variety of atheists is recognized,
from those who never knew the Christian way to God to
those who "never get to the point of raising questions about
God, since they seem to experience no religious stirrings"
(art 19). An article is devoted to "systematic atheism," which
"stretches the desire for human independence to such a point
that it finds difficulties with any kind of dependence on God"
and wishes thereby to give "man freedom to be an end unto
himself, the sole artisan and creator of his own history." For

people who embrace this view, such human freedom is considered irreconcilable with "the affirmation of a Lord who is author and purpose of all things" (art 20). Again the Church proclaims its ancient *kerygma*, "the mystery of the incarnate Word," "Christ, the final Adam," in whom "God reconciled us to Himself and among ourselves" (art 22).

Accepting atheism as a modern problem, the document calls for "sincere and prudent dialogue," at the same time advocating "that all men, believers and unbelievers alike, ought to work for the rightful betterment of this world in which all alike live" (art 21). In the hearts of "all men of good will" Christ's reconciliation has its effect, and "grace works in an unseen way." "For, since Christ died for all men, and since the ultimate vocation of man is in fact one, and divine, we ought to believe that the Holy Spirit in a manner known only to God offers to every man the possibility of being associated with this paschal mystery" (art 22).

In Chapter II, "The Community of Mankind," the Constitution begins by noting once more "the growing interdependence of men one on the other" as "one of the salient features of the modern world" (art 23) brought about by modern technical advance. This process, in which "reciprocal ties and mutual dependencies" increase, is called "socialization," a term from the works of Teilhard de Chardin (art 25). The process can be such that "the human person is greatly aided in responding to his destiny, even in its religious dimensions," but it can divert men from that destiny as well (art 25).

In the face of this development the Constitution advocates the "full spiritual dignity of the person" (art 23) and the common good of society as the conditions that will allow "social groups and their individual members relatively thorough and ready access to their own fulfillment" (art 26). Man "is the only creature on earth which God willed for itself." At the same time, man is by nature social and can only "find himself" in a "sincere gift of himself." All men are "called to one and the same goal, namely, God Himself" (art 24). Social institutions are justified in terms of their contribution to the fulfillment of the human person (art 25), but man possesses social responsibilities and must follow "the laws of social life which the Creator has written into man's spiritual and moral nature" (art 23).

The Constitution repeats the admonition of the gospel to love one's enemies (Mt 5:43–44) (art 28) and points to the importance of man's essential equality. It states that because of this "equal dignity of persons," which remains the case despite "rightful differences," it is necessary that "a more human and just condition of life be brought about" (art 29). Man cannot "content himself with a merely individualistic morality." Rather, it is a "sacred obligation to count social necessities among the primary duties of modern man and to pay heed to them" (art 30).

Chapter II closes with a call for self-cultivation in "the moral and social virtues" (art 30) and the careful education of youth "from every social background" (art 31). Only then can it be hoped that, "with the needed help of divine grace, men who are truly new and artisans of a new humanity can be forthcoming" (art 30). Only then "there can be produced . . . those great-souled persons who are so desperately required by our times" (art 31). The Fathers assert that man's personal dignity together with his "communitarian character" are fulfilled in Christ, "who sanctified those human ties, especially family ones, from which social relationships arise" (art 32).

By this time the Constitution has laid the ground for answering two of the three questions raised in article 2. It has presented its view of man, attempting to put together its classical heritage, the indications of modern thought and contemporary science, and the message of the Christian *kerygma*. It will develop these ideas further in Part Two, where are set forth more specific proposals. It has also stated its view of society, which will be enlarged upon in Part Two. In Chapter III of Part One the Constitution addresses itself to the third question, concerning the "significance of human activity throughout the world."

> Throughout the course of centuries, men have labored to better the circumstances of their lives through a monumental amount of individual and collective effort. To believers, this point is settled: considered in itself, such human activity accords with God's will. For man, created to God's image, received a mandate to subject to himself the earth and all that it contains, and to govern the world with justice and holiness; a mandate to relate himself and the totality of things to Him who was to be acknowledged as the Lord and Creator of all [art 34].

In all this men may be assured that "by their labor they are unfolding the Creator's work" and that their triumphs are "the flowering of God's mysterious design" (art 34). Moreover, by his work man not only changes things and society; he "develops himself as well," going beyond himself and developing his endowment and resources. Indeed, such growth "is of greater value than any external riches." The Constitution proclaims this "norm of human activity," that "in accord with the divine plan and will, it should harmonize with the genuine good of the human race, and allow men as individuals and as members of society to pursue their total vocation and fulfill it" (art 35).

Here we see how the Council strove to assert its recognition of "man's total vocation" (arts 11 and 35), how it attempted to combine its recognition of the importance, the legitimacy, and the nobility of man's worldly vocation with its own conception of the true calling of the Christian. To subdue the earth, to build community, and to develop himself—this is what man is doing on earth, and it "accords with God's will" (art 34). The Constitution can assert that legitimation; it can assert that it is consistent with man's destiny to "a divine life beyond all corruption" (art 13). Working out the implications of these assertions will be the task of a theology of history and of vocation. In this case too the Council is but the "beginning of a beginning."

We noted in a previous chapter that Christianity has never been able to solve this problem, that Catholicism never developed a model of the lay Christian, and that the only Reformation group achieving a measure of success attained it at the cost of two significant elements. First, in Puritanism it was achieved for a while at the price of massive repression, which could not but render the solution short lived. Such a repressive, overdisciplined, and narrowly focused solution had little to offer as a permanent answer to the long-range problems of man, society, and culture. The element of transcendence it strove to maintain does, however, point to an element in the Calvinist solution which must not be lost from sight. Second, the Calvinist solution also was attained in a way which led in a few generations to something rather like total secularization—to an odd combination, in fact, of secularization without emancipation.

Thus the problem involved in putting together the idea of a fully legitimate vocation in the world with the transcendent call of the New Testament is a difficult and complex one. The failures to solve it cannot be attributed simply to human stupidity or perversity—always ample, no doubt. There is a built-in ontological problem of how a religious life is harmonized with a life in the world, how the response to the call of something "beyond" can be maintained amidst concentrated concern with tasks. Some rhythm of involvement with the world and return to a relation to transcendence would seem to be required, a rhythm to be worked out concretely in different social and cultural settings. Troeltsch has suggested how this major point of tension and balance affected the history of the Church. We have found it a central element in the great problems faced by the Church since the Middle Ages. Catholic theology now faces the great task of working out the implications of the stand taken by the Council. It must come to appreciate and indeed illuminate the worth of the dramas acted out by individuals, by classes, by nations, and by larger groupings of men in the world.

The recognition of man's vocation at the same time justifies autonomous human activity. Vocation is seen to involve earthly affairs; that is, "created things and societies themselves enjoy their own laws and values which must be gradually deciphered, put to use, and regulated by men." Such activity possesses a rightful autonomy, "required by modern men" and in harmony with "the will of the Creator." Again the Council is dealing with an aspect of the problem which vexed Christians and plagued the Church for centuries. While temporal affairs do "depend on God," and man cannot participate in them "without reference to their Creator," nevertheless a sphere of legitimate autonomous human action in the world is proclaimed.

We have seen that in the 19th century the Church could not accept freedom of scholarship but sought to continue the long-obsolete situation of the Middle Ages, when all learning was conceived in a hierarchy of sciences with theology at the apex. Thus in the realm of learning was found the structural equivalent of the hierarchy in society in which the Church was preeminent. But now the Fathers recognize the freedom of the human mind.

> Therefore, if methodical investigation within every branch of learning is carried out in a genuinely scientific manner and in accord with moral norms, it never truly conflicts with faith. For earthly matters and the concerns of faith derive from the same God. . . . Consequently, we cannot but deplore certain habits of mind, sometimes found too among Christians, which do not sufficiently attend to the rightful independence of science. The arguments and controversies which they spark lead many minds to conclude that faith and science are opposed [art 36[.

This statement is followed by an official annotation to the two-volume study by Monsignor Pio Paschini, *Vita e Opere di Galileo Galilei*.

The Constitution raises the question of sin, noting that man's worldly accomplishments also bring temptation to evil and that "a monumental struggle against the powers of darkness pervades the whole history of man." "Caught in this conflict, man is obliged to wrestle constantly if he is to cling to what is good. Nor can he achieve his own integrity without valiant efforts and the help of God's grace." The Christian concern is not simply with the world as the arena for man's total vocation, which is activity in accordance with God's will. There is also that world of which Paul speaks in the Epistle to the Romans when he says, "Be not conformed to this world" (Rom 12:2). The Constitution defines that "world" as "that spirit of vanity and malice which transforms into an instrument of sin those human energies intended for the service of God and man" (art 37).

The Constitution sees man with his worldly vocation, his human capacities, his involvement in sin, and his call to grace. In trying to indicate how these characteristics of the human condition can be put together in a consistent piece, it recognizes a central element in man which the Church long resisted grasping. Here the Fathers retain their ancient Hellenic heritage of natural law, but they implicitly suggest its restatement in terms of personalism. The person —existence, development, and realization—is placed first as the core of man's earthly vocation and made one of the chief ends of the political and social community. This suggests that man has a structure, and whatever violates that structure is antipersonal and therefore unethical. In the best tradition of the Greeks, ethics is seen not simply as conventions agreed upon to maintain order but derived from genuine dimensions of the human situation—of man in his relation to the world. It is now restated, however, in terms of a personalism rather than the biologism of Aristotle.

Even more significant, the Church now sees that this structure has a certain openness and flexibility about it. Formerly the Church took the static view, saw man and society as a static — and historically a conservative — archetype. Right reason, with the aid of the magisterium, was thought capable of understanding that ahistorical model. Now man's unformedness, his open potential, his flexibility and many-sidedness are confronted. History reveals possibilities in him which, realized in part, in part have been suppressed by conditions, and even distorted in ways such that man is both "cause and victim." Man's entelechy is now perceived as open. The Church seeks to relate this openness to its own call to an ultimate destiny.

Yet the Council does not abandon the Christian insight concerning sin. Man is not simply foreshortened by the conditions of his existence which limit and distort his self-realization; he is not simply victim. He is also limited and truncated by his own short-circuited motivations; he is also cause. Self-interest, resentment, fear, the inordinate desire for security — these influence his action and its consequences. We earlier quoted the London *Tablet* to the effect that there was a danger of "taking the modern world too much at its own valuation," and of taking insufficiently into account "the way the world we live in has been made for us, in such great measure, by the sin as well as by the virtues of our predecessors" [quoted in 61:315]. It is not simply the world of the past that is so affected, the Council recognizes, but the present, evolving world. Men act out their hopes and aspirations in the dramas of earthly existence. Their efforts express elements of the greatest nobility. But they reflect those aspects of foreshortening which Christianity calls sin.

This section of the Constitution closes with a statement relating man's progress to the eschatological hopes of the Church. "Earthly progress must be carefully distinguished from the growth of Christ's kingdom. Nevertheless, to the extent that the former can contribute to the better ordering of human society, it is of vital concern to the kingdom of God" (art 39). For indeed, "Christ is now at work in the hearts of men through the energy of His Spirit. He arouses not only a desire for the age to come, but by that very fact, He animates, purifies, and strengthens those noble longings too by which the human family strives to make its life more human and to render the whole earth submissive to this goal" (art 38). "For after we have obeyed the Lord, and in His spirit nurtured the earth, the values of human dignity, brotherhood and freedom, and indeed all the good fruits of our nature and enterprise, we will find them again, but freed of stain, burnished and transfigured. . . . On this earth that kingdom is already present in mystery. When the Lord comes, it will be brought into full flower" (art 39).

Chapter IV of Part One deals with the role of the Church in the modern world. It sees that role primarily as one of exchange and dialogue with the world. The Church, "a visible assembly and a spiritual community" (art 40), "serves as a leaven." "That the earthly and the heavenly city penetrate each other is a fact accessible to faith alone. It remains a mystery of human history, which sin will keep in great disarray until the splendor of God's sons is fully revealed." But in this state of things, the Church should strive to have a "healing and elevating impact upon the dignity of the person, by the way in which she strengthens the seams of human society and embues the everyday activity of men with a deeper meaning and importance. Thus, through her individual members and her whole community, the Church believes she can contribute greatly toward making the family of man and its history more human" (art 40). The Church would contribute to human fulfillment.

After expressing its "high esteem" for "the things which other Christian Churches or ecclesial communities have done" for this goal, the "Council now sets forth certain general principles for the fostering of this mutual exchange and assistance in concerns which are in some way common to the Church and the world" (art 40). The Council believes that by revealing God to "modern man," who is "on the road to a more thorough development of his own personality," the

Church helps to meet "the deepest longings of the human heart." Only God "provides a fully adequate answer to these questions"—what is the meaning of man's life, of his activity, of his death (art 41). The Council holds that "the Church can anchor the dignity of human nature against all tides of opinion, for example, those which undervalue the human body or idolize it. By no human law can the personal dignity and liberty of man be so aptly safeguarded as by the gospel of Christ which has been so entrusted to the Church." The Church "proclaims the rights of man," yet eschews "any kind of false autonomy," while at the same time defending "the rightful autonomy of the creature, particularly of man." "For the gospel announces and proclaims the freedom of the sons of God, and repudiates all the bondage which ultimately results from sin" (art 41).

The Council sees the "union of the human family" as "greatly fortified and fulfilled by the unity, founded on Christ, of the family of God's sons," and states unequivocally that Christ "gave His Church no proper mission in the political, economic, or social order," but rather set before her "a religious one." But it is asserted that "out of this religious mission itself" can come "a function, a light, and an energy which can serve to structure and consolidate the human community according to divine law." Moreover, the "Church further recognizes that worthy elements are found in today's social movements, especially an evolution toward unity, a process of wholesome socialization and of association in civic and economic realms." The Church seeks to sustain what is best in man's nature and in his attempts to build community. "Bound to no particular form of human culture, nor to any political, economic, or social system," the Church "can inject into the modern society of man . . . faith and charity put into vital practice." It wishes to "assist and promote" the human institutions which men establish to increase human welfare (art 42).

The Christian laity are urged to perform as faithful

practitioners of their life's work and citizens of their countries. They are to be "citizens of two cities," capable of gathering "their humane, domestic, professional, social, and technical enterprises into one vital synthesis with religious values." In this way they will overcome the split between religious values and daily life, "which deserves to be counted among the more serious errors of our age."

Bishops and priests are exhorted to "preach the message of Christ" so that "all the earthly activities of the faithful may be bathed in the light of the gospel." At the same time it is humbly recognized "how great a distance lies between the message [the Church] offers and the human failings of those to whom the gospel is entrusted" (art 43).

Chapter IV thus puts before us the vision of a Church of service. It is appreciated, however, that the Church profits from the advance of modern society. By the science of our day, "the nature of man himself is more clearly revealed and new roads to truth are opened." Moreover, the Council advocates a "living exchange," to be developed "between the Church and the diverse cultures of people." The Constitution states, "Indeed, the Church admits that she has greatly and still profits from the antagonism of those who oppose or persecute her" (art 44). Service, dialogue, and exchange — these are the basis of the role of the Church. Humble, made up of sinners, needing to be purified while holy, being aided by antagonism — these are characteristics of the Church in the world today. Overcoming much in the heritage of its history and much in its contemporary situation, the Church approaches the world in genuine fraternity.

The first section of the Constitution closes by proclaiming anew that "while helping the world and receiving many benefits from it, the Church has a single intention: that God's kingdom may come, and that the salvation of the whole human race may come to pass," for the Church is asserted to be, in the words of the *Lumen Gentium*, "the sacrament of salvation" (art 45).

What is most striking at first about this document is the forthrightness, the lack of archaic language, and the humility —the lack of ecclesiastical arrogance—with which it sets forth the answers to the questions it raises. In terms of the background against which we have considered it, one is struck by the radical change in attitude and posture it represents. With utter realism it assesses both the situation of man today and the relation of modern man and his problems and aspirations to the historic Church.

Yet the questions posed earlier occur to us again. Is there here an equivalent of Barth's calling of modern man to transcendence? Is there here an attempt to shed the accretions of the centuries that is the equivalent to Bultmann's demythologization? The effects of the molting process, the uprooting of the Church from its embeddedness in the old order, are clearly apparent. Compared to the agonies of the past, the present situation seems to show the Church to be emancipated, freed. We are, of course, aware that the setting of the Council favors the intellectuals and gives those striving for a more liberal and up-to-date policy the support of world opinion. Yet once the bishops returned to their sees to be surrounded by the old bureaucracy, once the problems were faced again in the administrative mode of decision making, once the compromises of everyday ecclesiastical life were operative again, once the old habits and mental sets were reactivated—in short, once the Council was over—the forces recalcitrant to change were strengthened. But the changes have been started. The beginning of the beginning had been made.

The Church faces two sets of problems: the inner conflict between conservatives and the advocates of *aggiornamento*, and the evolving of its new positions without loss of the intensity and reality of its faith. A prime requisite for success is the preservation of its unity, the development of true inner dialogue. But the intellectual problems confronting Catholic theology are tremendous. It is to be hoped that it will be able to work upon them without too great a harassment from the rearguard of intransigent forces in the Church, some of whom, no doubt, are now after the Council more frightened than ever. We are entitled to ask whether the "very bold and far-reaching changes" necessary to the survival of Christianity in our day are forthcoming. Or, more modestly, do we have here the "beginning of the beginning" of such changes? Is the Church of Rome embarking upon the troubled waters of the great transition by which it may be able to lead Christianity to the contemporary relevance it has sought in vain and western men to a deeper and nobler vision of fulfillment? We shall attempt a preliminary assessment of the Constitution as representing the basic position of the Council in these respects in the following chapter.

VI

THE PASTORAL CONSTITUTION AND
THE RECONSTRUCTION OF THE CHURCH

THE *Pastoral Constitution on the Church in the Modern World* represents an immense effort on the part of the assembled Fathers to project a new image of the Church seen within the realistic setting of modern times, and to suggest the restatement of Christian teaching in a way that will find resonance in the minds and hearts of modern men. It builds upon the ground laid down in the *Lumen Gentium*. Among the conceptions of the Church presented in the latter was that of the "new people of God" (art 13), and the vision of the Church set forth there was markedly different from the one contained in the usual treatise on the Church found in theological manuals published prior to the opening of the Council in 1962. "Influenced by centuries of anti-Protestant polemics, the writers of this period placed heavy emphasis on the hierarchical and juridical aspects of the Church, including the supremacy of the Pope" [20:10]. Indeed, the document on the Church submitted by the commission which had done the preparatory work for this schema presented a similar treatment of the Church. But the Council revised the document drastically. The result has been called "more biblical, more historical, more vital, and more dynamic" [20:11]. As we have previously noted, the document was a compromise. It contained old and new ideas and pointed in old and new directions. Yet its general thrust was toward a redefinition that would understand the Church in the setting of its long theological reflections on itself, from patristic times on, but in terms of modern knowledge and in its modern setting. That attempt is carried farther in the present Constitution. Here the Church is seen in its new setting, shorn of the fictions and artificially sustained memories which clustered around definitions of the Church in the past.

We may characterize this Constitution as a mighty endeavor to project deinstitutionalization of myth in the Church of Rome, or, to put it in slightly different words, to begin the sociological demythologization of the Church. We use the word "myth" here in a precise sociological sense. We mean by it the use of human language to speak of divine things, a resort necessary to all religious thinking and all theology. But the myth of one age can well become incomprehensible to the next—become, indeed, the superstition of the next, the magic of the next—though it is the affirmation of Christian faith that what is embodied and communicated in the myth has not really lost its original significance but merely been obscured.

The Council begins the process of sociological demythologization. This is not to say that all at the Council were aware of the significance of the *aggiornamento* in depth on which they had embarked; nor does it mean that anyone can yet see the final solution to the problems involved. What was the myth with which Catholic Christianity entered the Second Vatican Council in 1962? It was this: *the vertical hierarchical Church serving as the sacramental mediator between God and man in a two-level universe in which what men did here below was significant simply in its moral dimension and all fulfillment represented the realization of timeless archetypes of man and society and finally full realization in the world to come.* It was a myth which summed up and embodied the faith as it came from the early Church. It was a subtle myth, expressed in creeds, in doctrine, in liturgy, in organization, in art, and in architecture in a highly proliferated and adumbrated complex of structures. The many volumes of the Denziger *Enchiridion Symbolorum*, in which Catholic doctrine is spelled out in detail, and the Code of Canon Law of 1917, represent only the theological and legal expressions worked out over centuries of this collectively developed, historically specific form of the Christian myth. In the liturgy and the sacraments its modalities of participation took shape, and in the theological definitions that grew up around them their explanation and justification as acts of God through Christ appeared. In the status divisions of clergy and laity—and among the clergy, of bishop and priest—the Church took on a set organizational structure.

All of this vast process bears the marks of the conditioning of the specific historical circumstances in which the Church developed. This is not to say that the Church, as a structure of cult, belief, and fellowship built over the centuries, can be either understood or explained as the mere product of the historical process. That the Christian could never concede. It would also be unsafe for the sociologist either to assume or to conclude such a proposition. Christianity rests upon a central religious insight, a basic message, concerning man's salvation—emancipation from the internal and external conditions which cripple or crush full personal existence. It proclaims certain events as acts of God effecting that liberation—his having sent Christ and established through his death and resurrection "the final man." It is a call to conversion, to a new kind of life. This message has been stated and worked out, expressed and related to human life, embodied in social forms and in ideas over the long period of Christian history. The result has been a process of institutionalization on three levels: cult, belief, and organization. The forms that have evolved bear the effects of the central Christian message, of which they are expressions, bearers, and instruments. As Troeltsch has convincingly indicated, the outcome is a certain autonomy of the religious element. But the forms show also the effects of the historical conditions under which they developed. They have been deeply influenced by the culture and social structure attendant upon their origin and growth. The ideas, the values, the interests, the allegiances, and the conflicts of the men who carried out those actions which gave them being made a profound impression upon them.

When the Church went into mission areas, it often tried to "deculturize" to some extent and to seek a new kind of expression in the new culture. Examples are many, from the celebrated charge of Pope Gregory the Great in 597 to Augustine (later St Augustine of Canterbury) on sending him to England, saying that everything in English culture not opposed to the faith should be accepted, to our own day. Such attempts gave rise, however, to serious problems. The Church had evolved in one culture—varied and many sided, to be sure, but, on deeper and more subtle levels, much of a piece. To relate the institutional Church as the expression of Christianity to other cultures was not simple. The Church came to the Scandinavians as a fully developed sacramental, dogmatic, and organizational system, but its sheer impressiveness, together with the remaining luster of antiquity, got it accepted pretty much as it was. When Christianity went to China, a more severe problem was confronted. For example, simply to translate the word "God" into Chinese was not easy, and Catholics and Protestants did it differently. The problem was twofold: First, can the message be detached from the concrete forms of expression in both discursive and presentational symbolism—in language and liturgy, in organization and architecture, etc.? Second, can the vested interests, the psychological securities, the conventions, large and small, of an established order be shed or put aside, or will the effort to do so undermine the religious faith of many clergy and laymen? It is, after all, in its culturally concrete form that the faith is understood and believed. Can the members of the Church sustain the great insecurity to which the process of molting subjects them? Such problems have appeared many times in Church history, particularly in modern times, from the effort of Matteo Ricci to establish Chinese Rites to "restate" Catholicism in a Chinese idiom (an effort condemned by Clement XI in 1715) to the attempt by Alfred Loisy, to make the Church face history (condemned by Pius X in 1908). They now arise not only in relation to non-European and non-European-derived cultures, to which the Church seeks for the first time to gain relevance, but also within western civilization itself, from which the Church has become estranged in significant respects.

In an earlier chapter (pp. 29–30) we made this statement:

> One of the great accomplishments of Catholicism is that it has succeeded—by its liturgy, by its sacramental practice, by its teaching, and by its discipline, within the context of a community of tradition—in maintaining in its adherents a quick sense and a deep conviction of the *reality* and *immediacy* of God. Closely related is the fact that it has kept unimpaired *a strikingly realistic understanding of the Church as mediator between God and man*, as the vessel or ark carrying through time the mediating function of Christ. The doctrine of the real presence of Christ in the Holy Eucharist has been central to this understanding. It is upon these two elements that the Church ultimately rests.

We also asked these questions (p. 10):

> Can the Catholic Church actually update Christianity? Can it adapt to the mentality of modernity Christian ideas and values, Christian conceptions of God and man, Christian convictions of the reality and seriousness of the religious life? Can it accomplish this by giving to the challenging aspects of modernity the full valence they demand and at the same time not lose its deeper character and basic identity? Can Catholicism confront the consequences, intellectual and spiritual, of modern developments in science and scholarship and in political, social, and economic life and adapt to them and still preserve its own lively sense of God's reality and presence?

Our consideration of the issues raised at the Council against the background of the rebuffed and suppressed efforts at *aggiornamento* of the previous century and a half now suggest what such questions involve. They involve the shedding by the Church of the concrete forms in which its central message had become externalized and made available to men. They suggest nothing less than the deinstitutionalization of the historic Church. They suggest a divesting of the formations and formulations of the past—a process that will not simply concern "externals" but enter into the deeper understanding of the content of faith.

We have questioned whether placing basic anchorage points of the historic faith in new settings represents a deeper probing of their meaning or a change of that meaning. Now we can see that in terms of spelled-out meanings, utilizing the intellectual vocabulary, the system of social relations, and the forms of participation of past ages, a change in meaning will have to take place. In its concrete statement and expression, in the structure and form of its earthly incarnation, Christianity will have to experience "very bold and far-reaching changes." A compartmentalization by which a community can live its religious consciousness in the 13th century and its everyday, its scientific, and its cultural life in the 21st will not prove viable. The time for such forms of "compromise" has passed. The central transcendent message of Christianity must now find radically new expression. It was this that the Second Vatican Council began to see; this that it was looking for in its renewal of the inner life of the Church and in its radical modification of the Church's relationship to the world.

What our analysis has showed so far is how fundamental, how thorough, how profound, "how bold and far-reaching" are the changes that will be involved in an *aggiornamento* in depth. We are no nearer to the answer to our other question: Can it be done?

Here let us merely make two observations. First, it will be recalled, the Catholic Church managed to preserve the reality and intensity of its faith within the overinstitutionalized Church that now must be radically reformed; the depth and reality of Catholic belief and practice were preserved by that dated myth which found concrete expression in the vertical Church in the two-level universe. An irony suggests itself here and it should make us uneasy. Is it not precisely those established expressions of Catholic faith, unchanged and defensively clung to, which rendered Catholicism increasingly irrelevant to the advancing western world that preserved within its own ranks the interior intensity and authenticity of faith? If so, is there not a great peril that any alterations in that structure of belief, cult, and organization sufficiently bold and far reaching to make it relevant to an unbelieving contemporary world might dilute the inner intensity and undermine the traditional convictions of Catholics enough to destroy the Church? This, of course, is what Catholic conservatives suspect and fear. It is not a question to be dismissed lightly.

Yet on closer examination some of the dangers apparent on first reading tend to carry much less threat if not to vanish altogether. The older myth in its large, adumbrated, institutional form was indeed the bearer and instrument as well as the expression of a deep and intense faith for many. It was in this form, however, that the Church lost so many of the strategic elements of western civilization, as well as large numbers of the common men. Nevertheless, it was effective for those who remained within the Church, who may be roughly classified in three categories. First, some people were insufficiently modern to be deeply upset by the cultural irrelevance of that complex, proliferated ideational, cultic, and institutional structure. Second, some were profound enough in their comprehension of what that complicated structure communicated and made available so that the increasing obsolescence of the forms did not cause major problems. Third, there were those who stood somewhere between these two categories. It was the last who often experienced great inner suffering and anguish. Today, we may expect that to the extent that Catholics are located near the first pole of the continuum they will be profoundly upset by fundamental change. To them the faith means the old forms of its expression; its inner content seems coterminal with and exhaustively expressed in the archaic formations and formulations. To the extent that Catholics stand near the second pole of the continuum they will feel liberated by the removal of impedimenta and of the cause of painful and needless scandal.

A second observation is more encouraging. Paul VI and numerous other commentators upon the attempt made by Vatican II to relate the Church to the world speak specifically of the "optimism" it displays. The spirit of Vatican II was hopeful, and the currents it has legitimated for *aggiornamento* also appear to be buoyed up by a real trust in the future. We must, however, note the substantial resistance to the changes set in train by the Council. The Fathers gathered at Rome, discovering their collegiality, experiencing the challenge to the Church in council and having to meet it in the discursive mode, having, moreover, to meet it with the eyes of the world upon them, were impelled to rise to a supreme occasion. In such circumstances they had to place great reliance upon those in their midst who had been thinking about the significant problems and upon the intellectual advisers they had brought with them. Thus liberal Catholicism reappeared; it reappeared brought up to date, made contemporary to this molting period of man's history, this time of a deeper taking stock and seeking direction.

We have said before that in attempting its great self-transformation Catholicism stands surrogate for western religion. We might also add that western culture as a whole is undergoing a serious value crisis. Raymond Williams, writing from London in *The Nation* of July 17, 1967, stated that the crisis within the Roman Church in Great Britain is "an essential part" of the "crucial intellectual argument now going on in Britain." In short, it is part of the crisis of British liberalism, which is of course a part of the crisis of values being experienced in the successful affluent societies of western Europe and America.

Catholic theology, in freeing itself from its ancient one-sidedness, its long-standing astigmatisms, must suggest ways for men to discern values, distinguish the authentic from the counterfeit, fulfillment from mere aggrandizement, and develop intelligently a sense of direction for working out their destiny in the world. In doing so it must rid itself of all the baneful consequences of its sectarian past while preserving the true spiritual riches which such defensiveness protected. It must keep its sense of and relation to transcendence and its ability to recognize significant ontological dimensions of man's existence. It must do this without retreating to a fixed and limited conception of human nature or to its old moralism, which saw human fulfillment only in terms of an ethic that was to a considerable extent a matter of repression and inhibition. It must keep and make more profound the sense of openness and creativity as part of human existence that was brought to the fore in Council discussions and documents. At the same time it must become able to suggest helpful guides for recognizing the imperatives of the human condition, which cannot be violated without severe damage to the individual and the community. It must work together with philosophy and the social sciences for a greater understanding of what in this Constitution is called "the transcendence of the person" and the "dynamically conceived common good." This means putting together the two perspectives on the world which were in bitter and prolonged conflict in the last century and a half. Transcendence, substance, ontology: what these words stand for must be related to what is signified by these: immanence, process, history.

In setting out on this course, Catholic theology attempts to accomplish not simply the *aggiornamento* in depth of Catholicism. That *aggiornamento*, if possible to achieve, will simultaneously be the strategic stroke in rendering all Christianity truly relevant to modern life. A general rediscovery of the existential message of Christianity would be nothing less than a great world historical renewal in a western civilization long in crisis. In this task, Catholic theology is in fact trying to bring insight and reason to bear upon a problem that the

West has never solved: how a man can live authentically as a person while mastering the external world, making that conquest serve his noblest aspirations within the context of a truly human community. The western past abounds with the wreckage of partial answers, from Christianity, from liberalism, from Marxism. Can Christians now sift, combine, and distill from them what in the light of Christian transcendence will prove to be a genuine guide to perplexed modernity?

In the face of that challenge, in the face of the openness and lack of a customary mental and spiritual landscape which it conjures up, in the face of the senselessness that threatens many when old complexes of meaning long seen as basic are questioned and analyzed, it is not surprising to perceive a reflex reaction of defensiveness among some in the Church. A long period of realignment, of deinstitutionalization and reinstitutionalization, of conflict lies ahead. Yet that in itself is not to be deplored. At worst it but represents the continuation in an open, more healthy form of the condition that has long existed beneath the repression and surface calm of an authoritarian atmosphere and structure. More hopefully viewed, it may be said to represent the coming of life and vitality to renew the body of the old Church. What is most significant is that the *aggiornamento* forces have won legitimation in the Council and that they maintain that status. It is doubtful whether all the attempts of the frightened or desperate can stop this long process once it has started. Next, it is very important that the unity of the Church be preserved; conflict should remain a form of dialogue and assume a condition in which freer and more profound dialogue can develop. What is sometimes called the "old Church" and the "new Church" must remain one Church so that in facing these great problems all the resources of the many-sided Catholic tradition will be involved. Such internal dialogue is as significant as is the already established ecumenical dialogue now taking place with those outside the Church.

We have already noted that the institutionalization of

religion is always a sociological dilemma. In their attempts to relate the transcendent to the immanent, the charismatic to the everyday, the sacred to the profane, religious institutions, like religious symbols, emerge with a basic conflict built in to their structure. The character of the Christian faith, its keen sense of transcendence, and the intensity and totality of commitment it demands combine with the age of the Church to make the dilemma of Christian institutions and Christian symbols most profound.

Institutions result from human action; they derive from precedents which have become normative and thereby provide the context for future conduct and thought. Thus they represent an objectification of what had originally been subjective, a stabilizing of what had originally been spontaneous. Institutionalization tends, in Henri Bergson's terms, to transform "dynamic religion" into "static religion" [6: chaps 2, 3]. It is this process that we see in the history of the Church. It is a process in which the concern with the welfare of an established institution and the vested interests of its functionaries become part of the concrete institutional structure. Christianity's original message is transformed in a subtle way. Moreover, the condition of institutional rigidity which develops in old institutions and the further rigidification which comes from defensiveness tend to cut off most genuinely creative efforts for a long time. This is the condition the Church was in when, after a century and a half of unsuccessful minority efforts, it turned to *aggiornamento* in depth.

The great insight toward which the *Pastoral Constitution* moves is that which we have found implied in its formulations —the sociological demythologization of the Church. Involved in that insight is a recognition of the "new age of mankind," and of the present crisis as a "crisis of growth," which is a prolegomena to that new age. The Council acknowledged that modern man is moving toward an open and indeterminate future, the making of which is his prime responsibility. Man's vocation in the world is both recognized and accepted. It is seen as involving the subjection of the earth to human welfare, the building of truly humane communities of men as the context of that welfare, and the development of the potential of the human person as its true fruition. We see here a great effort by the Fathers to divest the Church of that crypto Gnosticism and semi-Manicheanism which subtly suffused so much of Christian attitude and outlook throughout the centuries.

Protestants have usually leveled their criticism against what they regard as the semi-Pelagianism of the Church, which they consider (not altogether erroneously, let it be admitted) part of the tendency in Catholicism toward a somewhat idolatrous adulation of institution and office — toward ecclesiasticism or ecclesiolatry. They feel that the worth attributed by Catholics to Hellenic elements in the Christian tradition, by conceding to nature powers and possibilities which Protestant thought would prefer to ascribe to grace, makes for enhancing the institutional and authoritarian elements at the expense of spontaneity and liberty.

Shrewd as that insight may be, it is but part of the picture. The ecclesiolatry against which such criticism is directed is no less related to a disvaluation of the world, reinforced by the crypto-Gnosticism and semi-Manicheanism which have dogged the Church in the forms of hyper-Augustinianism for so many centuries. By emphasizing the communal and historical aspects of the Church and the worth of man's calling in the world, the Council moved away from these older forms of foreshortening to which the faith was subjected. Two things imply that the Fathers were seeking a more mature approach to the problems of human maturity: the critical reappraisal of the institutionalism and otherworldly emphasis inherited from the past, themselves to be explained as largely the products of a specific historical conditioning, as we have already suggested, and the new stress on the Church as a community of men in Christ and on man's worldly vocation.

Dietrich Bonhoeffer told us that in our century modern

secular man has come of age and having come of age has no
need for religion as it was known in the past [10]. The failures
of maturity in this so-called coming of age have quite justi-
fiably been pointed out [26:195ff]. It is not possible to make
claims for modern man's maturity of a very far-reaching kind.
The built-in obstacles to maturation in his social systems and
personality structures appear considerable. Yet many elements point to maturation and hold some promise of its
achievement. A greater individual self-realization, an openness to new experience, a degree of critical thinking—these
reflect the desire for a true maturation which would realize
man's possibilities. The overinvolvement in and dependence
upon institutions—Church or extended family—the limitation of experience to familiar contexts, and the acceptance of
beliefs on authority, characteristic of an older situation, are
disappearing. Yet too many still seek not a path to maturity
but escape from the dangers and threats that seem to lurk in
the insecurity of the new openness. The secular idolatries of
our times have grown large on this tendency and brought
untold calamity upon us.

The Fathers have, however, recognized the elements that
point to maturation and tried to do them justice. In its discussion of atheism, the *Pastoral Constitution* gave up an older
attitude of polemic and defensiveness for one of dialogue. The
Christian response to atheism is best given "by the witness of
a living and mature faith, namely, one trained to see difficulties clearly and to master them." Moreover, in its complete
acceptance of the legitimate autonomy of science and scholarship, the Constitution points to the approval of maturity as
the goal of men. It sees that "modern man is on the road to a
more thorough development of his own personality, and to a
growing discovery and vindication of his own rights" (art 41),
and it favors such a course. Man in our time tries to come of
age. The Fathers tend to accept, confirm, and identify themselves with that attempt. Furthermore, the attempt is made
in a situation characterized by the dissolution of the older

social structures in which man formerly lived. Their disappearance stimulates him to make the effort and at the same time seduces him to seek new securities which would retard it.

Certainly the traditional vertical Church, authoritatively teaching its myth with its overwhelming majority of membership in a state of intellectual and spiritual tutelage, occupied a most ambiguous position with regard to maturation. Certainly its hierarchical system and the kind of understanding of obedience it involved can—not alone among institutional structures, it is true—be described as in some ways institutionalizing immaturity through its forms of dependence. One important aspect of the one-sidedness of the Middle Ages which Trent and the Counter Reformation failed to dispel (and if anything consolidated) was the institutionalized immaturity of the laity in centrally significant religious respects. Seeing this problem, Karl Marx was led to state that the criticism of religion was the beginning of all criticism, the first step in the struggle toward maturity.

Today we realize that the full development of the human person involves his maturation. We have received from our new sciences new insights into what maturity means, though there is much about it that we do not yet understand. We know well that we are nowhere near as close to coming of age as Bonhoeffer thought. Yet in our time maturation is an aspiration. Man reaches for it, however, confusedly and with little success. Many elements which stand as obstacles to maturation are defined by the Church as sin. But the Church itself has often kept men children in things of the mind. To enable its own members to achieve maturity the Church must develop a Catholicism that does not demand a fundamentalist assent to items of intellectual definition unacceptable to the mature man today. There has long existed in the Church a kind of rundown hyperasceticism which sees the act of faith as "the submission of the intellect" and the "overcoming of intellectual pride." Such notions rest on personal formations well deserving psychoanalytic examination for they foster a kind of spiritual self-mutilation as the way to establish an archaic sense of security. In the frantic reaction to the modernist crisis that kind of attitude gained ground. The Church now faces the challenge of emancipating its faith from all such historically derived group neuroses, of making it once again an invitation to growth and enlargement of spirit through grace. The Church cannot become the sign of the transcendence of the human person, as the Council Fathers propose, if it fails to liberate its own members from outmoded fundamentalisms. In the summer of 1967 the *New York Times* reported that Pope Paul VI had abolished the antimodernist oath, that long-standing monument of ecclesiastical McCarthyism. The Vatican, the paper remarked, had denied the story but had "said that the oath was being shortened and heavily revised" [60]. The importance of this move can hardly be overestimated.

The sociological demythologization of the Church is at the same time the creation of conditions which will encourage mature faith among its members. The problems of institution, myth, and maturity are subtly intertwined. Myth speaks of divine things in human terms. To fail to grasp just how inadequate it is, despite its necessity, and to take it uncritically is to remain immature in important respects. Bergson has suggested the element of somnambulism in what he has called static religion [6: chaps 2, 3], and Cassirer comments that Socrates has shown us a way out of the somnambulistic effects of myth through self-knowledge [14: pt 2].

It is necessary to speak of the relations of God and man in mythic form, the only way it can be done, but once made, such statements can assume a most ambiguous character. They can point the way to transcendence or they can create a certain combination of exteriority and charismatic involvement which tends to elicit what we have just called somnambulism. They can come to provide a dream world, a fantasy universe, to replace the real world in which man must work out his destiny. Efforts to reach maturity, involving reality testing, then cause men to rebel against the fantasy world.

Christianity is the product of the original Hebraic break-through of myth in which the prophets dispelled much of the mythic somnambulism with the ethical call of the transcendent God. The Church, following this intuition, used Hellenic rationality further to dispel myth. Yet the Church could not escape history. It too finally involved myth in this pejorative sense, and this aspect of myth lies at the very heart of its great historic problems. The sociological demythologization of the Church begun at Vatican II represents the Catholic attempt to meet this challenge maturely.

We have seen that the Church began as a relatively sectarian religious movement of the interiorly turned in the empire; it became the spiritual source and central institution of the new civilization which arose in the Middle Ages upon the ruins of antiquity; and as such it became a "church" in Troeltsch's sense. We have seen that Church, on the defensive for four centuries, once again taking on an increasingly sectarian character—becoming a church in structure and a sect in spirit.

The Council points to a Church which in Troeltsch's sense will be neither church nor sect. The path opening before it is indicated in the *Pastoral Constitution* and in the *Lumen Gentium*. The Church no longer relies on an alliance with government or governing classes, no longer sees its future structurally bound up with any particular kind of political order, and consequently no longer has that familiarity exhibited by Pius X with what God intends human society to be. The harsh and cruel historical process by which the Church was literally torn out of its embeddedness in the older order of society and thought caused great suffering. It was, however, the process of emancipation. The Council recognized specifically the good done the Church by its opponents.

Now the Church begins seriously to explore the possibilities of a new kind of presence in the world. It seeks a presence that will no longer be the Church in the older medieval and Constantinian sense, in Troeltsch's sense, but one that also will not involve a sectarian posture of world rejection. This Constitution and the *Lumen Gentium* contain a number of leads: a Church which is the sign of personal transcendence, a Church which is in the world to serve, a healing and elevating Church, a Church which imbues everyday activity with a deeper meaning and importance, a Church engaged in mutual exchange and assistance with the world.

Acceptance of the autonomy of the human mind and of the sciences means that theology relinquishes its older role as queen of the sciences. Catholic thought long resisted seeing that modern thought recognized no such hierarchy but rather tended to seek enlargement of perspective in interdisciplinary dialogue. Modern universities with their equality of disciplinary departments embody this idea. Catholics, of course, long ago accepted it as practice in their own universities but failed to see that they accepted anything other than current administrative practices—it is a failure of perception not uncommon among ecclesiastical administrators and religious superiors. Now the Council understands the intellectual implications of modernity in this respect. The Church offers itself as an honest participant in the effort to serve man's welfare. Theology offers itself as a voice in the intellectual dialogue. Merit, not established status, is the criterion of worth. The Church states unequivocally that it has "no proper mission in the political, economic, or social order" (art 42). In the documents of the Council, in the appearance of Paul VI before the United Nations, in the meetings of Paul and Athenagoras we catch the hint of what the new direction of the Church's development must be. Before the United Nations, for instance, the Pope spoke with the dignity and charisma of his office yet in a spirit of human equality and fraternity and with a moving humility.

In this chapter we have introduced the term "demythologization" and used it in a larger and more inclusive sense than is usual. It is generally taken to mean the elimination of archaic and/or magical elements from the presentation of the Christian faith, referring chiefly to the 1st century version of the Babylonian cosmology to be found in the gospels. We have enlarged that meaning to include the elimination of all "dated" elements, not only in the thought of Christianity but in other forms of embodiment and external objectification of the Christian faith, which have become obsolete in the contemporary situation. We have seen all forms of external expression—all areas of institutionalization—as analogous to language. Religion as a sociological phenomenon exhibits three aspects, interrelated but differentiated, which represent the expression in thought, act, and relationship of the meaning of the religious message. Thus belief—creed, doctrine, and theology—cult, and organization may be thought of as different but analogous spheres of the objectification of religious meaning.

The sociological demythologization of the Church involves the dismantling of this vast superstructure, the disentangling of its essential, timeless elements from their historically and culturally conditioned expressions, and their new institutionalization. It is a process fraught with conflict, danger, and suffering, but it is the price of vitality and relevance. It is also related to and part of the attempt of man today to achieve maturity. The Council recognized that aspect of the modern experience that made for human maturation. "A more critical ability to distinguish religion from a magical view of the world and from the superstitions that still circulate purifies religion and exacts day-by-day a more personal and explicit adherence to faith" (art 7). Its end effect was to align itself with modern man's efforts to come of age. All this implies a new kind of Church, a new kind of community presence of the "people of God" in and with the world, calling it to transcendence and serving it.

We must now give some attention to religious language in a narrower and more precise sense—to language properly so called. We may regard religious language as consisting of two major elements. The first includes those aspects of religious language that "describe" the actions of God. "God called Abraham and Samuel, He spoke by the Prophets, He sent His Son." Such language is analogical, since we do not know any other way of speaking about God's acts except with the terms we use to describe human acts. This usage—analogical and therefore not, strictly speaking, "literal"—especially when the human words belong to an archaic mode of thinking, is mythical. To demythologize means to say these things in more contemporary or at least more contemporarily appropriate ways. We have no abstract language in which we can say them with timeless and "historyless" pure reason. Man does develop an ontology, but there is no "proto-ontological" language. To fail to see this is to repeat the mistakes of the past and find in the utterances of ecclesiastical authority and the expressions of scripture a kind of literalness which no discourse about God can ever have.

In the modernist crisis, the Church feared that the substance of its historic faith was being emptied out. Indeed, with the Church completely encased in the culture-bound mentality it had defensively maintained, any attempt to come to terms with the historical and timeless elements with the languages and modes of thought available was likely to lead a Catholic either to unbelief, as it did Loisy, or to recalcitrance and self-inhibition within the older established ways of thinking, as has since been normatively enforced in the anti-modernist oath. Yet Catholic theology always recognized that statements about God were analogical. In an earlier age, Catholic theologians had tried to work out a logic of analogy—an analogy of being of strict proportion. According to this, when we speak of the "living God" we neither make a literal statement nor assert a crude anthropomorphism. We declare that God lives according to his own mode, about which we know nothing; that we live according to a human mode, about which we know something; that our mode suggests attributes of God's but in God they exist totally differently, in a way unknown and mysterious to us. Analogicity asserted things by analogy and recognized how minimal and suggestive were the assertions. Dogmatic teaching and popular thinking, while always using analogy (and its related principle of eminence, which attributed created perfections "analogically" to God, and which is dependent upon the character of human knowledge of such created "perfections"), tended to under-emphasize and even lose sight of the significance of the distinction between the language of theology and that of everyday experience. Indeed, a thorough examination of the implications for knowledge of the medieval doctrine of analogy, if carried out in relation to the present state of our knowledge of nature and our knowledge of the knowing process, might have proved as upsetting to Pius X as did Loisy's extreme historicism.

A second element in religious language proper concerns man's actions—his hearing the call and his response to it. There a different kind of language is possible. When the gospel tells us that as the twig is inclined so the tree is bent, that it does not profit a man to gain the whole world and lose his own soul, that sufficient for today are today's troubles, it speaks of characteristics of human existence. (When it makes such statements as "to those who received him, to them gave he the power to become the sons of God," it uses both kinds of language, describing man's embracing of faith in a new life and attributing the cause to God's initiative.) Speaking of human characteristics in this way may be little different from scientific language—the twig quotation does not differ fundamentally from what may be found stated in a behavioral psychology text—or it may call for a more existential language, a language which sees the matter from the point of view of man as actor, participant, and responder. Most of our religious assertions combine both kinds of language—the analogical, about God, and the existential, about man. The ways of putting both analogy and existential statements are highly conditioned by the culture and epoch. Such statements may be thought of as the mythic in the narrower sense.

Demythologization means to free the "real content" from the dated forms of expression. In any attempts to do this the Church has always been concerned to preserve the historical element in the Christian faith, a concern that would appear to be entirely essential. The "mythic" statement "God sent His Son" is identified with the earthly career of Jesus of Nazareth, who, the creed asserts, "suffered under Pontius Pilate." Those who knew this man experienced the existential call of his person, message, and mission. They stated it in the original *kerygma* in the two kinds of language spoken of above. They were not writing "objective history" but they were talking of experiences rooted in an objective historical event. Yet the question of what it means to speak of "objective history" raises new problems, for history is not simply a recording of everything that happened, but only of everything significant that happened. To put it that way brings up the question, Significant for what and to whom? Elements of subjective understanding—of *verstehen*—are introduced. Moreover, existential aspects not so easily objectified come into the picture. In this area, history, the social sciences, and psychology are at present far from having achieved any profound clarification.

Human life presents a many-sided spectacle involving quite diverse kinds of experience. The experience of personal relations is different from the disciplined experience of the scientific laboratory. There are also ethical experience and aesthetic experience. We are suggesting that in these realms — in religious experience, in human existential experience, in the experience of scientific observation, in ethical experience, and in aesthetic experience—the modalities of experience call for specific modes of expression. Whatever the classification used, each area requires a specific language to do justice to the specific mode of experience, the specific perspective upon and way of relating to reality. True, all these modes of experience are experiences and ways of relating to reality typical of the human person and are also experiences of and relations to a world. In the unity of the person and the context of person–world they receive a kind of integration. But human personal existence is not an objectified metalanguage, despite its subjective unity. Each realm involves a different kind of experiencing and a different kind of problem for utterance and communication —for formulation.

Looking at the modernist crisis after more than half a century, one gets the uneasy feeling that both sides thought they had the "metalanguage" for handling the vast complex — Loisy in history, Pius in scholastic theology, or even common-sense language. With such a complete failure to comprehend the complexity of knowing, it is little wonder that events assumed a tragic cast. Conservativism placed its adherents in the embarrassing situation of insisting upon a fundamentalist literalness in the gospel as history and thereby losing the sense of what is meant by history. Modernism advocated demythologization before there was any language (or any sense of the need for a language) to sort out the elements in the complex assertions of faith as they had come into existence. Only in this Council do we see the Church developing a sense of history of the modern kind.

In a very insightful criticism of the *Pastoral Constitution* Dr. Joseph Sittler believes the "problematic of the *historical* mode of man's being in the world" too lightly touched upon [81:424]. He says,

> When Sören Kierkegaard asked "is a historical point of departure possible for an eternal consciousness; how can such a point of departure have any other than a mere historical interest; is it possible to base an eternal blessedness upon historical knowledge," he blasted open a problem that had been gathering pressure ever since the Enlightenment. This question today torments both Roman and non-Roman thought, constitutes the profoundest anguish of modernity as it weighs the Christian gospel, and is the awesome but promising context for our common reopening of the meaning of tradition [81:425].

The *Pastoral Constitution* represents a great advance in the

Catholic attempt to understand the historical. But it leaves unsolved the problem of ontology and history, of substance and process, of structure and openness. There is much work for Catholic theology here.

Sittler pushes the question farther. He raises in historical form the matter of immanence and transcendence. Pius X in the *Lamentabili* appears now so nearly entirely the creature of an age and a sociological situation that one asks where transcendence is in relation to this document. Is it not concerned rather with defending a historically specific mode of apprehending what Christian tradition teaches? Sittler impels us to think about the radical problem of historicity and a relation to something out of history, to see man in his full relativity, his complete historicity. Only then can we understand this problem. But the considerations on language introduced above—tentative and suggestive in themselves—are significant here. To seek to understand what is involved in man's simultaneous historicity and relation to transcendence without sorting out experiences with appropriate languages is to impose a Babel of tongues upon an already subtle and anguish-laden area.

The question of immanence and transcendence is the form the problem assumed in the modernist crisis. Immanence, experience, subjectivity (motivation, aspiration, response, resolve), openness of potentiality, evolution and emergence, creativity—these are the very stuff of the human drama. But they open out upon, seek for, point toward, and are involved with transcendence, formulated knowledge and tradition, structure—both ontological and historical.

Sittler raises a second question. He asks whether the *Pastoral Constitution* does not take too optimistic a view. Does it not overlook and underplay the way the advance of technology and the passing of traditional society undermine human belief and hope? Karl Mannheim pointed out that in the modern West men tended to become incapable of religious or utopian enthusiasm and to develop a mentality of "fact mindedness" [53:230ff]. The critical character of modern thought, the mechanization of life by technology, and its routinization in urbanization seemed to be cutting off modern western man from the deep wellsprings of spiritual creativity. Sittler makes a comparable observation on what he calls "the soul of modernity":

> What is involved is rather a total dubiety about the real, and a sense of the end of those promises that the Enlightenment held out. For by a strange irony, the very scientific enterprise that has so deeply shaped modernity now falters in its confidence that it can fulfill such promises. The very structure and process of the world recedes from the penetration of the scientific gaze so that correspondences between human thought and actuality are questioned in fact, and, more importantly, in principle. The modern intellectual is thus characterized by what may be termed the pathos of intellection, and the sardonic as a total mood displaces the pilgrim gallantry of an earlier generation [81:425].

There is more here than sheer Niebuhrian rhetoric. It is reflective of the mood of many. Yet in terms of the two cultures of C. P. Snow, one wonders whether the dissolution of scientifically based hope is not more characteristic of the humanist intellectuals derived from the Enlightenment than of scientists themselves. No one is any longer a fundamentalist about physics—no one considers its formulas photographic in their representative realism—but a sophisticated common sense can hardly doubt in this age of spectacular advance in macro and micro physics that there are some fairly accurate "correspondences between human thought and actuality." The Council remained realistic in its epistemology, though not dogmatically so. It affirmed that men can know reality but did not commit itself in any scientific or philosophical language. Epistemologically the Council remained "naive," but sophisticatedly naive. It affirmed the reality of knowledge and left open the whole epistemological area for study and exploration. It remained optimistic in this area as well.

The Enlightenment was a secession from Catholicism — a violently rebellious one in many ways. It was based upon the Hellenic side of the older Catholic culture. In this Council the Church sought rapprochement with its rebellious child and its offspring in science and social thought. In returning to a wholeness it had failed to preserve historically, it fittingly enough accepted that earlier optimism. Unlike certain Protestant neoorthodox trends which see the religious experience as appropriate to the experience of disillusionment, the Council took a more hopeful stand.

Sittler's second question points up the complexity of the situation of western man today. Western man has come through a long period of relative demythologization —centuries of uprooting, of molting, of technical progress, of increased knowledge, of advancing anomie. He has generally made two responses to the disorganizing effects of this dynamic history: tried desperately to cling to his old beliefs and shore up his old structures —to clutch his gods —and tried also to find new myths to give him security, to enable him to escape the burden of freedom —whored after new gods. A few people have sought to face the world eschewing all escapes from freedom and to respond as men of awareness and responsibility. The process of demythologization was at first the carrier of a great hope, the bearer of great promise. More recently disappointment and disillusionment have clouded the outlooks of many. The Council has attempted to face this modern challenge and to prepare the Church to face it in the light of the Christian message.

The historical problem and the epistemological problem must both be met by Catholicism as part of its theological problem. This Constitution recognizes the role of natural and social science in forming the mentality of modern men, notes that the "scientific spirit exerts a new kind of impact on the cultural sphere and on modes of thought." This brings men "hope of improved self-knowledge" (art 5), but also it "can foster a certain exclusive emphasis on observable data, and an agnosticism about everything else." "For the methods of investigation which these sciences use can wrongly be considered as the supreme rule for discovering the whole truth. By virtue of their methods, however, these sciences cannot penetrate to the intimate meaning of things" (art 57). Further, "the intellectual nature of the human person is perfected by wisdom and needs to be. . . . Steeped in wisdom, man passes through visible realities to those which are unseen" (art 15). The Council Fathers saw that modes of human knowing — modes of man's response to his world and to a beyond reached through it — could be lost in a culture whose forms of expression were only "scientific" and "technological." Here too they remain optimistic and assume the reality of knowledge.

Their discussion of science and wisdom brings us to the problem we discussed earlier. No scientific or philosophical language, nor yet the modes of experience to which such languages are linked, comprises either the "really real" or the metalanguage into which all the rest can be translated as into a common denominator. When we add to these considerations our earlier observation of the openness of man's entelechy, and the profundity of man's historical conditioning affecting his modes of thought, feeling, and experience, we see how radical is the problem here.

Western thought in our times is showing a new, deeper self-consciousness, one that can often lead to confusion and anguish. Man has embarked upon the examination of himself in depth. He will often find himself blocked. A number of the blocks come from the vested interests of entrenched ideologies — or rather of ideologues (and cryptoideologues masked as "scientists and scholars"!) who are threatened by the openness required by the examination. These may be religious, as in the many cases of intransigence, from Galileo to Loisy; but they can equally well be nonreligious and even antireligious. Schools of thought in science and scholarship become quasi myths protecting men from an encounter with openness. Scientism performs a role in this respect similar to that of religion.

Still, man has begun his self-examination, though he may often seek to escape the logic of the effort to find refuge in confessional, scientific, or scholarly halfway houses. This extension of self-awareness comprises the forward thrust of the historically developing consciousness of our period. In the history of human consciousness we have reached the stage of demythologization early foreshadowed in Socrates. It is, as we have suggested, a demythologization not simply of religious belief but of all cultural and institutional forms inherited from the past, from religion to the relationships of the sexes. The Council seemed to have a sense of this, as reflected in the *Pastoral Constitution*. It opened up the basic questions. It needs to be followed by fearless, tolerant, and patient work to meet, understand, and work toward solution of the great problems involved. Catholic theology, in dialogue with other forms of religious thought and with science and scholarship, must enter into the main stream of western intellectual history at this strategic point and in this strategic area. There is an enormous amount of catching up to do.

The new venture on which the Council set theology will be a difficult one. There will be many shocks; the growing pains will bring much suffering to individual souls; it will from time to time rock the Church. But should this venture be once again suppressed in fear and hysteria as in 1907, the Church will have lost its historic opportunity. *Aggiornamento* will have proved a vain hope; to pretend it any longer in such circumstances, a hoax.

That Catholicism has entered upon this course with optimism is itself a promising omen. Some 20 years ago F. S. C. Northrop suggested that great hope for Western culture may indeed lie in the potential of Roman Catholicism for self-examination and reformulation of its beliefs in the light of the modern scientific experience. He spoke of the precedent for this revolutionary development in the revolution in Catholic thinking made by Aquinas in accepting Aristotelianism in the 13th century and relating it to Christian belief. At the time of writing, the statement seemed at best a forlorn hope, perhaps simply a well intentioned wish [64:254ff]. Now the possibility has emerged as a most significant historic challenge. It is a phenomenon of our time; it is on the frontier, on the farthest reaches, of western man's painful effort to come of age. For the Church to meet this challenge the changes will have to be very bold and far reaching, transcending anything that has yet been achieved by any denomination. In this effort the Roman Catholic Church bears the future of Christianity as a whole.

VII

THE PASTORAL CONSTITUTION
AND PROBLEMS OF SPECIAL URGENCY

THE second part of the Constitution was drawn up to present guidelines for Church policy and Catholic action. It was conceived as more practical, less theoretical than Part One, a fact reflected in its title, "Some Problems of Special Urgency." It is not, however, to be looked at as a matter of specific programmatics, although it is more concretely conceived and more problem-oriented than Part One. It is divided into five chapters: Fostering the Nobility of Marriage and the Family; The Proper Development of Culture; Socio-Economic Life; The Life of the Political Community; and The Fostering of Peace and the Promotion of a Community of Nations. It will be noted that these five topics correspond to the four subdivisions introduced by Troeltsch in his study of the history of the Church's relation to the world—family, learning, economic life, and political life—and that in our times a new global dimension is added to the consideration of political life.

Chapter I, dealing with the family, emphasizes conjugal and personal relationship. While admonishing against "excessive self-love, the worship of pleasure, and illicit practices against human generation" (art 47), the Council Fathers state the Church's approval of married love and declare that such love, together with the good of the children, "imposes total fidelity" and argues for "an unbreakable oneness" between the spouses (art 48). The love of men and women is seen as "eminently human." It represents in marriage a "merging of the human with the divine" which excels by far "mere erotic inclination" (art 49).

Two remarkable characteristics of this section are the personalist emphasis on the love of the spouses and the absence of the older abstract and legalistic discussion of primary and secondary ends. Adolf Harnack thought of the Roman Church as in some major way continuing the Roman Empire, especially as continuing the Roman tradition of legality. The importance of law in the history of the Church in the West has been enormous; many of the great popes of the Middle Ages were canonists. Some historians have admired this aspect of the Church, seeing in it a kind of triumph for principle and rationality. Others, however, and a large number of theologians as well, have considered the dominance of law in the ecclesiastical mentality the mental concomitant of the transformation of the Church from a community into a juridical structure. That it routinized ethics and objectified community in ways at times calamitous to spiritual life can hardly be denied. In its dealing with marriage, as with other matters, the Church codified its law. Canon law defined marriage as a "contract," in which the spouses grant each other the right to certain acts—"to those acts which are capable to procreate new life" [34:440]. In spite of pressure from conservatives, the preparatory commission refused to use the word "contract" in the Constitution. The declaration presents marriage after the Pauline metaphor of the relation between Christ and the Church. It stresses personal relationship consistent with the personalist emphasis of the document as a whole.

In the past Catholic thought on marriage had typically been legalistic and presented in terms of an ververbalized scholasticism. There were the "primary" and "secondary" ends of the relationship to be taken into account. The primary end was the procreation of children; the secondary, the relationship between husband and wife. Here the Manichean minded saw less the development of love than a remedy for concupiscence. The new theology of the period following World War II explored this area and introduced the personalist notions that came to the fore in the Council treatment. Here too the new theology met obstacles and opposition; a number of works which attempted to revise the approach to marriage were put on the Index in the 1950s. The Constitution avoids the older terminology altogether. It states that "marriage and conjugal love are by their nature ordained toward the begetting and educating of children," but adds, "while not making the other purposes of matrimony of less account." The commission which drafted the final text wished to avoid settling this question in the document.

We have already noted that despite Troeltsch's statement that the Church came to terms with the world easily in the area of family relations, and despite the fact that the Church always gave the family a strong emphasis, it never was able to combine sex and spirituality without marked strain. We have indicated the depth of this problem and the relation of it to the basic formation of the human person and his development of freedom and the capacity to direct himself. We have suggested that the conditions of life in late antiquity—both social and physical, and including, indeed, sanitary conditions—tended to exacerbate the problems involved here. As the model of the Christian took form, it left little room for incorporating sexuality. It was a monastic model trimmed down for the laity.

Officially, of course, the Church did not condemn sex. Its creationist theology and its resistance to the Manicheanism that haunted it throughout its career made that impossible. Yet sex was highly suspect. Throughout Christian history there were those who, like many conservatives in the Council, "did not see how married love in its sexual expression could be related to a sacrament. They explained that the sacrament pertains only to the spiritual friendship of the spouses, while sexual life is only a remedy for concupiscence" [34:442]. Such thinking reminds one of the picture of Christian spouses given by Calvin in the *Institutes*. The Calvinist was indeed admonished to procreate children in soberness. The Catholic

Church has always officially held the line on this matter; the Council of Trent taught that the sacrament of matrimony "sanctifies the natural love" of the spouses, and much of Catholic theology came to see the sacrament consummated in the act of sexual intercourse. But the deeper suspicions remained. The Church could not really see how to put sex together with its conception of spirituality. A quotation from Pope Pius XII will suggest that felt incongruity:

> As St. Thomas very rightly asserts, the deepest natural instinct is the instinct of conservation; the sexual instinct comes second. In addition, it is for the rational inclination, which is the distinguishing privilege of our nature, to regulate these fundamental instincts and by dominating them to ennoble them. . . .
>
> In order to acquire this perfect mastery of spirit over the senses, it is not enough to refrain from acts directly contrary to chastity, but it is necessary also generously to renounce anything that may offend this virtue nearly or remotely; at such a price will the soul be able to reign fully over the body and lead its spiritual life in peace and liberty. Who then does not see, in the light of Catholic principles, that perfect chastity and virginity, far from harming the normal unfolding of man or woman, on the contrary endow them with the highest moral nobility [75:302].

The fact that the interpretation of Catholic teaching as well as its theological and legal formulation was carried out for centuries in this atmosphere of thinking explains the caricature which specific Catholic teaching of sex often became. (It should also be noted that, even before the Council, many confessors attempting intelligent prudential counsel and respecting the responsibility of the spouses for decisions in conscience, showed remarkable sensitivity and often gave advice which in practice amounted to policies much more liberal than the officially stated teaching would lead one to expect.) The fact that it was the work of celibates makes the consequences even more predictable. Let us merely cite the questions raised by Maximos IV, Patriarch of Antioch, during the third session of the Council on October 29, 1964: "Do we not have the right to ask ourselves whether certain official positions do not follow from obsolete conceptions, and possibly even from the psychosis of celibates who are strangers to this sector of life? Are we not, unwittingly, weighed down by that Manichaean concept of man and of the world whereby the carnal act, evil in itself, is tolerated only for the sake of the child?" [45:223]

This kind of basic attitude toward sex found its formulations in canon law, where an additional institutional bias saw the institution of "family" as superior to the individual persons who made it up, and in theology, where the biology of Aristotle—repeated in 1954 by Pius XII—saw man as an organism ordained to the ends of its nature. Yet it is important to grasp that beneath the abstractions and legalism still lurks a substantial psychological problem which the Roman Church has never come close to clarifying, either existentially or theoretically. In its personalist approach and in its eschewing of older "spiritualisms" of a Manichean kind, the Council did important pioneer work. But there remains much to be done.

The Fathers of the Council agreed with the pope to remove the question of "birth-control" from the Council discussions. On June 23, 1964, Paul VI established a special commission to study the issues with respect to licit and illicit methods of regulating conception. The history of this commission, which has experienced considerable internal conflict, is beyond the scope of the present work. The Constitution itself states that "sons of the Church may not undertake methods of regulating procreation which are found blameworthy by the teaching authority of the Church in its unfolding of the divine law." In the Latin text a footnote (footnote 14 of Chapter I in Part Two) states that "certain questions which need further and more careful investigation have been handed over, at the command of the Supreme Pontiff, to a commission for the study of population, family, and births, in order that, after it fulfills its function, the Supreme Pontiff may pass judgment. With the doctrine of the magisterium in this state, this holy Synod does not intend to propose immediately concrete solutions" (art 51). Yet the document does teach the idea of "human and Christian responsibility" in parenthood (art 50). "They [married couples] will thoughtfully take into account both their own welfare and that of their children, those already born and those which may be foreseen. For this accounting they will reckon with both the material and the spiritual conditions of the times as well as of their state in life. Finally, they will consult the interests of the family group, of temporal society, and of the Church itself" (art 50).

While, as we have seen, the Catholic must not regulate procreation in ways "which are found blameworthy by the teaching authority of the Church" (art 51), decisions concerning responsible parenthood are to be made by the spouses concerned. "The parents themselves should ultimately make this judgment in the sight of God" (art 50). It has been commented that the Council "teaches the principle of responsible parenthood in article 50, in spite of the loud warning of Cardinal Ottaviani that by doing so the Church would also have to change her doctrine on infallibility" [34:443].

The question of the methods of regulating births is left as it was before the Council. Yet it was recognized that "certain modern conditions often keep couples from arranging their married lives harmoniously, and that they find themselves in circumstances where at least temporarily the size of their families should not be increased" (art 51). This may injure their love and the "full intimacy of married life," and thereby endanger the family in important ways (art 51). Again the older idea of natural law is restated in a personalist idiom finding the "objective standard" which should be brought to bear "based on the nature of the human person and his acts" (art 51). It has been observed that although the Council declares "that a true contradiction cannot exist between divine laws pertaining to the transmission of life and those pertaining to authentic conjugal love" (art 51), the Constitution "did not fully resolve the problem" [34:443].

The document also seeks to exclude the public authority from the decision regarding the size of family. Such judgment derives from the "inalienable right to marry and beget children" and belongs "to the honest judgment of the parents" (art 87). The family is "a kind of school of deeper humanity" and "the foundation of society" (art 52). The "presence of the father" is "highly beneficial" to the children. Moreover, "the children, especially the younger among them, need the care of their mother at home. This domestic role of hers must be safely preserved, though the legitimate social progress of women should not be underrated on that account." Attention is given to the proper education of the children and a plea made for support and aid of the family by Church, state, and private agencies. In an interesting abandonment of an earlier stance and with a new humility in these matters, it is stated that those "who are skilled in other sciences, notably the medical, biological, social and psychological, can considerably advance the welfare of marriage and the family, along with peace of conscience, if by pooling their efforts they labor to explain more thoroughly the varying conditions favoring a proper regulation of births" (art 52).

Looking at the social transformation which technology is spreading throughout the world in its historical perspective, we should not be surprised to find among its results an upsetting of the patterns of relationships between the sexes. Modernization on one level uproots men from older established cultural contexts; it "liberates" them from the bonds of traditional social groups. Such liberation is at the same time a kind of psychological deracination causing anomie—a state in which loss of consensus on basic values coincides with loss of membership in stable groups. On another level modernization introduces people to attitudes of conscious criticism of tradition. In this kind of situation the sexual drive becomes emancipated from that complex of social and psychological inhibitions and canalizations which direct, contain, and hold it in check in more stable social and cultural conditions. The strength and centrality of sexuality in the human makeup tend to make the resulting condition one of turmoil and even chaos. In the midst of this profound cultural confusion about sexuality—a confusion which the West encourages for its market value, while the communist East still attempts to enforce the more puritanical mores inherited from the past—a search is going on for genuineness of relationship and for a pattern of meaning, a search for value.

How well does this document succeed in relating the Church to the modern sexual revolution? Undoubtedly it moves away from an earlier hyper-Augustinianism as the dominant mood of Catholic attitudes on sex. But there is here, perhaps more than elsewhere, a need for serious study and investigation in Catholic theology. Man today looks for meaning as a sexual being. Can Christianity aid his quest?

Part One of this Constitution recognized man as a historical being located in time and involved in the processes of social change, development, and transformation. It attempted to put together traditional Christian teaching on man—his having been made in God's image, his fall from grace, his redemption by Christ, and his eternal destiny—with a newer concept of man as he stands revealed to himself in this age of transition, in which the processes of history and his own scholarly and scientific efforts have brought him to a higher self-consciousness. It concedes that, after a long and arduous struggle, man has the means to transform the earth and make it a fit habitation for himself and his posterity. It realizes that he is on the verge of developing an understanding of himself which will enable him to shape himself. It sees both of these capacities as having been brought about by historical developments that have upset traditional norms, institutions, and establishments and uprooted man from earlier unquestioned securities. It sees the misery and grandeur of man increased and intensified many times over as he stands on the edge of either self-apotheosis or self-annihilation.

But can it be said that the Council Fathers faced the fact of sexuality—the fact that "male and female created he them" (Gen 1:27)—with the same profundity as it faced the fact of historicity? Moreover, can it be concluded that the Council showed the same insight into the peculiar problems of women, the role of women in the family and in the working world, the problems of feminine identity, the problem of personal development as it presents differing aspects to men and women? The sexual revolution and the emancipation of women represent genuine historical achievements. On these bases new patterns of human behavior and a new, more satisfying human identity need to be developed. Recognizing the worth and ultimate mystery of man's earthly vocation involves also recognizing the worth and ultimate mystery of his sexual identity—of maleness and femaleness, and of the relationships between male and female.

The Constitution seeks to infuse man's earthly activity with the sense of transcendence to the here and now, to relate his activity in the world to a destiny that lies beyond it. Thus the Fathers hope to show modern man the Christian orientation to an eternal life with God, to share with him the Church's anticipation of the return of the Risen Lord to inaugurate his messianic kingdom. While attempting to overcome the ancient bias against the world, the Constitution tries to reveal man's deepest purpose and ultimate destiny as Catholicism conceives it. In this document the Fathers in effect spell out a new "Summa Contra Gentiles" in the spirit of fraternity and dialogue. They proclaim, as Aquinas had done in the 13th century, man's final goal and the insufficiency of merely earthly realities, of whatever spiritual nobility, to fill man's basic need. But they do so, not in terms of Aristotle's relatively static conception of man's entelechy; they do so in terms of man as a historically evolving being. Historical man becomes eschatological man.

Man seeks fulfillment on earth—in his earthly activities, his courting and marrying, his establishment and support of a family, his community development and nation building, his economic activity, and his pursuit of knowledge. He changes his world at the same time that he makes himself. But, according to the Church's teaching, he is still a stranger and a sojourner here below. He is still called to a farther destiny. Where Aquinas saw this relation in static terms, the *Pastoral Constitution* recasts the whole thing in dynamic terms.

We have already seen that the dynamic approach introduces an awareness of the unstructuredness and openness which modern man experiences. It is interesting that in Chapter II of Part Two, in the course of the more practical consideration of some urgent problems, a question of the utmost theoretical significance arises. One reason is that the document, being the product of commissions, committees, and floor debate, does not exhibit the unity to be expected from individual authorship. But there is a more cogent reason. It is precisely in the consideration of practical matters that the most significant theoretical questions appear in our day. It is precisely in terms of practical implications that theoretical advances take on their greatest import. The development of nuclear weapons has made this clear with respect to the natural sciences, and it is rapidly becoming true for the social sciences.

Chapter II, Part Two is entitled "The Proper Development of Culture." In its introduction the Fathers for the first time make use of the concept of culture as it is understood in sociology and anthropology. Here, rather than in the theoretical section, Part One, it is recognized that man lives not only in a physical environment and a social environment, but also in an environment of meaning which he himself develops. Man is further defined as a being that "can come to an authentic and full humanity only through culture, that is, through the cultivation of natural goods and values." Culture is "all those factors by which man refines and unfolds his manifold spiritual and bodily qualities." Culture has "a historical and social aspect." In consequence we can speak of "a plurality of cultures," which involve "various conditions of community living, as well as various patterns for organizing the goods of life," which form "for each human community its proper patrimony." In culture so understood, "throughout the course of time man expresses, communicates, and conserves in his works great spiritual experiences and desires, so that these may be of advantage to the progress of many, even of the whole human family." Culture provides "the specific historical environment which enfolds men of every nation and age" (art 53).

Where previously the Constitution placed great stress—and quite properly—on the role of technology in bringing about profound and rapid social change, it is now observed that "the enormous growth of natural, human, and social sciences," as well as progress in technology, has "profoundly changed" the "living conditions of modern man." Indeed, these changes are initiating "a new age in human history." Thus

> . . . the so-called exact sciences sharpen critical judgment to a very fine edge. Recent psychological research explains human activity more profoundly. Historical studies make a signal contribution to bringing men to see things in their changeable and evolutionary aspects. Customs and usages are becoming increasingly uniform. Industrialization, urbanization, and other causes of community living create new ways of thinking, acting, and making use of leisure. The growth of communication between the various nations and social groups opens more widely to all the treasures of different cultures. Thus, little by little, a more universal form of human culture is developing, one that will promote and express the unity of the human race to the degree that it preserves the particular features of the different cultures [art 54].

Clearly, the Council has gone a long way toward accepting many of the insights of historicism and the social sciences.

But it still hopes to be able to hold on to transhistorical truth in two spheres. One is reminded of the work of Ernst Troeltsch, who with personal anguish probed the implications of historicism for religion. At first he sought to find a transhistorical basis for truth and value in the inner experience of the Christian and its effect upon his action. He also thought he detected an evolution in the world religions toward a universal religious point of view that would be like liberal Protestantism [87]. Later he took a more pessimistic attitude: "The actual history of religion knows nothing of the common character of all religions, or of their natural trend toward Christianity" [88:77f]. In his *Historismus und Seine Probleme* Troeltsch concerned himself with the "relation of individual historical facts to the standards of value within the entire domain of history in connection with the development of political, social, ethical, aesthetic, and scientific ideas." He found that "even the validity of science and logic seemed to exhibit, under different skies and upon different soil, strong individual differences present even in their deepest and innermost rudiments" [88:52f]. He felt that culture, though the "source of all nobility and all greatness," was in every case a unique historical product, the result of a "molding which is peculiar, unique, and *sui generis*," and that it remained in a state of "permanent dependence on the natural basis and the temporary and special historical basis of that basis" [88:105ff].

This Constitution, while admitting the dependence upon local conditions, accepting with approval the specific differences in cultures which make up the particular patrimony of peoples, and recognizing the historical and cultural conditioning of men, still sees in this historical period a "more universal form of human culture . . . developing" (art 54). The communications revolution and the development of interdependence—"socialization," to use the conciliar term—tend to produce uniformity. Moreover, granting an openness and a range of possibility unrecognized in the past, the

Fathers continue to see a basic oneness in human nature which makes the most diverse cultures variations upon the theme of human possibility conditioned by a great variety of historical circumstances. Hence the element of unity and consistency in all cross cultural phenomena.

The social sciences have placed heavy emphasis upon the differences between cultures and on the relativity of cultural norms and values. But the social sciences have always rested upon two assumptions—that all societies and cultures could be analyzed in terms of one kind of theoretical categorization, and that no matter how great the cultural differences a social scientist from one culture could come to understand a radically different one with time, patience, effort, and sympathy. These assumptions imply the further premises that there is a psychic unity of the human race despite all the variation and that the human situation, however different in various settings, exhibits a basic analogousness.

The assumptions of modern social science tend to support the more optimistic position of the Council with respect to the implications of historicism. The Fathers see cultures as the creation and expression of a human nature much more flexible, open, and unformed than was recognized by previous Church positions, but they believe that a common set of tendencies is nevertheless characteristic of human nature. Cultures, they feel, are conditioned by vastly different historical circumstances in the experience of different peoples. Yet as long as men are men and the human condition has some elements of invariance, all cultures must exhibit a common or analogous set of typological characteristics, despite the greatest variation of concrete content. Further, the Fathers perceive an inclination toward religious profundity and genuine truth in all cultures. In the *Decree on the Church's Missionary Activity*, they admonish nonwestern Christians to "be familiar with their national and religious traditions, gladly and reverently laying bare the seeds of the Word which lie hidden in them" (art 11).

Culture is a human creation; it "flows immediately from

man's spiritual and social nature" (art 59). It has "an eminent place in the integral vocation of man," but one still not completely understood; its meaning has yet to be fully uncovered (art 57). By cultural development of himself, man also spiritualizes himself and helps to "elevate the human family" toward "universal values" (art 57). The Church is "sent to all peoples of every time and place" and is "not bound exclusively and indissolubly to any race or nation, nor to any particular way of life or any customary pattern of living, ancient or recent. Faithful to her own tradition and at the same time conscious of her universal mission, she can enter into communion with various cultural modes, to her own enrichment and theirs too" (art 58). While coming to a recognition in depth of the historicity of modes of thinking, feeling, and acting and the relativity of cultural products, the Fathers assert a naturally based potential universalism and proclaim the Christian gospel as its leaven and crown. Catholic theology will have much to do to explore and spell out the problems involved in this stand.

In the Fathers' view, not only do different cultural perspectives divide men and introduce particularisms into their modes of thought and relationship, but the different specializations which come from science and Western learning do the same thing on another level of sophistication and organization. It is not simply the matter of the two cultures—one based in science, the other in humanities; one optimistic about man's capacity, the other tending to a profound disillusionment— discussed by C. P. Snow, but rather a more proliferated particularism of separate scientific and scholarly disciplines. Interdisciplinary communication in our day is often more difficult than intercultural communication. The historian who has managed to understand the Assyrians often cannot communicate with the anthropologist who has managed to communicate with the Australian aborigines!

Today it is more difficult than ever for a synthesis to be formed of the various branches of knowledge and the arts. For while the mass and diversity of cultural factors are increasing, there is a decline in the individual man's ability to grasp and unify these elements. Thus the ideal of "the universal man" is disappearing more and more. Nevertheless, it remains man's duty to preserve a view of the whole human person, a view in which the values of intellect, will, conscience, and fraternity are preeminent [art 61].

It cannot be doubted that here the Constitution deals with a subject of strategic significance in our world. The Council recognized the serious danger of "the loss of living fidelity to the heritage of tradition" which is an effect of our "enormous scientific and technical progress" (art 56). It recognized too the threat to a genuine humanism, as well as to man's realization of his capacity for spirituality, should the methods of observation of phenomenon come to dominate higher education (art 57). The close communicability between people of different cultures, instead of leading to "a true and fruitful dialogue between groups and nations," can be an element "disturbing the life of communities, destroying ancestral wisdom, or jeopardizing the uniqueness of each people" (art 56). A scientistically inclined and earthbound humanism threatens to truncate the potential of the Christian vision of man and may lead to a foreshortening of humanism itself. There is also the problem of "mass culture," of making it possible for "all men on earth" to be participants and to "share in cultural values, when the culture of the more sophisticated grows ever more refined and complex" (art 56).

Yet the document exhibits a kind of humanistic optimism in dealing with culture. Tracing the origin of culture to the nature of man, it asserts as well man's capacity to know reality (art 15), another basis for sharing perspectives in intercultural relations. It even sees in modern culture a number of items of great value:

> . . . scientific study and strict fidelity toward truth in scientific research, the necessity of working together with others in tech-

nical groups, a sense of international solidarity, an ever clearer
awareness of the responsibility of experts to aid men and even
to protect them, the desire to make conditions of life more
favorable for all, especially for those who are deprived of the
opportunity to exercise responsibility or who are culturally poor.

It adds, "All of these values can provide some preparation for
the acceptance of the message of the gospel—a preparation
which can be animated with divine love by Him who came to
save the world" (art 57).

Thus does the Council point a way to uniting those
things which have always been badly split off from each other
in Christian history. Spirit and flesh, otherworldly destiny
and earthly vocation, the possession of a final religious answer
and humble work to expand human understanding. Culture
is thus seen as the medium, the meaningful environment, in
which man lives. It is to be judged on the basis of a personalist
interpretation of natural law—in terms of its relation to the
personal realization of the individual. It is the central element
and the enabling condition of human vocation. It is thereby
strategically pertinent to the "divine plan . . . that man
should subdue the earth, bring creation to perfection, and
develop himself" (art 57). Man becomes a cooperator with
God, a cooperator in creation. The cultivation of himself and
the provision of the cultural atmosphere and social structure
conducive to such cultivation are considered primary. The
"human spirit must be cultivated in such a way that there
results a growth in the ability to wonder, to understand, to
contemplate, to make personal judgments, and to develop a
religious, moral and social sense" (art 59).

Man in culture but expressing, in different cultures differently, potentially universizable human propensities; man
in history and conditioned by historical circumstances but
tending to transcend history and to reach beyond it; man
embedded in the historical stream with its unique events and
at the same time a part of a sacral history moving toward fulfillment in God's time; man the creature of the earth whose

earthbound but also destined for relationship to God—these are the ideas the Council Fathers attempt to bring together in this document in accepting modern ideas of evolutionary change, of historical specificity, and of cultural relativity.

In all of this they are not unaware of the dangers from intercultural confusion, from phenomenalism and scientism, from overspecialization and the loss of a general humanism, from technicism deriving from the strategic centrality of technology, from the loss of tradition, from the materialism and superficiality that could come from increasing affluence. The Constitution states that "although the Church has contributed much to the development of culture . . . it is sometimes difficult to harmonize culture with Christian teachings." But it adds significantly,

> These difficulties do not necessarily harm the life of faith. For recent studies and findings of science, history, and philosophy raise new questions which influence life and demand new theological investigations. Furthermore, while adhering to the methods and requirements proper to theology, theologians are invited to seek continually for more subtle ways of communicating doctrine to the men of their times. For the deposit of faith or revealed truths are one thing; the manner in which they are formulated without violence to their meaning is another [art 62].

The Fathers admonish,

> May the faithful live in very close union with the men of their time. Let them strive to understand perfectly their way of thinking and feeling, as expressed in their culture. Let them blend modern science and its theories and the understanding of the most recent discoveries with Christian morality and doctrine. Thus their religious practice and morality can keep pace with their scientific knowledge and with an ever-advancing technology. Thus too they will be able to test and interpret all things in a truly Christian spirit.

Finally, "In order that such persons may fulfill their proper function, let it be recognized that all the faithful, clerical and lay, possess a lawful freedom of inquiry and of thought, and the freedom to express their minds humbly and courageously about those matters in which they enjoy competence" (art 62).

Here the Fathers face significant problems concerning modern culture. First is the problem of developing a genuine contemporary humanism and thereby maintaining awareness of the possibilities of the human spirit. We noted earlier that the secularization of culture was both a process of human emancipation and an emptying out of the substance of the older culture, whether Christian or humanist. Christopher Dawson has observed, "The old domination of classical humanism has passed away, and nothing has taken its place except the scientific specialisms which do not provide a complete intellectual education, and rather tend to disintegrate into technologies" [19:132]. Max Weber, commenting upon what became of the inner-worldly asceticism of Calvinism, said over half a century ago,

> Since asceticism undertook to remodel the world and to work out its ideals in the world, material goods have gained an increasing and finally inexorable power over the lives of men as at no previous period in history. Today the spirit of religious asceticism—whether finally, who knows?—has escaped from the cage. But victorious capitalism, since it rests on mechanical foundations, needs its support no longer. The rosy blush of its laughing heir, the Enlightenment, seems also to be irretrievably fading, and the idea of duty in one's calling prowls about in our lives like the ghost of dead religious beliefs. Where the fulfillment of the calling cannot directly be related to the highest spiritual and cultural values, or when, on the other hand, it need not be felt simply as economic compulsion, the individual generally abandons the attempt to justify it at all. In the field of its highest development, in the United States, the pursuit of wealth, stripped of its religious and ethical meaning, tends to

become associated with purely mundane passions, which often actually give it the character of sport.

No one knows who will live in this cage in the future, or whether at the end of this tremendous development entirely new prophets will arise, or there will be a great rebirth of old ideas and ideals, or, if neither, mechanized petrifaction, embellished with a sort of convulsive self-importance. For of the last stage of this cultural development, it might well be truly said: Specialists without spirit, sensualists without heart; this nullity imagines that it has attained a level of civilization never before achieved. [101:181f].

The broad cultural emphasis of this Council would seem to offer some way out of the impasse in which strategic elements of western society find themselves. Perhaps here we have a stimulus far beyond the religious sphere, strictly speaking, for a "rebirth of old ideas and ideals" brought up to date and shorn of the limitations attending them in the past. It is interesting to note the response of one Catholic theologian to this problem:

Let it suffice to state that, in our opinion, a culture that wants to serve toward the promotion of the human person in the technological age must emphasize above all "pure" intellectual values; it must develop man's ability to think both in abstract and in general terms; it must lead man to think "universally": it must liberate man from the commonplace, from slogans, and teach him to think personally. This cannot be achieved, however, except through constant contact with the classics, not only the Greek and Latin classics, but also the classics of every age and people, ancient and modern, Western and Eastern— not only from the field of literature and art, but from every field: philosophical, political, scientific, juridical and religious [90:473].

In the discussion of the problems involved here the Constitution joins the sociological and anthropological notion of culture as the matrix determining man to the equally important recognition that man creates culture and makes history. If man makes history and is the creator of culture, and if history and culture are vital factors in making man what he is, then obviously man can make himself with a greater self-consciousness the more he understands and is able to take responsibility for history and culture. The Fathers believe this kind of enhanced self-awareness is emerging in our day and consider it full of promise as well as fraught with peril. The Church, they declare, seeks to lead men "toward interior liberty." They affirm the "legitimate autonomy of human culture and especially the sciences" (art 59). Putting together the newer idea of culture and the older meaning of the term, which referred to the conscious cultivation of the human potential, they state that "the possibility now exists of liberating most men from the misery of ignorance" and see the effort to do so "a duty most befitting our times" (art 60). They add that "energetic efforts must also be expended to make everyone conscious of his right to culture and of the duty he has to develop himself culturally and assist others" (art 60).

The possibility of developing a greater measure of control over his own development is the fruit of the new self-consciousness with which modernity has endowed man. The value confusion of our age, however, makes human comprehension and responsible action in this respect extremely difficult. It is a value confusion derived from the same developments that brought about our increased self-consciousness.

The first problem concerns the content that culture ought to have and the values it should promote in our technological age. In other words, it is a question of what type of man we should now create, so that today's man may live as *man* in a world increasingly dominated by technology. The really crucial problem in today's world is that of preserving man's characteristics of *homo sapiens*, of *human personality*, in a world that tends to make him only a *homo faber*, a robot, a machine—yes, a link in a gigantic assembly line [90:472].

The emphasis of the Constitution on freedom is significant since, as we have seen, Catholicism came into the modern world fearing cultural freedom as a threat to its established beliefs and values. It is stated that

> . . . it is not the function of public authority to determine what the proper nature of forms of human culture should be. It should rather foster the conditions and the means which are capable of promoting cultural life among all citizens and even within the minorities of the nation. Hence in this matter men must insist above all else that culture be not diverted from its own purpose and made to serve political or economic interests [art 59].

The Constitution emphasizes its advocacy of liberty for culture, the arts, literature, and science.

Speaking of the acknowledgment of this liberty of culture, "and especially of the sciences," a Catholic theologian has said,

> This assertion is of great importance. First of all, it ought to dispel the conviction of many non-Catholics and non-Christians that faith deprives Catholics of the necessary cultural and scientific freedom, and that a scientist cannot accept faith without renouncing his free scientific research. According to them, faith would condition the scientist both in his process of research as well as in his conclusions, since he is required to conform the latter to the data of faith. These convictions have been greatly reinforced by some deplorable facts of the past, like the Galileo case. However, we must assert with emphasis that the Catholic enjoys the same freedom of research and investigation that his non-Catholic colleagues enjoy.

The same theologian points out the importance of the Constitution's recognition that "all the faithful, clerical and lay" possess such freedom (art 62).

> The Council's assertion of the freedom of culture and scientific research must be brought to bear even within the Church, where some want to put a muzzle on culture and scientific

investigation for fear that certain limits, established more or less arbitrarily, might be transgressed or that faith itself might be put in danger. In this respect, it is proper to observe that one must not confuse the truths of faith, absolutely certain in virtue of the authority of God who revealed them and the confirmation of the Church which defined them, with the presentation that has been made of those truths during the course of centuries. Nor should they be confused with what has been more or less legitimately added to them, to the point of giving the impression either that the additions form a singular body with those truths or that *aut simul stabunt aut simul cadent*. Actually, we ought to point out that, in the area of faith, there are relatively few doctrines that are absolutely certain, while many points—even those believed to be definitely established—are open to investigation. The clearest proof of this is the fact that the Council reopened questions that seemed forever closed [90:466].

In the face of the Council Fathers' perception of the positive and negative aspects of modern man's relative "deculturation," his uprooting from provincial traditionalisms, and the consequent increase in self-consciousness and loss of security it has entailed, they seek to develop a Christian humanism—indeed, a Christian Prometheanism. How successfully does the attempt to put forward a kind of Christian Promotheanism, directed to man's growth and fulfillment and his mastery of his environment, offer modern men an attractive alternative to autonomous human self-sufficiency? That question can hardly be answered at this time.

In Chapter III of Part Two the Fathers turn their attention to socioeconomic life. In the words of the conclusion, they present "teaching already accepted in the Church." There is no doubt that the Constitution's treatment of socioeconomic matters continues the Roman Catholic Church's concern with social welfare for three quarters of a century, but it particularly reflects the two encyclicals of Pope John XXIII, who "in his brief reign" actually changed papal teaching, "both its spirit and its content" [33:40].

Hales states that "part of the charm of Pope John was his refusal to pontificate on public affairs; one feels he is only giving advice; with Leo XIII and with Pius XI one is not allowed to forget that they are laying down the law" [33:40f]. Here we see, as in the behavior of Pope Paul VI before the United Nations General Assembly, the hint of what a new Catholicism might be—neither church nor sect. Hales also speaks of John's acceptance of liberal Catholicism: "Since Pope John endorsed the political principles of the liberal Catholics they have become at last a part of the official attitude of the Church" [33:42]. Hales shows that John was a genuine innovator—a Catholic Mazzini [33:189ff]. Hales' *Pope John and His Revolution* is a remarkable book about a remarkable man.

Both spirit and content of the Constitution as it deals with socioeconomic life (and later with political problems) do indeed echo the basic principles and aspirations of *Mater et Magistra* and *Pacem in Terris*. The Constitution also explicitly recognizes that specific remedies cannot be proposed, that these are "matters in a constant state of development" (art 91). They are taken up in the Constitution in order that Christians may "be led, and all mankind enlightened, as they search for answers to questions of such complexity" (art 46). Thus this section reinforces the goal of the Constitution as a whole of entering into a genuine dialogue with the modern world.

The chapter records man's increased "dominance over nature," his intensified "mutual dependence," to be seen among both individuals and groups, and, as a consequence of this more complex situation, the "more frequent intervention on the part of government." It deplores the contrast evident in our day between wealth and poverty. While economic development, "if guided and coordinated in a reasonable and human way," could meet the "intensified needs of the human family," the fact is that "all too often it serves only to intensify the inequalities" (art 63). The Constitution advocates "meeting the rising expectations of the human race" and urges that "the mere multiplication of products" not be made "the fundamental purpose of this productivity." Not "profit" or "domination," but the "service of man" and "indeed of the whole man, viewed in terms of his material needs and the demands of his intellectual, moral, spiritual, and religious life" must be the end of economic activity (art 65). People today feel inequalities "with ever sharper awareness"; such inequalities "seriously jeopardize the peace of the world" (art 63). Thus "an enormous mass of people still lack the absolute necessities of life," while "some, even in less advanced countries, live sumptuously and squander wealth" (art 63). Reforms are needed, "along with universal changes in ideas and attitudes" (art 63).

"Economic development must be kept under the control of mankind" and "at every level the largest possible number of people" should have "an active share in directing that development." The Constitution states that "growth must not be allowed to follow a kind of automatic course resulting from the economic activity of individuals. Nor must it be entrusted solely to the authority of government" (art 65). It is advocated that "immense economic inequalities" be removed and that the "life of individuals and their families" be kept "from becoming insecure and precarious" because of the hazards of development (art 66). There is a brief reference to "automation" and the need to prepare for it, but some in the advanced countries will be disappointed that it is dealt with only in passing (art 66).

The dignity of labor is recognized. Labor is considered superior to the other factors of production since "labor comes immediately from the person." Every man has the "duty to labor faithfully" and the "right to work" (art 67). "Among the basic rights of the human person must be counted the right of freely founding labor unions." Although "peaceful settlement" of labor disputes is advocated, the strike is "a necessary, though ultimate, means for the defense of the workers' own rights and the fulfillment of their just demands" (art 68). The Fathers assert,

God intended the earth and all that it contains for the use of every human being and people. Thus, as all men follow justice and unite in charity, created goods should abound for them on a reasonable basis. Whatever the forms of ownership may be, as adapted to the legitimate institutions of people according to diverse and changeable circumstances, attention must always be paid to the universal purpose for which created goods are meant [art 69].

In using private property, a man "should regard his lawful possessions not merely as his own but also as common property in the sense that they should accrue to the benefit of not only himself but of others" (art 69). The Constitution speaks favorably of a broad sharing in the management and profits of enterprises (art 68).

It is asserted that "private ownership or some other kind of dominion over material goods provides everyone with a wholly necessary area of independence and should be regarded as an extension of human freedom. Finally, since it adds incentives for carrying on one's function and duty, it constitutes a kind of prerequisite of civil liberties." These words repeat the teaching of encyclicals since *Rerum Novarum*, with the interesting qualifying phrase "or some other kind of dominion over material goods." The document states immediately, "The forms of such dominion or ownership are varied today and are becoming increasingly diversified. They all remain a source of security not to be underestimated, even in the face of the public funds, rights and services provided by society" (art 71). These lines were added to the final draft "to meet the objections of those African and Asian bishops who had complained, with good reason, that earlier drafts were too Western or too European in tone and outlook and did not give due recognition to the various community patterns of ownership that are found in their particular countries" [36:495]. In an earlier article appears the following:

In economically less advanced societies, it is not rare for the communal purpose of earthly goods to be partially satisfied through the customs and traditions proper to a community. By such means the absolute essentials are furnished to each member. If, however, customs cannot answer the new needs of this age, an effort must be made to avoid regarding them as altogether unchangeable. At the same time, rash action should not be taken against worthy customs, which, provided that they are suitably adapted to present-day circumstances, do not cease to be very useful [art 69].

Thus the document attempts to avoid some of the errors of Catholic economic prescriptions in the past: overemphasis on private property and ethnocentric interpretation of European forms of private property as natural law. In this area, however, the Constitution does not seem as imaginative as in others. One must agree with Monsignor George G. Higgins, who said, "On balance, I think it must be said that the Constitution's treatment of the problem of private ownership barely scratches the surface of an enormously complicated problem."

Having been drawn up in the 1960's, when a great variety of economic forms had already evolved in the West, when there was an increased awareness by the West of other cultures, and when some two decades of economic experimentation had taken place in the nonwestern lands, the Constitution has the advantage of seeing the possibility of diversity and therefore of avoiding doctrinaire adherence to economic forms for ideological reasons. Here too the deinstitutionalization of traditionalism and the progress of new developments proved a boon. Moreover, the Constitution seeks impartiality in major ideological economic conflicts. Overemphasis upon economic approaches and values to the exclusion of more general human ones is recorded as true of "nations which favor a collective economy as well as in others" (art 63). Evidently the "others" are the western European countries and the United States. The Constitution advocates a broad sharing of management and profits but does not proclaim this a natural right. It repeats the old teaching on private property but qualifies it in two directions: Modern public ownership may be necessary to the common good, and traditional forms of group ownership are to be respected. Those who hold back their capital from productive uses "gravely endanger the common good" (art 65), a reference to traditional upper class behavior in less developed countries—many of them Catholic. Land reform is espoused despite the opposition to it of traditional Catholic upper classes in a number of countries. Catholics are called to "make a great contribution to the prosperity of mankind and the peace of the world" (art 72).

Chapter IV of Part Two declares that "the political community exists for that common good in which the community finds its full justification and meaning, and from it derives its pristine and proper right. Now, the common good embraces the sum of those conditions of social life by which individuals, families, and groups can achieve their own fulfillment in a relatively thorough and ready way." Moreover, the "political authority . . . must always be exercised within the limits of morality and on behalf of the dynamically conceived common good" (art 74). While political mores "can vary according to the particular character of a people and its historic development," nevertheless "it is in full accord with human nature that juridical structures should, with ever better success and without any discrimination, afford all their citizens the chance to participate freely and actively in establishing the constitutional bases of a political community, governing the state, determining the scope and purpose of various institutions, and choosing leaders" (art 75). Independent groups, such as the family and social and cultural groups, must not be deprived "of their own lawful and effective activity," but "because of the increased complexity of modern circumstances, government is more often required to intervene in social and economic affairs." Though the state can assume unusual powers to meet emergencies, normal exercise of right "should be restored as soon as possible after the emergency passes." The document states further, "In any case it harms humanity when government takes on totalitarian or dictatorial forms injurious to the rights of persons or social groups" (art 75).

Citizens are admonished to "develop a generous and loyal devotion to their country, but without any narrowing of mind." They are told to look always "simultaneously to the welfare of the whole human family." Christians have a "special and personal vocation in the political community . . . that they give conspicuous example of devotion to the sense of duty and of service to the advancement of the common good." They should "recognize that various legitimate though conflicting views can be held concerning the regulation of temporal affairs." Politics is a "difficult but most honorable art." Those who embrace it should work to exercise that art properly. "Prudently and honorably let them fight against injustice and oppression, the arbitrary rule of one man or one party, and lack of tolerance. Let them devote themselves to the welfare of all sincerely and fairly, indeed with charity and political courage" (art 75).

The Constitution states that "the role and competence of the Church" should "in no way be confused with the political community, nor bound to any political system. For she is at once a sign and safeguard of the transcendence of the human person." The Church

... does not lodge her hope in privileges conferred by civil authority. Indeed, she stands ready to renounce the exercise of certain legitimately acquired rights if it becomes clear that their use raises doubt about the sincerity of her witness or that new conditions of life demand new arrangements. But it is always and everywhere legitimate for her to preach the faith with true freedom, to teach her social doctrine, and to discharge her duty among men without hindrance [art 76].

In Chapter V of Part Two the Constitution deals with the problems of peace and the international community. It shows a keen awareness of the urgency of these problems, seeing "the whole human family" as having reached "an hour of supreme crisis in its advance toward maturity" (art 77). It attempts "to summon Christians to cooperate with all men in making secure among themselves a peace based on justice and love, and in setting up agencies of peace" (art 77). It discusses curbing the savagery of war and condemns total war as well as the arms race (arts 79, 80, and 81). It looks forward to freeing man "from the age-old slavery of war" (art 81) through "the establishment of some universal public authority acknowledged as such by all, and endowed with effective power" (art 82).

It advocates measures for the "international common good" (art 82) and with respect to "food, health, education and employment" (art 84). "If an economic order is to be created which is genuine and universal, there must be an abolition of excessive desire for profit, nationalistic pretensions, the lust for political domination, militaristic thinking, and intrigues designed to spread and impose ideologies" (art 85). The Church stands forth as "a sign of . . . brotherliness which allows honest dialogue and invigorates it," and seeks to "foster within the Church herself mutual esteem, reverence, and harmony, through the full recognition of lawful diversity." The Fathers call for "unity in what is necessary, freedom in what is unsettled, and charity in any case" (art 92). "Christians cannot yearn for anything more ardently than to serve the men of the modern world ever more generously and effectively" (art 93).

The document ends with the statement of Pope Paul VI promulgating it: "each and every one of the things set forth in this Pastoral Constitution has won the consent of the Fathers of this most sacred Council. We too, by the apostolic authority conferred on us by Christ, join with the Venerable Fathers in approving, decreeing, and establishing these things in the Holy Spirit, and we direct that what has thus been enacted in synod be published to God's glory."

The conclusion of Part Two of the document concedes that the program "is but a very general one," and "deliberately so." Nevertheless the Fathers of the Council "entertain the hope that many of our proposals will be able to bring substantial benefit to everyone, especially after they have been adapted to individual nations and mentalities by the faithful, under the guidance of their pastors" (art 91). This reference to the guidance of the pastors does not, presumably, represent a retreat from the earlier recognition of autonomy of lay vocation, which, it will be recalled, was differentiated from the apostolate of the hierarchy in the *Lumen Gentium* itself. It may be assumed also that it does not contradict in any way the Fathers' realization of the need for unity in diversity and for dialogue within the Church. It is, however, a reminder of the hierarchical structure of the Church even as a Church of dialogue, as a Church seeking a new form of relation to the world and a new mode of living in the world.

The Constitution is admittedly a long and at times even wordy document, and much more of a beginning than a definitive statement. It shows a new desire to learn from the world and takes a new positive attitude toward the world. It seeks to understand what man is doing in the world and starts the process of relating Catholic ideas and values to man's life on earth in a way that breaks with the semi-sectarian otherworldliness of the past. In what is said and what is left unsaid, it shows a new openness and a new wish to shed outmoded attitudes and positions, to evolve a new kind of presence in the world.

The question arises, How much here is new and how much represents simply a continuity with the past? This question must be answered on two levels. There is first of all the theoretical level. How much is new thinking here, how much represents a new perspective, how much involves real change from the older immobilist stance of the siege mentality, how much of it successfully accepts the new ideas of history and the empirical sciences and the new facts of the emancipation of man from tradition against which Catholicism so long put up a stubborn and uncomprehending resistance, comprehending only that it was a threat? Then there is the practical level, the level of effectiveness in life of what has been formulated in words. Indeed, one of the characteristics of the preconciliar Church was to mistake words for life. Even for many "liberals" *Rerum Novarum* constituted a Catholic position on labor whereas it was simply a statement very often ignored on the practical level by pastors. What will happen today on the practical level? Surely there is a profound division between the "old church" and the "new church." One is reminded of the Bavarian pastor who told his congregation one Sunday morning in 1965, "No matter what they do in Rome, here in Bavaria we remain Catholic!"

How much continuity and how much discontinuity exists on the theoretical level? How new are the positions taken at the Council and especially in this Constitution, which deals with many items long neglected by Catholic thought altogether? It must be recalled that the Roman Catholic Church propagated the image of itself as "unchanging," which on a popular level was seen as a mark of its authenticity. Consequently, the changes introduced by the Council and those suggested in its enactments are a cause of scandal—of problems of faith—for some persons nurtured in the older forms. Concretely, faith was highly involved in its own formulations; what was believed tended to be believed in the terms of its literal statement. The institutional forms may all be seen analogously as "statement" of faith and attitude. Hence the call for deinstitutionalization implicit in much of the work of this Council constitutes a threat to many. The result is a defensive reaction against the new. So even in practical terms the question of the extent of theoretical continuity becomes an important one.

Moreover, as part of the changelessness in terms of which the preconciliar Church taught its members to think of it, there exists "a whole method of writing in the Church that always appeals to preceding popes and councils in order to show the continuity. But in fact the contrary is true." It is "a kind of method at work that is quite disagreeable to modern minds" [38:554]. Father Häring has remarked in discussion, "I think some people have an impression of continuity in the Church that is too optimistic." He points to the discontinuity between the church and state policy of Boniface VIII and the conciliar declaration on religious liberty as an example [34:554].

The stance of the Council represents a major discontinuity with the closed defensiveness of the past; its receptivity to a new relation to the world is discontinuous with its earlier reserve and even hostility; its attempts to confront and appropriate the intellectual conquests of modernity are discontinuous with its earlier sectarianism; its rediscovery of the layman within the Church and his vocation within the world is discontinuous with its earlier clericalism; its efforts to shed ethnocentric European and Western characteristics and to seek new forms of life in new cultures is discontinuous with much of its earlier thought and practice. The list could be prolonged, but it would be needless. All that is new has had its precursory appearances within the Church, often to be condemned or suppressed. The problem of continuity and discontinuity becomes a major theological one as well as a practical one for the postconciliar Church.

Actually, the elements of discontinuity will have to be given heavy emphasis in the postconciliar period if *aggiornamento* is to be a success and if the Roman Catholic Church is to play the historic role that will devolve upon it—if it is to stand surrogate for Christianity as a whole in its encounter with modernity. The second section of this Constitution suggests a further importance of the Church's effort toward *aggiornamento*. The West has long lived upon its illustrious past, has long made strides based upon the spiritual capital stored in the past, and in so doing has often dissipated that capital. Who can doubt that the West experiences a value crisis! Western civilization as a whole must develop forms of dialogue with a world it formerly dominated and need not be surprised to find not well disposed toward it. This necessary readjustment of the West bears a profound structural analogy with the attempt by the Church to create a new form of presence which is neither "church" nor "sect" in the old sense. Moreover, the ideals of the Enlightenment—the "blushing heir" of secularization—require a more profound existential rooting than they can any longer be given by the shallow rationalism of the period or the naturalism which followed. Even Marxism, which attempted to secularize Christian chiliasm into a historicist apotheosis brought about by man-becoming-Prometheus, stands in need of deeper grounding to produce a true and profound humanism [30]. Western science and learning, the crown of our civilization, require a profound rethinking to relate them to the present condition of Western man as he struggles toward maturity in the context of a history threatening to overwhelm him or pass him by.

If Roman Catholicism is to serve the world, it must offer something of direction, of inspiration, of example. Only by accentuating its new departures will this be possible; only by developing the elements of discontinuity introduced in the Council can it bring its ancient message, shorn of its culturally and historically specific limitations, into contact with the minds of men today. Earlier we spoke of the sociological demythologization of the Church as the great task of the postconciliar period. A European priest who is at the same time an American-trained sociologist and who was a *peritus* at the Council concerned in the preparation of this document has said this:

The motivation behind the Church's adaptation must be profoundly rooted in the salvation of mankind and not in a simple adaptation of an institutional system. It means a complete *remise en question* of the Church's whole life—going as far as a revision of the theological concept of mission; of the pattern of authority in the Church; of the relationship between hierarchy and laity, between bishops and priests; and of the contacts with other Christians, with other religions and with atheists, and among them with Marxists [39:548f].

He urges the "institutionalization of change" as prerequisite for any degree of success [39:548]. He urges the Church to pay attention to the social sciences, especially psychology and sociology.

There is a need for the Church to institutionalize research concerning relations between theology and the human sciences. Universities have a vital role to play in *basic* research. Without their help any progress in thought will be accidental and episodic. I consider it to be one of the most important tasks of Catholic universities today to establish permanent centers, with an interfaculty character, for interdisciplinary research [39:547].

The present author anticipated this suggestion in 1956 in an article entitled "The Catholic Immigrant and the American Scene": "What is called for in the circumstances is nothing less than a large program of research dedicated to scholarly and scientific study of the American Catholic experience. Leadership for such research should lie with the graduate departments in history and the social sciences in the leading Catholic universities in this country" [65:268]. The proposal received no response whatsoever—not even a letter to the editor!

But Houtart cautions, "Merely to use modern tools to better ensure the Church's power over society, or to manipulate mass media in order to create an artificial image of a dynamic Church, to put a computer at the service of an autocratic and conservative chancery office, would only make things worse" [39:549]. Genuine deinstitutionalization is necessary. But it must be carried out in such a way that the unity of the Church—the unity in diversity and in charity envisaged by the Council Fathers—is maintained. Interior dialogue in the Church, ecumenical dialogue without, and further presence to and dialogue with those of other religions and of no religion—this is the difficult task or set of tasks facing the postconciliar Church. It faces it in a state of considerable confusion, for the new experience of uncertainty and indeed of vitality has produced an interior anomie in the Church itself.

Can the Church emerge successfully and thus genuinely make its historic contribution to Christianity and authentically serve the western world—indeed, all the world? This is the question no man can answer.

VIII

THE DOGMATIC
CONSTITUTION ON DIVINE REVELATION

A FULLER consideration of the significance of the Council and of the postconciliar crisis of Roman Catholicism would have required a careful examination of the 16 documents discussed and enacted by the Fathers and of the various books which have appeared on the background of these documents in commission and in the floor discussion. We have so far confined ourselves to a brief analysis of the *Dogmatic Constitution on the Church* and a much fuller examination of the *Pastoral Constitution on the Church in the Modern World*. No doubt a detailed consideration of the 16 documents and of their background at the conciliar sessions would reveal the many sides of the consensus which was achieved in Rome and at the same time suggest the variety of pressures and strains attendant upon conciliar decision-making. That many at the Council did not realize the implications of what they were enacting is clear enough from what we have considered so far. That the documents dealt with here open up realms for future development beyond our present comprehension is also quite apparent. But the detail provided by a fuller treatment would itself yield some idea of the kinds of conflict that will continue to mark the period of crisis, change, and growth now in progress. Such an undertaking, however, would require many volumes.

We have taken a short cut to what it is hoped may prove a satisfactory approximate result. Recognizing the ecclesiological character of the Council, the fact that, as Pope Paul observed, the Council concentrated on trying to understand more thoroughly the Church itself and its position in the world today, we have focused so far on the two basic ecclesiological documents and have given our major attention to that dealing with the great historic problem of the Church and the world. We turn now to a consideration of the other dogmatic constitution enacted by the Second Vatican Council—the *Dogmatic Constitution on Divine Revelation*, the *De Revelatione*.

The Church claims to be founded upon a special intervention of God in human history, to be based upon and be the bearer of divine revelation. Our concern with the Church must therefore also be a concern with how the Church understands revelation and its own relationship to revelation. Since the 2d century the Church has lived in a state of reciprocal dependency with the Bible. The Church compiled the Bible, accepting the Hebrew scriptures and deciding among the writings produced during its own history which should be recognized as worthy of full canonical status. Thus in a sense the Church created the Bible. Yet the events of the Old Testament seen as the history of God's self-revelation to men and as the long, historical propaedeutic for the coming of Christ, and the books of the New Testament written within the community of the infant Church itself, record and reflect what Christians consider the mighty acts of God in his converse with man. They represent those acts which brought the Church into existence. How precisely to define this reciprocity in theological terms has long been the cause of conflict. Indeed, that conflict will be seen reflected in the Constitution we are to consider in its treatment of the relation of scripture to tradition.

Promulgated on November 18, 1965, the Constitution is divided into six chapters following a very brief preface. Chapters I and II deal with revelation—"Revelation Itself" and "The Transmission of Divine Revelation." The next four chapters deal with the scriptures—"The Divine Inspiration and the Interpretation of Sacred Scripture," "The Old Testament," "The New Testament," and "Sacred Scripture in the Life of the Church." Chapter I states that "Through divine revelation, God chose to show forth and communicate Himself and the eternal decisions of His will regarding the salvation of men" (art 6). Chapter II proclaims, "God has seen to it that what he revealed for the salvation of all nations would abide perpetually in its full integrity and be handed on to all generations" (art 7). What is this divine revelation in the light of the Second Vatican Council?

Revelation involves the "hidden purpose of His will" (art 2). God has made known "those divine treasures which totally transcend the understanding of the human mind" (art 6) "out of the abundance of His love" in order to speak "to men as friends and live among them so that He may invite and take them into fellowship with Himself" (art 2). What this is, called by *De Revelatione* the "plan of revelation" (art 2), "is realized by deeds and words having an inner unity: the deeds wrought by God in the history of salvation manifest and confirm the teaching and realities signified by the words, while the words proclaim the deeds and clarify the mystery contained in them" (art 2).

In addition to this special revelation in which God acts in history and communicates with men, there is a natural revelation—although these terms are not used in the document—in which God "gives men an enduring witness of Himself in created realities" (art 3). God "ceaselessly kept the human race in His care, in order to give eternal life to those who perseveringly do good in search of salvation." Then in his own time God called Abraham and his descendants and "through the patriarchs, and after them through Moses and the prophets," he taught this chosen nation to "acknowledge Himself as the one living and true God, provident Father and just Judge, and to wait for the Savior promised by Him" (art 3). "Then after speaking in many places and varied ways through the prophets, God, 'last of all in these days has spoken to us by his son' (Heb. 1:1–2)," who is "the Word made flesh." "The Christian dispensation, therefore, as the new and definitive covenant, will never pass away, and we now await no further new public revelation before the glorious manifestation of Our Lord Jesus Christ (cf. 1 Tim. 6:14 and Tit. 2:13)" (art 4).

Since patristic times the Catholic tradition has shown a marked tendency to see the content of revelation as "truths," and almost from the beginning of its contact with Hellenic culture the Church has tried to state that content in intellectual formulations—to construct dogmatic definitions. It is interesting that this document reflects the general tendency of the Council to take a more historical approach and to recognize the significance of process. The emphasis on both *acts* and *words* as constituting revelation opens up an area for theological development in the attempts by Catholics to probe their new insights into the meaning of historicity.

Concomitant with the Catholic emphasis upon the intellectual formulation of articles proposed to the believer for his assent has been the emphasis upon the element of intellectual assent in the Catholic understanding of the act of faith. In this respect the Council returns, somewhat at least, to an earlier and more holistic conception of what is signified by faith. " 'The obedience of faith' (Rom. 16:26; cf. 1:5; 2 Cor. 10:5–6) must be given to God who reveals, an obedience by which man entrusts his whole self freely to God, offering 'the full submission of intellect and will to God who reveals,' and freely assenting to the truth revealed by Him." Such faith requires the assistance of God's grace and "the interior help of the Holy Spirit who must precede and assist" affecting the heart and mind (art 5). The quotation within the Council statement—"the full submission of intellect and will to God who reveals"—is from a document of the First Vatican Council, *Dogmatic Constitution on the Catholic Faith* [28]. Its general tone contrasts with Vatican II statements, as in this case, where the contemporary document speaks of man entrusting "his whole self freely to God" in faith. There is here no logical contradiction but rather a kind of incongruity of connotation which juxtaposes the old and the new in Catholic thinking about faith. We see submission versus gift, discipline versus generosity, and holistic process versus an older faculty psychology which too often tended to lose sight of the whole person. The notions of entrusting oneself and submission bear a significant relation to the pair we noted earlier—deeds and words, entrusting with deeds, submission with words. What is suggested here is in fact a major area of the rethinking faced by Catholic theology in the postconciliar epoch, an area of conflict and development.

Having thus dealt with revelation itself, the Constitution next takes up its transmission, which is regarded as guaranteed by special divine assistance. The document states that the "full revelation of the supreme God is brought to completion" in Christ, who "fulfilled and promulgated with His own lips" the gospel "that had been promised in former times through the prophets." Christ "commissioned the apostles to preach to all men that gospel which is the source of all saving truth and moral teaching, and thus to impart to them divine gifts" (art 7). The Constitution continues,

> This commission was faithfully fulfilled by the apostles who, by their oral preaching, by example, and by ordinances, handed on what they had received from the lips of Christ, from living with Him, and from what He did, or what they had learned through the prompting of the Holy Spirit. This commission was fulfilled, too, by those apostles and apostolic men who under the inspiration of the same Holy Spirit committed the message of salvation to writing [art 7].

Again revelation is not seen as consisting of words alone. Christ reveals not only in words, but in deeds, in his effect upon his associates, and in the reflection of the apostles. The transmission of revelation takes place also in the example and ordinances (presumably the sacraments) of the apostles as well as in their preaching. The Fathers are here taking a more genuinely historical approach to Christian origins. Also, it should be noted, in the above section the idea of tradition is introduced. We have first the apostolic preaching (the *kerygma*), then its transmission by word of mouth (by tradition) and in written works (in canonical scriptures).

> But in order to keep the gospel forever whole and alive within the Church, the apostles left bishops as their successors, "handing over their teaching role" to them. [Here the document quotes Irenaeus.] This sacred tradition, therefore, and sacred Scripture of both the Old and the New Testament are like a mirror to which the pilgrim Church on earth looks at God, from whom she has received everything, until she is brought finally to see Him as He is, face to face (cf. 1 Jn 3:2) [art 7].

> And so the apostolic preaching, which is expressed in a special way in the inspired books, was to be preserved by a continuous succession of preachers until the end of time. Therefore the apostles, handing on what they themselves had received, warn the faithful to hold fast to the tradition which they had learned either by word of mouth or by letter. . . . This tradition which comes from the apostles develops in the Church with the help of the Holy Spirit. [The Constitution speaks of the] preaching of those who have received through episcopal succession a sure gift of truth [art 8].

A third vital Catholic conception has thus been introduced — that of the teaching office of the Church and especially its hierarchy, which is called technically the magisterium. In these four — *revelation, scripture, tradition, magisterium* — are to be found the acts and words of God properly proclaimed and interpreted to men.

The question of the relation of scripture and tradition has long been a cause of conflict both within the Roman Catholic Church and between Catholics and Protestants. Some Catholics have emphasized what they call "the two sources" of revelation, the Bible and tradition, while others have tended to see these as two parts of a larger interdependent whole. The Council of Trent, reacting against the Reformers who played down tradition, held that they were two sources and could be treated in relative isolation from each other. Either may be a source of dogma, and statements of dogma may indeed be formulated from tradition alone without their having visible basis in scripture. In recent years the new theology has revived what was presumably an earlier view of the matter, that all doctrine is really contained in the Bible, at least by implication, but that the implied dogmatic content may not be visible without interpretation in the light of tradition. The commission of the Council which did the final editing of this Constitution was under strong and steady pressure explicitly to affirm that the Bible does not contain all the content of the divine revelation. The Constitution did affirm that "a close connection and communication between sacred tradition and sacred Scripture" exists and, apparently at the request of Paul VI, that it was not from scripture alone that the "Church draws her certainty about everything that has been revealed." However, the Fathers preferred not to settle the old "two sources versus one source" controversy. They say "both sacred tradition and sacred scripture are to be accepted with the same sense of devotion and reverence" (art 9). The two "form one sacred deposit of the word of God, which is committed to the Church" (art 10).

> The task of authentically interpreting the word of God, whether written or handed on, has been entrusted exclusively to the living teaching office of the Church. . . . This teaching office is not above the word of God, but serves it, teaching only what has been handed on, listening to it devoutly, guarding it scrupulously, and explaining it faithfully by divine commission and with the help of the Holy Spirit. . . . It is clear, therefore, that sacred tradition, sacred Scripture, and the teaching authority of the Church, in accord with God's most wise design, are so linked and joined together that one cannot stand without the others, and that all together and each in its own way under the

action of the one Holy Spirit contribute effectively to the salvation of souls [art 10].

We have, then, the four chief reference points necessary to a discussion of the Catholic conception of revelation and its place in the Church—revelation itself, the two vehicles of its transmission, scripture and tradition, and the magisterium. The magisterium interprets the scripture and passes on authentic tradition. Yet the "tradition which comes from the apostles develops in the Church with the help of the Holy Spirit. For there is a growth in the understanding of the realities and the words which have been handed down" (art 9). In this the magisterium, which has a "sure gift of truth," is important, but it is not the sole agency of transmission to be recognized. The tradition is also transmitted and developed "through the contemplation and study made by believers, who treasure these things in their hearts" (art 8). Here a wider version of tradition is introduced. The factors involved now appear to have become five—revelation itself, its two embodiments and means of transmission, scripture and tradition, another way of transmission and development (a broader concept of tradition but checked by the bishops), and the magisterium. The Fathers obviously avoid two sets of problems bristling with difficulties when they say nothing in this context about either the status of recent Mariological dogmas, particularly the Assumption, which would appear completely unscriptural, and the role of papal infallibility, as defined by the First Vatican Council, in the transmission of tradition. To mention these two modern dogmas in the context of this discussion is to suggest the rocky path awaiting Catholic theology as it attempts to hold on to the basic insights of its faith and to overcome the consequences of its latter-day fundamentalism.

In Chapter III the Fathers turn to the problems of inspiration and interpretation. They hold that "the books of both the Old and New Testament in their entirety, with all their parts, are sacred and canonical because, having been written under the inspiration of the Holy Spirit (cf Jn 20:31; 2 Tim. 3:16; 2 Pet. 1:19–21; 3:15–16) they have God as their author and have been handed on as such to the Church herself" (art 11). The Constitution goes on, "In composing the sacred books, God chose men and while employed by Him they made use of their powers and abilities, so that with Him acting in them and through them, they, as true authors, consigned to writing everything and only those things which He wanted" (art 11). Since the things asserted in scripture "must be held to be asserted by the Holy Spirit, it follows that books of Scripture must be acknowledged as teaching firmly, faithfully, and without error that truth which God wanted put into the sacred writings for the sake of our salvation" (art 11). "However, since God speaks in sacred Scripture through men in human fashion, the interpreter of sacred Scripture, in order to see clearly what God wanted to communicate to us, should investigate what meaning the sacred writers really intended, and what God wanted to manifest by means of their words" (art 12).

Here the Constitution joins the traditional teaching of the Roman Catholic Church concerning the inspiration and inerrancy of Holy Writ to the recognition that the Bible is to be understood properly only by an understanding of the human authors and the circumstances under which they actually wrote. We have already seen that modern biblical research and its critical interpretation have in the past been the occasion of defensive reactions by the Church and its conservative leadership. We have paid some attention to the situation during the pontificates of Leo XIII and Pius X. A French theologian has summarized this history as follows:

> The Church has been dealing with this problem for more than a century. It has vacillated in its approach: sometimes it has taken a negative outlook, constructing barriers (certain decrees of the Biblical Commission), condemning books, temporarily suspending the teaching faculties of a given professor, or forbidding exegetical work in a particular field; at other times it has taken a

constructive position encouraging and organizing scientific exegesis, and giving it a sense of direction [44:420].

Biblical scholarship in Roman Catholic circles virtually ceased in terms of anything genuinely creative or critical following the modernist crisis. But work was gradually resumed, and its quality gradually improved. By the early 1940s a considerable recovery had been made. In September of 1943, Pope Pius XII issued an encyclical which "may be justly regarded as a *magna charta* for the Catholic Scriptural scholar by reason of its liberating attitude toward biblical science and the urgency of its appeal for the advancement of Scripture studies within the Church" [84:172]. This encyclical, *Divino Afflante Spiritu*, "urged Catholic biblical scholars to study the various literary genres that were used by the inspired authors of Sacred Scriptures" [35:75].

Said Pius XII,

What is the literal sense of a passage is not always as obvious in the speeches and writings of the ancient authors of the East, as it is in the works of writers of our own time. For what they wished to express is not to be determined by the rules of grammar and philology alone, nor solely by the context; the interpreter must, as it were, go back wholly in spirit to the remote centuries of the East and with the aid of history, archeology, ethnology and other sciences, accurately determine what modes of writing, so to speak, the authors of that ancient period would be likely to use, and in fact did use. [The Catholic exegete] ought not by any manner of means debar himself from taking in hand, and that repeatedly, the difficult questions which have found no solution up to the present time ... in an attempt to find a well-founded explanation in perfect harmony with the doctrine of the Church, in particular with that of biblical inerrancy, and at the same time satisfying the certain conclusions of the secular sciences [73].

Yet this encyclical did not end the problems of Catholic biblical scholars in their relationships with conservatives in the Church. Indeed, some of the latter never seemed to accept the papal teaching embodied in the *Divino Afflante Spiritu*. In 1961 the Supreme Sacred Congregation of the Holy Office, not yet reduced in importance by the Council, issued a *monitum* to Catholic biblical scholars which was variously interpreted but seemed a clear warning against the dangers to the faith lurking in genuine biblical science. Not long after this a conservative and conventional schema on Revelation was submitted to Vatican II for its consideration in November of 1962. The text was severely criticized, and in a few days a vote was taken on whether this draft should be returned to the commission to be rewritten. The result was 1,368 to return it against 822. This was somewhat short of the two thirds required by the Council rules which had previously been adopted to return a document to the preparatory commission. The pope, intervening, set up a new commission to rewrite the text [44]. There were further revisions on the floor and some at the request of Pope Paul.

The Constitution restates the two emphases of Pius XII, that on comprehension of the human author and his intentions and that on understanding the literary forms—conventions, idioms, figures, types of composition. In addition to investigating carefully "what meaning the sacred writers really intended," the biblical scholar should "have regard for 'literary forms.'"

For truth is proposed and expressed in a variety of ways, depending on whether a text is history of one kind or another, or whether its form is that of prophecy, poetry, or some other type of speech. The interpreter must investigate what meaning the sacred writer intended to express and actually expressed in particular circumstances as he used contemporary literary forms in accordance with the situation of his own time and culture. For the correct understanding of what the sacred writer wanted to assert, due attention must be paid to the customary and characteristic styles of perceiving, speaking, and narrating which prevailed at the time of the sacred writer, and to the customs men normally followed at that period in their everyday dealings with one another [art 12].

The Bible, however, is not simply an ancient collection of books. It "must be read and interpreted according to the same Spirit by whom it was written." Therefore, "serious attention must be given to the content and unity of the whole of Scripture." In this there will be revealed "the harmony which exists between elements of the faith." Moreover, the "living tradition of the whole Church must be taken into account," and all "is subject finally to the judgement of the Church," by which is meant the teaching office (art 12).

Again we have the distinction between the broad tradition of transmission ("the living tradition of the whole Church") and the narrower meaning of the term ("the judgement of the Church"). As in all conciliar documents, there are in this Constitution quotations and references from the Fathers and from past popes and councils to construct a continuity while moving in new directions. In a footnote this document quotes Aquinas: "Any knowledge which is profitable to salvation may be the object of prophetic inspiration. But things which cannot affect our salvation do not belong to inspiration" [1:119, n 31]. The text contains many references to Augustine and others. This chapter closes with a quotation from St John Chrysostom's "On Genesis," "that we may learn the gentle kindness of God, which words cannot express, and how far He has gone in adapting His language with thoughtful concern for our weak human nature" (art 13).

These three chapters present the Church's conception of revelation and of its own relation to revelation. The document is indeed admirable in its attempt to spell out guidelines in a subtle and difficult area. Yet the student of the Second Vatican Council cannot help feeling somewhat let down. He expected to encounter the supreme mystery of the *kerygma* proclaimed by the Christian Church. Earlier we quoted the statements of the *Lumen Gentium* and of Pope Paul on the mystery of the Church. Although the word "mystery" is used once in these three chapters, the sense of mystery conveyed in the *Dogmatic Constitution on the Church* is missing. The supreme mystery of biblical religion, that God should have communicated with man, is treated almost professionally. One feels that the concern with the categories in which the Church wishes its members, and particularly its scholars and exegetes, to understand the revelation usurps the sense of largeness and wonder characteristic of other documents — and in precisely the place where such a sense is perhaps most appropriate. Revelation is here made rather cut and dried, with emphasis upon inerrancy, scholarship, patristic and theological guidelines, and episcopal guaranteed authenticity of interpretation. Also mentioned are the inspiration of the Spirit and the need for reading the Bible in the same Spirit, and the inspiration of the meaning revealed to those who study and ponder scripture in their hearts. But these seem somewhat overshadowed by the technical and protective guidelines set forth by the Constitution.

Moreover, if the *De Revelatione* does not convey as keen a sense of mystery as does the *Lumen Gentium*, neither does it convey as living a sense of historicity as does the *Gaudium et Spes*, the *Pastoral Constitution on the Church in the Modern World*. The latter document showed an acute awareness of the way man's thinking, feeling, and action are shaped by the culture in which he lives, and how that culture is itself shaped in relation to historically specific circumstances. In the *De Revelatione* this process is recognized, and the need for scholars and exegetes to penetrate into and understand the forms of thought and feeling of the past is emphasized. What is lacking is some hint of a realization by its authors of the openness of this historicity so fully felt in the *Gaudium et Spes*. The old understanding of the Church within the Roman communion stressed a hierarchical Church — juridically structured, sacramentally set — and the supremacy and infallibility of the pope. The new understanding which emerged in the two constitutions on the Church brought to the fore the pilgrim people of God in history. The first saw Church and society as matters of fixed structure; the second, as process, interpenetrating each other in a variety of modes. In the *Pastoral Constitution on the Church in the Modern World* man appears as a developing being playing a role as junior partner in creation—as a kind of cocreator, realizing himself and God's intentions. Commentators on the *Gaudium et Spes* have pointed out the great tasks it opens up of developing a theology of creation that will attempt to grasp the mystery of man's life in the world. That older, fixed notion of the Church seems congruent with set guidelines—fathers, theology, secular sciences, tradition, infallible episcopy—for the comprehension of what is involved in revelation, and with the odd notion, so subtly qualified, of biblical inerrancy.

We have seen that the Constitution attempts to get away from the fundamentalist position on the understanding of scripture. Revelation is perceived as consisting not just of deeds but also of words. To see revelation as God's initiating communication with men, as a communication which involves both words and deeds (deeds as the context in which the words take on their real significance), would appear to require a language to express a revelation that is both mythic and existential, as we used those terms in a previous chapter. However, this kind of understanding of revelation alternates in the Constitution with an older, more substantializing interpretation. The opening preface quotes 1 John 1:2-3 "that our fellowship may be with the Father, and with his son Jesus Christ." The document speaks of "deeds and words having an inner unity" (art 2); it says that man has "access to the Father in the Holy Spirit"; and it sees in scripture and tradition the glass in which "the pilgrim Church on earth looks at God" (art 7). These all point to an understanding of revelation that is existential and that implies process. There are also the references to "plan of revelation" (art 2), the taking over from Vatican I of the idea of submission of mind and will (art 5), the references to "truths," the "deposit," and others which point to a more substantializing conceptualization. The first kind of characterization connotes a living process; the second often leads to seeing what is here involved as a matter of transmitting verbal formulations. This is the old conflict of process and history versus a pseudo-transcendent ontology which we have met many times throughout our analysis.

Christianity became institutionalized on the three levels of cult, belief, and organized fellowship, and this institutionalization has long provided the context for western man's religious experience. It is one of the peculiarities of its history that the Church came to emphasize the verbal content of belief—the aspects of the religious response that could be intellectually formulated as dogma and doctrine. This was the effect of the "naturalization" of a religion originating in Semitic Palestine in the world of the Greeks.

Adolf Harnack attributes the marked intellectualization of the Christian attitude to the consequences of the anti-Gnostic reaction of the 2d century. In his view, its resistance to the intrusions of Gnosticism, which represented for the early Church a threat of "acute hellenization," caused the Christian community to take on certain attributes of that against which it fought. Having to fight the hellenization with Greek philosophical weapons, it became hellenized itself. The results, as Harnack reconstructs them, were a strong emphasis upon the content of belief, the transformation of the clergy into a cadre of intellectual specialists with the laity in tutelage, and a rigidity of adherence, expression, and organization which curtailed much of an earlier liberty. Whether or not Harnack has exaggerated the dangers and effects of the Gnostic crisis, he has certainly described important circumstances conditioning the evolution of the Church, the emergence of that adumbrated sociological mythic expression whose demythologization has become the task of our period.

Wilfred Cantwell Smith has pointed out the dangers involved when the student of religion reifies and hypostatizes the living realities of religious life into fixed, substantialized categories. He sees this tendency derived from basic characteristics of western culture. He observes that

> . . . in the Christian tradition, radically more so than is true of most others, there has been a sustained and central emphasis on formulating the faith in prose, from the Apostles' Creed to the most recent volume of Tillich's systematic theology. Much more attention in the Western world has been paid to the evolving content of this particular form of expression, than to the fact of it, which has tended to be taken rather uncritically and un-self-consciously for granted [83:163].

If this western tendency to intellectualize and turn experience into an "it" is deleterious to scholarly comprehension, how much more profound are the problems it raises for theology within a tradition and community of faith! The document here shows itself as a compromise in the way most conciliar documents are compromises. In some passages it suggests a view of revelation as a process—and as a process in relation to transcendence which cannot be finally objectified in any culture, even a Christian culture. In other places it uses the older, objectified manner.

Smith distinguishes faith and tradition, seeing tradition as the cumulated oral and written materials which come into existence in a community of faith. It is tradition that is made the object of study by scholars. This concept of tradition is much the same as the conceptions of tradition, broad and narrow, and scripture put forward in the *De Revelatione*. It too is of interest to the theologian, but he is concerned with it in the modes and with the tools of systematic thought and in the spirit and light of faith. Faith itself is not observable; it is not immediately presented to the scrutiny of the scholar or social scientist. Its consequences may be noted, but they are likely to be ambiguous. Smith states that "each man's faith is his own, is partly free, and results from an interaction within the personality between that confronting tradition along with all other mundane circumstances, external and inner, and the transcendent" [83:143]. Thus faith—unless it be one's own personal faith—is known partially and indirectly by both scholar and theologian. A Catholic theologian has suggested characterizing a vital, in contrast with a merely verbal, notion of revelation as "a reality-in-communication, a being-manifest in Christ himself . . . an intelligible . . . active presence of eschatological realities in human forms . . ." [24:70f]. Some such notion of what revelation is would appear essential to do justice to the dynamic reality of the contact of faith with transcendence. A Protestant scholar commenting upon this Constitution notes that "The concept of revelation as God's action in giving life to his people calls for the use of a language that will be congenial to such a reality, words that convey a sense of ontological depth and of personal immediacy. . . . The Constitution seems to utilize such a language in some articles then to forsake it in others, without full recognition of the confusion aroused by shifting from one perspective to another" [56:70f].

The shifting is the indication of transition, the effect of compromise, and the reflection of genuine confusion. Faith sees revelation as the mighty deeds of God and his speaking through the prophets (and in the latter days through his son) which call forth a response in men. The expression of revelation requires the utilization of what we have called both mythic and existential language. In post-Tridentine Catholicism the ancient intellectualization of revelation was increased by defensiveness. During the post-Tridentine centuries the Roman Church conceived of revelation as truths verbally defined to which the mind and the will must be submitted.

The demythologization of the Church, the historic task of the postconciliar epoch, will demand the rediscovery of revelation as process and a liberation from verbal fundamentalism. It will need much help from biblical scholarship and from theologians aware of such scholarship and its implications. The dynamic character, the openness, the historical conditioning, and the consequences of a many-factored causality upon the interpretation and transmission of the import of revelation (and upon the formation, development, and communication of tradition) raise the most difficult problems, both methodological and substantive. This document suggests as guidelines the canons of scientific research, the tradition of the Fathers, the decisions of the magisterium, the use of the totality of scripture as context, and the idea of inerrancy. Relating them to a comprehension of the Bible in our day will pose innumerable subtle difficulties—even enormous ones.

It is curious that the *De Revelatione* makes but brief reference to liturgy and sacrament (arts 21 and 26) and their relation to revelation. In the *Constitution on the Sacred Liturgy* (*Sacrosanctum Concilium*) it is stated that "in the earthly liturgy by way of foretaste, we share in that heavenly liturgy which is celebrated in the holy city of Jerusalem toward which we journey as pilgrims" (art 8). The relation of liturgy and sacrament to revelation is recognized not only in that "the liturgy is considered as an exercise of the priestly office of Jesus Christ" (art 7) but also in that "before men can come to the liturgy they must be called to faith and to conversion" (art 9). The *Constitution on the Sacred Liturgy* takes account of the analogy between liturgy and sacrament and revelation and employs the existential language of the Epistle to the Hebrews to assert that "the word of God is living and efficient" (Heb 4:12).

The Constitution insists upon the Catholic idea of scriptural inerrancy. Before we consider the problems involved in this notion, it will be helpful to consider the typical situations in which transmission of the message of revelation takes place through the centuries. Let us start with Smith's conception of faith–tradition. Faith is the apprehension of the call of the transcendent and the response to it on the part of the believer. Tradition—oral and written—is made up of the accumulated records and lore, proclamations and commentaries, which are developed and passed on in a religious community. It usually consists of a body of texts and an oral tradition. The latter exists as the setting for reading and study of the texts and is itself affected substantially by the content of the texts.

Tradition actually is not homogeneous; it is essential, in fact, to consider at least two kinds of components making up the stream of tradition. They stand in close relation to each other in often invisible and subtle ways. First is the tradition of the learned, subject to scholarly and institutional checks and to occasional reform. There is the popular tradition as well, fed by the narrower tradition but in turn providing the larger community setting for that more learned tradition. Then there is a set of established forms of religious participation—cult and prayer—which is influenced by text and oral tradition and which in turn influences the interpretation and understanding of text and oral tradition. The total religious phenomenon, constituting the context for the transmission of tradition, also involves established avenues of that transmission—hierarchies, schools, approved teachers, etc. Through them the texts are transmitted and the oral tradition is passed on and interpreted. Finally there is the form of community, which supplies the context for all the rest. This may be of a special and segregated sort, as in the Christian Church, or it may be coterminal with the general society, as in Hinduism. Even in societies having separate religious communities, a general milieu may exist, shared by all, which has many characteristics of a single religious community [see, for example, 4]. This general religious phenomenon must at any rate be seen in the setting of the total society. It will be affected in important ways by the nature of that society—traditional or modern, rural or urban, simple or highly differentiated, hierarchical or egalitarian, etc. It will also be affected in important ways by its relationship to the total society—it may be a sect withdrawn from it, as in the early Church, or the central and dominant institution in it, as in the society in the Middle Ages.

It is in this topological setting that one must place the four basic anchorage points proposed in this Constitution: revelation, scripture, tradition (narrow and broad), and magisterium. The Council Fathers recognized that the scriptures were written by men whose modes of thought and feeling were quite different from those of western men in our day. Consequently they recognized the need for critical scholarship of scripture.

But we must consider the parallel and analogous problems in the transmission of tradition. Even within the Christian stream of thought and awareness the modalities of thought have changed from epoch to epoch—from the 2d century to the 5th; from the 5th century to the 13th; from the 13th to the 16th; from the 16th to our own day. The *Pastoral Constitution on the Church in the Modern World (Gaudium et Spes)* communicated to us a lively sense of historical process and of the specific cultural and historical conditioning to which men are subject. We must recall that in considering the total religious phenomenon as the setting for the transmission of tradition. In such a setting transmission would appear to be a matter of both continuity and transformation — a complex combination of the two. Problems of transmission of tradition would seem to offer a field for scholarship and critical evaluation as vast and significant as those of biblical studies.

What takes place in this setting is process. There is the interpersonal process of communication among those occupying positions in all the parts of that elaborate structure, and between the generations within that setting. And there is the intraindividual process of memory. It is communication and memory that make us men, providing us with an identity, a past, a projected future, and a present relationship to our human and nonhuman surroundings.

The social sciences have revealed something of these processes to us. We know that meaning undergoes change in communication and in recall. We must look at cultural transmission both in terms of how meaning is affected by the conditioning effects of situations and in terms of how it is affected by these aspects of process. Moreover, the *Dogmatic Constitution* itself calls attention to an interesting facet of this problem when it states that elements of scripture must be understood in the context of the whole Bible (art 12).

Men create meaning systems, going beyond the evidence. The systems reflect men's situations, men's relations to others, men's aspirations and interests, petty and large. Such systems become part of and embedded in the institutional structure of societies. Institutions with their defined goals and means, their stable statuses and roles, subtly and reciprocally interpenetrate with the systems of meaning. A creed and a theology exist in the setting of a religious community and in specific relation to its inner structure and its total relation to its setting. We recognized this earlier when we noted that beliefs, forms of worship, and organization were all expressions of religion analogous to language.

Communication and memory are processes, and they take place within the topological structure we have outlined. The reference points of this structure, if examined closely, show themselves again as process. Nature indeed is motion, as Aristotle said, but much more open-ended motion than he realized. Magisterium is an element in the process of transmission, but magisterium is itself a complex set of processes: the sociological process of becoming a bishop influenced in a hundred subtle ways by the situation within the Church and the general society, the processes of relation and conflict among the bishops and between them and other elements in society, the general processes of memory and communication as they are specifically conditioned under the given historical circumstances. Similarly with the other components of our outline. Process involves contradictions, ambiguities, conflicts, and alignments which result in transformation as well as preservation and transmission.

It is in this general setting that one must see the transmission of scriptures, the production of new redactions and renditions, as well as the passing on of oral tradition, although writing introduces a kind of control not present in wholly oral transmission. What can it mean to speak of scriptural "inerrancy" in such a setting? It would seem that beneath this term lurks a fundamentalist idea that there is a language which "really" preserves the "proper statement" of the "truth," an idea that truth is a matter of words and the Church has the right words.

Minear has remarked on the primacy of interest given to this concept in the document: "Inerrancy is taken to be an essential corollary of inspiration and is necessary to the certitude which the Church must have as the ark of salvation" [56:83]. Catholics seem to move here in a context whose basic anchorage points are historicity, inerrancy, certitude, verbalism, objectification. Despite the attempts to come to grips with historicity, this setting seems to emphasize words rather than acts and the passing on of formulated beliefs rather than the living experience of faith. The idea of a formulated deposit and an inerrant scripture coming down through the ages in the sociological–historical setting we have suggested appears highly artificial. It is little wonder that Minear concluded, with respect to the Constitution's presentation of transmission, "The historian will experience difficulty in adapting this picture to the actual course of Christian history, with its endless ambiguities, dilemmas, and detours. The social psychologist may well wonder how it reflects the baffling mixture of honesty and deception in every human heart and every social situation, and may be led to ask whether it springs from anxious wishful thinking or authentic trust" [56:83].

What is suggested here is that it derives from the great fear on the part of Catholics to let go of a minimal mooring of literalism, without which the popular Catholic mind finds it hard to understand authenticity of tradition and achieve the certitude of trust. The Catholic Church is afraid that giving up its fundamentalism in these respects would mean giving up its authority; it fears further that a weakening of its authority would mean a loss of that sense of God's reality and of his relation to men through Christ which has been the core of its strength and very existence. For this reason this scriptural area will remain a difficult one in the postconciliar period. It will also prove a strategic one. Within the Church two rival models are in subtle conflict. One clings to the old Church—authority, submission, verbal deposit, closedness; the other seeks to renew the Church and fulfill its present promise in leadership, cooperation, living faith, and openness. In the area of the meaning of revelation the battle is profoundly joined in the souls of men.

The doctrine of biblical inerrancy stressed by recent popes seems to inflict upon the Church a needless fundamentalism and one difficult to credit in the light of science and history.

> With grave words did [Pope Leo XIII] proclaim that there is no error whatsoever if the sacred writer, speaking of things of the physical order "went by what sensibly appeared" as the Angelic Doctor says, speaking either in figurative language, or in terms which were commonly used at the time, and which in many instances are in daily use at this day, even among the most eminent men of science. For "the sacred writers or to speak more accurately—the words are St. Augustine's—the Holy Ghost who spoke by them, did not intend to teach men these things— that is the essential nature of the things of the universe—things in no way profitable to salvation."

Here we have Pope Pius XII quoting Pope Leo XIII in a statement in which they both avoid one kind of fundamentalism to fall into another [73:275]. The *De Revelatione* states that the books of scripture teach "without error that truth which God wanted put into the sacred writings for the sake of our salvation" (art 11). The Catholic scholar R. A. F.

MacKenzie states in his annotation to the document at this point,

> The Bible was not written in order to teach the natural sciences, nor to give information on merely political history. It treats of these (and of all other subjects) only insofar as they are involved in matters concerning Salvation. It is only in this respect that the veracity of God and the inerrancy of the inspired writers are engaged. This is not a quantitative distinction, as though some sections treated of salvation (and were inerrant), while others gave merely natural knowledge (and were fallible). It is formal, and applies to the whole text. The latter is authoritative and inerrant in what it affirms about the revelation of God and the history of salvation. According to the intentions of its authors, divine and human, it makes no other affirmations [1:119, n 31].

We now begin to see the kind of subtle and ambiguous use of nuance to which Catholic scholarship is condemned by official fundamentalism in the approach to this subject. The above statement wishes to avoid any cutting up of the Bible into "inspired and inerrant" parts and other parts not so privileged, a wise caution. But the meaning of "formal" raises more than a few empirical and epistemological difficulties.

To suggest the former let us consider Genesis 41:50–52: "Before the year of famine came, Joseph had two sons, whom Asenath, the daughter of Potiphera priest of On, bore to him. Joseph called the name of the firstborn Manasseh, 'For,' he said, 'God has made me forget all my hardship and all my father's house.' The name of the second he called Ephraim, 'For God has made me fruitful in the land of my affliction' " [7]. Actually the Hebrew meanings of the two names are uncertain and John L. McKenzie, SJ, in his *Dictionary of the Bible* states that the etymology of Genesis 41:51 is popular. Inerrancy obviously does not mean what it sounds like. We now enter the realm of increasingly fine distinctions.

However, in the *Humani Generis*, after taking a position

that leaves the issue of evolution "an open question" as long as it is the evolution of the body and not the soul, and after hedging the whole matter with elaborate cautions, Pius XII states,

> There are other conjectures, about polygenism (as it is called), which leave the faithful no such freedom of choice. Christians cannot lend their support to a theory which involves the existence, after Adam's time, of some earthly race of men, truly so called, who were not descended ultimately from him, or else suppose that Adam was the name given to some group of our primordial ancestors. It does not appear how such views can be reconciled with the doctrine of original sin, as this is guaranteed to us by Scripture and tradition, and proclaimed to us by the Church. Original sin is the result of a sin committed, in actual historical fact, by an individual man named Adam, and it is a quality native to all of us, only because it has been handed down by descent from him (cf Rom. v 12–19; Conc. Trid, sess. v, ca, L-4) [74:298].

Here evidently the book of Genesis teaches both history and biology, presumably necessary to our salvation. (It is interesting to ask what inerrancy means with respect to Genesis 6:2 in this context.) Since Pius XII, Catholic thinking has developed; some theologians suggest that there was no historical Eden and find it possible to present the implications of the doctrine of original sin in a less fundamentalist manner [see, for example, 40].

There is no doubt that the holding on to fundamentalism is a consequence of the desire to proclaim the content of a doctrine "truly true," and it is seen as possible only by means of a literalist declaration. Further, in perceiving in some scholars of the past a cavalier disregard of the sum and substance of the Christian tradition and even a desire to overthrow it, the Church sees reality and reacts with justified defensiveness to real problems. Yet it is to be wondered whether or not this spirit of fundamentalism does not burden

Catholic scholars unnecessarily, distracting their attention to and wasting their energies upon false problems. One is tempted to quote Plato:

In the *Phaedrus* Socrates and Phaedrus discuss the myth associated with the altar of Boreas, which they encounter in their walk along the Ilissus. Phaedrus asks Socrates whether or not he believes the tale. Here is the reply:

The wise are doubtful, and I should not be singular if, like them, I too doubted. I might have a rational explanation that Orythia was playing with Pharmacia, when a northern gust carried her over the neighboring rocks; and this being the manner of her death, she was said to have been carried away by Boreas. There is a discrepancy, however, about the locality; according to another version of the story she was taken from Areopagus, and not from this place. Now I quite acknowledge that these allegories are very nice, but he is not to be envied who has to invent them; much labor and ingenuity will be required of him; and when he has once begun, he must go on to rehabilitate Hippocentaurs and chimeras dire. Gorgons and winged steeds flow in apace, and numberless other inconceivable and portentous natures. And if he is sceptical about them, and would fain reduce them one after another to the rule of probability, this sort of crude philosophy will take up a great deal of time. Now I have no leisure for such enquiries; shall I tell you why? I must first know myself, as the Delphian inscription says; to be curious about that which is not my concern, while I am still in ignorance of my own self, would be ridiculous. And therefore, I bid farewell to all this; the common opinion is enough for me. For, as I was saying, I want to know not about this, but about myself: am I a monster more complicated and swollen with passion than the serpent Typho, or a creature of a gentler and simpler sort, to whom nature has given a diviner and lowlier destiny? [76]

There is no intention of comparing the scriptures, whether of the Old or the New Testament, with the popular mythology of 5th century Greece. But the sociologist and analyst of culture will do well to mark the analogies for what they are worth. A concern to reduce mythic language to the descriptions of fact and then to explain the mythic narrative by analogy has the effect of destroying completely the religious content of the myth. Moreover, it opens up a difficult, ingenious, and unenviable task which is neverending. Such necessities inflicted upon the biblical critic would appear to serve mostly to distract him from more important questions. The defense of a specious verbal literalism represents a kind of straitjacket inflicted upon biblical scholarship by the frightened.

That the platonic quotation is not completely out of place may be seen from the following passage from a study of the book of Job by a Catholic scholar published in 1953:

> Much in the book is clearly not intended to be taken as corresponding closely to historical fact. The poetic form of the speeches excludes the idea that the reader is given a transcript of the dialogue that passed between Job and his friends. The double scene in heaven with the consultation between God and Satan is a device to admit the reader to the secret which lies at the root of Job's troubles. The arrangement by which the news of the multiple calamities pours in on the sufferer in quick successive blows is artificially planned to heighten the impression produced by his catastrophic change of fortune. But these opinions are not adequate to justify the opinion that Job never existed and is presented merely as a type. The reasons which led the unnamed Rabbi to hold this view are not recorded (TB Baba Bathra 15a). The ancients were wont to weave their stories about real personages; and had Job and his story been the product of imagination, would a non-Israelite be chosen as the hero? Moreover, Job is introduced in Ex 14:14–20 as a man renowned for his uprightness side-by-side with Noe; cf. Jas 5:11. Even a nursery rhyme like "Little Jack Horner" has its historical basis. And the tradition of the Church has always regarded Job as an historical personage [85:319].

This paragraph appears in what is in fact a very fine study of the scriptural work. It reads like the necessary tribute demanded by authoritarian fundamentalism of objective scholarship as the price of its existence. What we have said suggests the importance of this area for the future development of Catholicism and the kind of problem which will provide the material of conflict and growth. How to preserve its sense of the reality and immediacy of God in his converse with man without holding on to an outmoded fundamentalism; how to adopt and utilize with their full implications the methods and instruments of modern research and the insights of the modern consciousness which guides research without losing its sense of God's reality and immediacy—these are the two problems underlying all the subtle and complex questions inherent in this area of study.

Chapter IV of the Constitution is devoted to the Old Testament. The historical development of the Hebrew religion is recognized. "To this people which He acquired for Himself, He so manifested Himself through words and deeds as the one true and living God that Israel came to know by experiencing the ways of God with men, and with God Himself speaking to them through the mouth of the prophets, Israel daily gained a deeper and clearer understanding of His ways and made them more widely known among the nations" (art 14). The chapter states that "the principal purpose to which the plan of the old Covenant was directed was to prepare for the coming both of Christ, the universal Redeemer and of his messianic kingdom" (art 15). While the New Testament is "hidden in the Old" and the Old "made manifest in the New" (art 16), despite some things "incomplete and temporary," the books of the Hebrew Bible express a "lively sense of God" and contain "a store of sublime teachings about God, sound wisdom about human life, and a wonderful treasury of prayers" (art 15). "Christians should receive them with reverence."

It is curious, however, how much this chapter subordinates interest in the Old Testament to its prefigurement of the New and how little is said with respect to Jewish religious life itself. In this document we find little of the kind of theological attitude toward the Jews which is to be seen in the *Declaration on the Relationship of the Church to Non-Christian Religions*. The latter comments, "As this sacred Synod searches into the mystery of the Church, it recalls the spiritual bond linking the people of the New Covenant with Abraham's stock" (art 4). Moreover, it states that "according to the Apostle, the Jews remain most dear to God because of their fathers, for He does not repent of the gifts He makes or of the calls He issues (cf. Rom. 11:28–29)." And "Since the spiritual patrimony common to Christians and Jews is thus so great, this sacred Synod wishes to foster and recommend that mutual understanding and respect which is the fruit above all of biblical and theological studies, and of brotherly dialogues" (art 4). This spirit seems curtailed in Chapter IV of the *De Revelatione* devoted specifically to the Hebrew Bible.

Chapter V, on the New Testament, sees the revelation of God set forth and showing its power "in a most excellent way in the writings of the New Testament" (art 17). It gives the gospels "a special pre-eminence" and declares that "The Church has always and everywhere held and continues to hold that the four Gospels are of apostolic origin." It "unhesitatingly" asserts their "historical character." This chapter also speaks of revelation as consisting of deeds and words (arts 17 and 19). "The sacred authors wrote the four Gospels, selecting some things from the many which had been handed on by word of mouth or in writing, reducing some of them to a synthesis, explicating (*explanantes*) some things in view of the situation of their churches, and preserving the form of proclamation but always in such fashion that they told us the honest truth about Jesus" (art 19).

Chapter VI deals with the place of the Bible in the life of the Church; the Church "has always regarded the Scriptures together with sacred tradition as the supreme rule of faith, and will ever do so" (art 21). "Easy access to sacred scripture should be provided for all the Christian faithful," and for this reason the Church originally adopted the Septuagint. This is certainly the first time in many centuries that a document of such ecclesiastical status urged the availability of scripture. The Church desires "to move ahead daily toward a deeper understanding of the sacred Scriptures so that she may unceasingly feed her sons with the divine word" (art 23). The document speaks also of the "watchful care of the teaching office of the Church." Yet the old popular idea of "sacrament versus Bible" as the issue between Catholics and Protestants, and the many institutional checks enacted by the Church to keep unapproved texts away from its membership tend to become things of the past in the light of this declaration. It quotes St Jerome to the effect that "ignorance of the Scriptures is ignorance of Christ" (art 25) and states that "theology is most powerfully strengthened and constantly rejuvenated" by contact with the written word (art 24). Study of the Bible, as well as of the "holy Fathers of East and West and of sacred liturgies," by both clergy and laity is encouraged. In addition to its specific approval of the modern methodology of biblical study, "This sacred Synod encourages the sons of the Church who are biblical scholars to continue energetically with the work they have so well begun, with a constant renewal of vigor and with loyalty to the mind of the Church" (art 23).

The idea of the "mind of the Church" is used a good deal in Catholic discussion. To think with the Church and according to the mind of the Church has been held up as an ideal of loyalty in the defensive post-Tridentine period. What is meant by such terms? They appear to refer to a kind of thinking which takes its guidelines and anchorage points from the active understanding of tradition current in the Church and especially subject to the checks of the magisterium.

But what of the distinction we have suggested between popular and learned tradition? One might suggest also a kind of functionary's tradition, not necessarily attuned to the most learned aspects of the theological tradition but not the tradition of popular piety either. It is a kind of bureaucratic tradition which often reflects specifically conditioned attitudes of defense and the pursuit of organizational interests of a varied sort.

The notion of the mind of the Church requires much study. It must be viewed within the complex topological structure of transmission we have suggested and in relation to the processes going on within it. It is a state of existence of and relationship among what the Church sees as the four corner pillars of its edifice of belief: revelation, tradition, scripture, and magisterium within the setting of that larger framework. In the period ahead there will take place an enormously complicated and difficult restructuration of the mind of the Church on all the basic issues considered in our analysis. The study of the Bible and its implications will occupy a central and strategic position in this conflict-laden evolution.

The *De Revelatione* has been seen to be less expressive of the mystery of faith than was the *Lumen Gentium*, less historical than the *Gaudium et Spes*, and less ecumenical than the *Nostra Actate*. It is also less eschatological than a number of other conciliar documents. If the *Pastoral Constitution on the Church in the Modern World* attempts to suggest an interpenetration between eschatology and historicity, thereby relating the processes of sacred and secular history, one does not feel that spirit in this document. The "truth" about the past rather than the "anticipation" of the future seems the dominant interest. And while making a series of signal and significant concessions to modern methodology and the modern mentality, it evinces concern with maintaining a kind of mooring in an inerrancy understood as a qualified literalism and another in "the watchful care of the sacred teaching office of the Church." Yet the serious and genuinely scientific and scholarly study of the Bible has been embraced by an ecumenical council. It is a course which contains its own demands and which will re-present at many turns the basic issues compromised in the formulation of this conciliar document.

IX

EPILOGUE

THE ecumenical council of our era, known now as Vatican II, the call to which was announced by Pope John XXIII in January 1959, was opened by that pontiff on October 11, 1962, after over two years of preparation. In that period many feared that the Roman Curia would so emasculate the coming council that little would be accomplished. In his opening speech John himself repudiated those "prophets of gloom, who are always forecasting disaster," who think "that our era, in comparison with past eras, is getting worse," and who "behave as though they had learned nothing from history, which is none the less, the teacher of life." John saw, rather, in "the present order of things" Divine Providence "leading us to a new order of human relations, which, by men's own efforts and even beyond their very expectations, are directed toward the fulfillment of God's superior and inscrutable designs" [1:712f]. He affirmed as well that "everything" in our day "leads to the greater good of the Church" [1:713]. He proclaimed that

> ... the Catholic Church, raising the torch of religious truth by means of this Ecumenical Council, desires to show herself to be the loving mother of all, benign, patient, full of mercy and goodness toward the brethren who are separated from her. To mankind, oppressed by so many difficulties, the Church says, as Peter said to the poor who begged alms from him: "I have neither gold nor silver, but what I have I give you; in the name of Jesus Christ of Nazareth, rise and walk" [1:716].

243

Until December 8, 1965, when the Council was closed by Paul VI, there took place some 10 public sessions in which were enacted 16 conciliar documents dealing with a great variety of issues. In his formal closing brief, Pope Paul stated that this Council "must be numbered without doubt among the greatest events of the Church." It was the largest ever held, as Paul noted, and "the richest because of the questions" which it "discussed carefully and profoundly." It was, moreover, the "most opportune, because, bearing in mind the necessities of the present day, above all it sought to meet the pastoral needs and, nourishing the flame of charity, it has made a great effort to reach not only the Christians still separated from communion with the Holy See, but also the whole human family" [1:738].

Our consideration of three major Council documents has shown that the Council did face the issues before the Church, did attempt to formulate direction with respect to them, and found it necessary in doing so to compromise newer perspectives and newer understanding with older ideas and mental postures characteristic of the Church for a long time. The documents of the Council show the results of compromise. They exhibit the stresses and strains which were experienced in the effort to inaugurate a profound updating of Catholic Christianity.

The inner content of conciliar documents indeed offers to content analysis a much more reliable index of the kinds of conflicts and the nature of the dangers to be faced in the postconciliar epoch than does the actual voting record of the assembled Fathers. The final voting on Council documents recorded a near unanimity. On December 4, 1963, the Fathers enacted the decree on Communications (*Inter Mirifica*) by a vote of 1,960 to 164; on October 28, 1965, they enacted the *Declaration on the Relationship of the Church to Non-Christian Religions* by a vote of 2,221 to 88. On an earlier vote on the proposition concerning the Jews there were 1,821 affirmative as against 245 negative votes. The vote on the declaration on

Religious Liberty in December 1965 was 2,308 to 70, and the vote for the *Gaudium et Spes*, to which we devoted major consideration in this analysis, on the same day was 2,309 to 75. The *De Revelatione*, despite the earlier division of 1,368 to 822, finally was approved in November 1965 by a vote of 2,344 to 6. Obviously the conciliar vote tally fails to represent the distances separating viewpoints in the Church and fails to register the various groupings among the episcopacy and their advisers.

It appears that every issue of significance in Christian history, and indeed in religious life, came before the Council. What is man's ultimate destiny? What is his earthly vocation? How are they related to each other? What is man's relationship to God? What is human community? How are the two interrelated? What is meant by saying that God speaks to man? What is the Christian Church? What is the relationship of God's call to man's earthly drama? What is the relation of the Church to the world? What is religious participation, and how is it related to man's quest for ultimate meaning and relationship? These questions or their equivalents arise in every culture and find their answer —implicitly or in explicit beliefs —in every religion. Historically, Catholicism has spelled out a complex of answers, embodied them in its creeds and liturgies, and built around them its communal and hierarchical structure. This set of themes, institutionalized within the Church, provided the basic answers to western man's problem of meaning for centuries. The answers were guaranteed and underwritten by the sense of the immediacy and reality of God and of man's relationship to him and participation with him in the Church which long characterized Catholic faith and remains its greatest source of strength.

This institutionalized form of Christianity became the tutor of Europe and provided European civilization with its basic consensus. But the forms of intellectual expression, of liturgical participation, and of organized membership that came into existence hardened little by little and became alienated to one degree or another from important elements in the dynamic society of the high and late Middle Ages. We have seen how the Church, once mother and schoolmistress of Europe, gradually became a stranger and an alien in the midst of the civilization her children brought into being.

First came the Reformation, which attempted to renew and purify Christianity outside the unity of the old Church and in contradiction to many of its doctrines. At the same time there took place the rise of humanism, rooted in the Hellenic culture which the early Church had embraced and brought into synthesis with its own religious world view. In the Renaissance men sought a more this-worldly religion, and in the Enlightenment they revolted in the name of reason against the religious institutions of the past, seeing them as the fabrications of priestcraft and superstition.

Marxism presented western man with a new and dynamic counter gospel invoking history and science and interpreting in a this-worldly manner the memories of Christian transcendence which Hegel has historicized. In the 17th century Europe saw the rise of modern science, and since then western man has experienced its demythologizing effects upon the modes of his most intimate thought. Protestantism, humanism, Marxism, and scientism—against all these the Roman Church attempted to maintain and defend the forms of Christianity it had evolved in the first thousand years of Christian history.

In the meantime lay elites and finally many of the common people seceded from the Church and its ecclesiastical and clerical culture and constructed a dynamic western civilization. Never before had man achieved so much control over the means and circumstances of life. Technology introduced a laicized society in which traditionalism was dissolved. Urbanization created a wholly new kind of culture. The intellectual effects of science and the sociological consequences of the technology made possible by science destroyed the old world of rural peculiarity and cultural isolation. All this came to a head in the 20th century in the communications revolution, which continues swiftly to uproot men from older cultural settings. There was a secularization of culture, a vast and deep inner transformation of the modality of western experience marked by a loss not simply of traditional guidelines and anchorage points but of the religious motivation and substance of large numbers of people, both mass and elite. Furthermore, this dynamic, antitraditional, technologically based urban world is torn by conflicts—old conflicts inherited from the past and new ones brought to realization in the difficult conditions of the transition.

Robert Merton has suggested that in our times a new differentiating criterion exists which is more significant than the older structural differences that distinguished groups of men in the past. More important than social class, or religious affiliation, or even national and ethnic allegiance is whether one is rooted in particular provincial cultural settings or is part of the larger translocal world brought about by science, technology, social mobility, and the communications revolution. To Merton the distinction between "locals" and "cosmopolitans" is perhaps the most strategic one of our day.

In a study of the Middle East a decade ago, Daniel Lerner found that people could be divided into three types depending upon how much they were a part of a provincial setting or how much a part of the larger world of modernity. His categories were "traditionals," "transitionals," and "moderns." In that transitional and conflict-ridden part of the world, he says, it was "transitionals," the men "in motion," upon whom the destiny of the region would ultimately depend. They had altered their mode of consciousness; they had developed a "psychic mobility" which made them pursue goals and aspirations far transcending the ideas of rural provinciality.

Both Merton's and Lerner's classifications point to the communications revolution as the most significant agent in

247

modern societies. The world of the moderns, the transitionals, the cosmopolitans is the world of tomorrow, and it is this world which the Church tried to take into account, with which it tried to enter into genuine and authentic relation in the *Gaudium et Spes*. It is a world compounded of the elements against which the Church has always acted in a defensive manner. Yet it was this modern world which also looked to Vatican II with hope.

Protestantism had tried to reform and renew Christianity and later to render it relevant to modernity. Its achievements were impressive, but it was not successful on the whole. Humanism, Marxism, and scientism had proposed substitutes for Christianity, but, in the form in which they have come down to us from the 16th, 17th, 18th, and 19th centuries, these are as obsolete and outmoded as the traditional forms of Christianity. A this-worldly humanism or a historic apotheosis which consists in a collective control of the conditions of life is a necessary ingredient of any viable system of values western man may evolve, but they are insufficient. Men are beginning to look beyond the simple, limited, and provincial this-sidedness of the Enlightenment and of its child and heir Marxism. They raise again the deeper problems of meaning and the questions of ultimacy and transcendence. The development of modernity which has enhanced man's powers has also removed his securities. It has brought him face to face with the challenge of understanding himself and his situation, no longer as the adolescent rebel of the Enlightenment, but with a mature responsibility capable of responding adequately to the problems of human survival in the third quarter of the 20th century.

What do the perennial religious questions mean in this setting? What does the Christian answer mean in this new situation? In the face of the greater anomie which has been the obverse side of emancipation many attempt to withdraw into older securities, no longer securely believed—Christian securities, humanist securities, Marxist securities, scientistic securities. But such halfway houses cannot last out the contemporary crisis.

We have seen in the documents of the Vatican Council the intellectual and existential problems in the encounter of the Christian tradition with a rapidly unfolding modernity. History and ontology, process and substance, immanence and transcendence, openness and structure; self-expression and realization and discipline and directed development for individuals—these indicate sides of reality which western man must confront and relate together. As a consequence he can evolve a view of himself and his world that will do justice to his situation as his enlarged consciousness can now grasp it. Western man has brought himself to that point where he must self-consciously opt for self-consciousness and its inherent responsibilities or vanish before the Pandora's box of technical achievement and detraditionalized human aspiration which his efforts have opened up. He faces the challenge of genuinely coming of age.

The development of human personalities—of stable personal organization for individual human beings—that can achieve maturity requires some enduring context of beliefs, values, and social structures. It requires the building of genuine community. But the communications revolution, the growing affluence, and the inherent dynamic involved in science-based technology threaten to make community in the old sense—stability in the old sense—impossible. Man's expanding knowledge makes specific and fundamentalist traditional lore obsolete and thereby undermines one of the cornerstones of traditional stability. Can modern men learn to build community on the basis of this dynamism? Can they evolve a religious consciousness which will provide the orientation and guidance in relation to the total human situation necessary for this great task?

We stated earlier that in its effort to update itself, to achieve an *aggiornamento* in depth, Catholicism stands surrogate for Christianity as a whole, and upon the success or failure of this effort depends the future of Christianity. We may suggest too that the success or failure of Christianity in this crisis may well prove the strategic element in determining whether western civilization will continue its remarkable career of developing man's potential or whether it and many of its most precious human values will vanish from the scene, to be rediscovered by what suffering and at what time no one knows.

The Catholic Church has returned to relevance. What happens within its confines from now on will be the concern of all. In returning to relevance from its long, defensive withdrawal, it has taken on a new responsibility. Can the Church maintain its unity and bring about its sociological demythologization? Can it shed the forms evolved historically and find new modes of thought, expression, and participation relevant to the new age which is advancing upon us? Can it bring into the future the spiritual wealth of its ancient tradition? Can it achieve all this and maintain its faith—its deep conviction of God's immediacy and reality, and its sense of the meeting of immanence and transcendence in Christ? Can it find *aggiornamento* in depth without loss of depth and intensity of its faith? Can it do so and evolve the new form of organization and presence—neither "church" nor "sect"—requisite to its mission in tomorrow's world?

It is at any rate on trial before the world to bend its every energy in the attempt. It must make the attempt by aiding man's advance to maturity. While it preserves and guards what used to be called the simple faith of the people, it must recognize, prepare for, and contribute to the new world of the communications revolution and mass higher education which technology will bring into being, a world in which "simple faith" will be transformed beyond our every expectation.

Max Scheler wrote a half century ago,

Christianity, some say, is bankrupt; No—simply the Churches, say others; Just this Church and that one, say others yet again. All these theses were prevalent long ago—long before the war. Among the older voices only *one* is almost wholly unheard today —the one which says, Religion itself is bankrupt: it is only an atavism in historical evolution. That this voice is missing shows that we should expect at all events an age of extreme *vitality* in matters of religion, an age characterized by quite new kinds of mighty spiritual conflicts. But for precisely that reason, in the coming age every positive religion and Church must cease to be a mere ice-box for old truths—as it was recently put by a Swiss theologian. No doctrinal position—unless it wishes to surrender entirely—will be able to content itself with a mere wish to maintain its *status quo;* every such position will have to exert itself in addition to demonstrate positively to the world its overriding worth—and to be the warrant of its own truth. There we have certainly a new situation, to which none may remain blind. Consider the person who wishes merely to *preserve*, or at the most *defend*, his religious position: if he dare not see in it the positive means of salvation for suffering humanity, and will not extend to humanity this means in a gift of joy and love, then he will find even his more modest goal of self-preservation *no longer* attainable. As men reckon, his cause will vanish from the face of the earth. For this is how things stand: neither mass-indifference, however widespread, nor even heresy and unbelief, nor sham piety nor superstition were ever a real, an ultimate danger to the existence of a positive religion and Church. Rather the opposite—the outworn, the decadent, custom and inertia were never so mightily propped and preserved in Church-religion as by—*inter alia*—indifference and unbelief. Especially among the educated. Only one true possible danger threatens the existence of a positive religion—the greater enthusiasm and the deeper faith of those who practice *another religion*. It was skeptic indifference and unbelief which enabled the Churches to live such an easy life before the war and to be so content with "maintaining" their position. But the time will come when unbelief's sterile negation and the apparent tolerance of religion by lazy indifference will come to an end. Then religion will once again be recognized and attacked from all sides for what it is—the highest concern of man. Then will be an end of the easy life. And with it there will cease the perfunctory frontier-patrol of one's values and ideas, or the airtight, quasi-paralyzed self-mummification in the coffin of exclusive organizations and places apart. Only one alternative will then be valid—either one must gird up one's loins and with open, succoring arms, *give*, present or lavish something on humanity, heal its heart's open wound, or one must be prepared to find that the world, though thirsting feverishly for religion, believes one has nothing to give; to find, even, that one no longer feels oneself wholly in the right or in possession of the true and the good—of, in short, the divine verities. But in the latter case one must also be prepared to find that this catalytic conviction also penetrates one's own ranks, and that the mere policy of "holding fast"—that gesture of pride and avarice—brings on the destruction of the very things which one wished to preserve. Any positive religion which today fails in the above sense to carry out its spiritual mission, to bear new and living witness to its cause in every way, is most certainly doomed to defeat and decline in the spiritual struggles which we have before us. Not in the sense of outward power and might, but in the sense of proofs of heart and soul, every positive religion must win victory *or* suffer defeat. He who has nothing to give in *this* crisis of the world will lose what he possesses [80:121f].

The hour of Scheler's challenge has indeed arrived. Christianity is becoming a serious thing again; Christians and especially the Christian leadership must be serious about it. Is it "now only the dawn," as Pope John declared, "a forerunner of most splendid light?" [1:718] Will there, in response to intelligent and responsible human effort, be given a new outpouring of the spirit?

NOTES

1. Abbott, Walter M, SJ, general ed, and Gallagher, Joseph, translation ed: *The Documents of Vatican II* (Guild Press, Inc, America Press, Association Press, New York, New York) 1966.
2. Aubert, Roger: The Catholic Church, in Guy S Metraux and François Crouzet, eds, *Religion and the Promise of the Twentieth Century* (The New American Library, Inc, Mentor Books, New York, New York) 1965.
3. Baum, Gregory, OSA: *De Ecclesia: The Constitution on the Church* (Paulist Press, Deus Books, Glen Rock, New Jersey) 1965.
4. Bellah, Robert N: *Tokugawa Religion: The Values of Pre-industrial Japan* (The Free Press, New York, New York) 1957.
5. Belloc, Hilaire: *The French Revolution* (Henry Holt & Co., Inc, New York, New York) 1911.
6. Bergson, Henri: *The Two Sources of Morality and Religion*, R Ashley Audra and Cloudesley Brereton, trs, assisted by W Horsfall Carter (Doubleday & Company, Inc, Anchor Books, Garden City, New York) 1954.
7. Bible, Revised Standard Version, Catholic ed.
8. Billington, Ray Allen: *The Protestant Crusade* (Rinehart & Company, Inc, New York, New York) 1952.
9. Blondel, Maurice: *L'Action* (F Alcan, Paris) 1936–37, 2 vols.
10. Bonhoeffer, Dietrich: *Letters and Papers from Prison*, Eberhard Bethge, ed, Reginald H Fuller, tr (The Macmillan Company, New York, New York) 1953.
11. Bouyer, Louis: *Newman: His Life and Spirituality* (Meridian Books, Inc, New York, New York) 1960.

12. Butler, Abbot Christopher: The Aggiornamento of Vatican II, in John H Miller, CSC, ed, *Vatican II: An Interfaith Appraisal*, International Theological Conference, University of Notre Dame, March 20–26, 1966 (University of Notre Dame Press, Notre Dame, Indiana) 1966.

13. Campion, Donald R, SJ: The Church Today, in Walter M Abbott, SJ, general ed, and Joseph Gallagher, translation ed, *The Documents of Vatican II* (Guild Press, Inc, America Press, Association Press, New York, New York) 1966.

14. Cassirer, Ernst: *The Myth of the State* (Doubleday & Company, Garden City, New York) 1955.

15. Charlier, Celestin: *The Christian Approach to the Bible* (The Newman Press, Westminster, Maryland) 1958.

16. Congar, Yves M J, OP: *Lay People in the Church*, Donald Attwater, tr (The Newman Press, Westminster, Maryland) 1957.

17. Dansette, Adrien: *Religious History of Modern France*, John Dingle, tr (Herder and Herder, Inc, New York, New York) 1961, vol II.

18. Cross, Robert D: *The Emergence of Liberal Catholicism in America* (Harvard University Press, Cambridge, Massachusetts) 1958.

19. Dawson, Christopher: *The Crisis of Western Education* (Sheed & Ward, New York, New York) 1961.

20. Dulles, Avery, SJ: The Church, in Walter M Abbott, SJ, general ed, and Joseph Gallagher, translation ed, *The Documents of Vatican II* (Guild Press, Inc, America Press, Association Press, New York, New York) 1966.

21. Durkheim, Emile: *The Elementary Forms of the Religious Life*, Joseph Ward Swain, tr (The Free Press, New York, New York) 1954.

22. Dyson, R A, and MacKenzie, R A F: Higher Criticism of the Bible, in Bernard Orchard, Edmund F Sutcliffe, SJ, Reginald C Fuller, and Ralph Russell, DD, eds, *A Catholic Commentary on Holy Scripture* (Thomas Nelson & Sons, London) 1953, secs 43–46.

23. Eliade, Mircea: *The Sacred and the Profane*, Willard R Trask, tr (Harcourt, Brace & Co, New York, New York) 1959.

24. Ernst, C: In *Vatican II: The Theological Dimension* (Thomist Press, Washington, D C) 1963, quoted from Paul S Minear, A Protestant Point of View, in John H Miller, CSC, ed, *Vatican II: An Interfaith Appraisal*, International Theological Conference, University of Notre Dame, March 20–26, 1966 (University of Notre Dame Press, Notre Dame, Indiana) 1966.

25. Fackenheim, Emil L: *Metaphysics and Historicity* (Marquette University Press, Milwaukee, Wisconsin) 1961.

26. Fackenheim, Emil L: On the Self-Exposure of Faith to the Modern Secular World: Philosophical Reflections in the Light of Jewish Experience, *Daedalus*, Winter, 1967, pp 193–219.

27. Ferré, Frederick: *Language, Logic and God* (Harper & Brothers, New York, New York) 1961.

28. First Vatican Council: On Faith, in *Dogmatic Constitution on the Catholic Faith*, Denz. 1789 (3008) chap 3.

29. Fremantle, Anne, ed: *The Papal Encyclicals in Their Historical Context*, ptg 5, expanded (The New American Library, Mentor-Omega, New York, New York) 1963.

30. Garaudy, Roger: *From Anathema to Dialogue: A Marxist Challenge to the Christian Churches*, Luke O'Neill, tr (Herder and Herder, Inc, New York, New York) 1966.

31. Hales, E E Y: *The Catholic Church in the Modern World* (Doubleday & Company, Inc, Image Books, Garden City, New York) 1958.

32. Hales, E E Y: *Pio Nono* (Doubleday & Company, Inc, Image Books, Garden City, New York) 1962.

33. Hales, E E Y: *Pope John and His Revolution* (Doubleday & Company, Inc, Garden City, New York) 1966.

34. Häring, Bernard, CSsR: Marriage and the Family in John H Miller, CSC, ed, *Vatican II: An Interfaith Appraisal*, International Theological Conference, University of Notre Dame, March 20–26, 1966 (University of Notre Dame Press, Notre Dame, Indiana) 1966.

35. Hartman, Louis F, CSsR: The Great Tree and Nabuchodonosor's Madness, in John L McKenzie, SJ, ed, *The Bible in Cur-*

rent Catholic Thought (Herder and Herder, Inc, New York, New York) 1962.

36. Higgins, George G: Economic and Social Life, in John H Miller, CSC, ed, *Vatican II: An Interfaith Appraisal*, International Theological Conference, University of Notre Dame, March 20–26, 1966 (University of Notre Dame Press, Notre Dame, Indiana) 1966.

37. Hobsbawm, E J: *The Age of Revolution: 1789–1848* (The World Publishing Company, Cleveland, Ohio) 1962.

38. Houtart, François: Discussion, in John H Miller, CSC, ed, *Vatican II: An Interfaith Appraisal*, International Theological Conference, University of Notre Dame, March 20–26, 1966 (University of Notre Dame Press, Notre Dame, Indiana) 1966.

39. Houtart, François: Suggestions for Doctrinal Development, in John H Miller, CSC, ed, *Vatican II: An Interfaith Appraisal*, International Theological Conference, University of Notre Dame, March 20–26, 1966 (University of Notre Dame Press, Notre Dame, Indiana) 1966.

40. Hulsbosch, A, OSA: *God and Creation and Evolution* (Sheed & Ward, New York, New York) 1965.

41. Journet, Charles: *The Church of the Word Incarnate*, A H C Downes, tr (Sheed & Ward, New York, New York) 1955.

42. Kane, John J: *Catholic-Protestant Conflicts in America* (Henry Regnery Co, Chicago, Illinois) 1955.

43. Küng, Hans: In *Journal of Ecumenical Studies*, 1964, vol 1, p 111.

44. Laurentin, Rene: Vatican II: Report on the First Session, *Cross Currents*, 1963, vol 12, no 4, p 420.

45. Leahy, William K, and Massimini, Anthony T, eds: *Third Session Council Speeches of Vatican II* (Paulist Press, Deus Books, Glen Rock, New Jersey) 1966.

46. Lenski, Gerhart: *The Religious Factor* (Doubleday & Company, Inc, Garden City, New York) 1961.

47. Lindbeck, George A: A Protestant Point of View, in John H Miller, CSC, ed, *Vatican II: An Interfaith Appraisal*, International Theological Conference, University of Notre Dame, March 20–26, 1966 (University of Notre Dame Press, Notre Dame, Indiana) 1966.

48. Loisy, Alfred: *Autour d'un Petit Livre* (A Picard et fils, Paris) 1903.
49. Loisy: Alfred: *L'Évangile et l'Église* (A Picard et fils, Paris) 1902. English edition: *The Gospel and the Church* (Charles Scribner's Sons, New York, New York) 1912.
50. Lubac, Henri de, SJ: Lumen Gentium and the Fathers, in John H Miller, CSC, ed, *Vatican II: An Interfaith Appraisal*, International Theological Conference, University of Notre Dame, March 20–26, 1966 (University of Notre Dame Press, Notre Dame, Indiana) 1966.
51. McGrath, Mark G, CSC: The Constitution on the Church in the Modern World, in John H Miller, CSC, ed, *Vatican II: An Interfaith Appraisal*, International Theological Conference, University of Notre Dame, March 20–26, 1966 (University of Notre Dame Press, Notre Dame, Indiana) 1966.
52. Macquarrie, John: *An Existentialist Theology: A Comparison of Heidegger and Bultmann* (Harper & Row, Publishers, New York, New York) 1965.
53. Mannheim, Karl: *Ideology and Utopia* (Harcourt, Brace & Co, New York, New York) 1949.
54. Martin, James A, Jr: *The New Dialogue Between Philosophy and Theology* (The Seabury Press, Inc, New York, New York) 1966.
55. Miller, John H, CSC, ed: *Vatican II: An Interfaith Appraisal*, International Theological Conference, University of Notre Dame, March 20–26, 1966 (University of Notre Dame Press, Notre Dame, Indiana) 1966.
56. Minear, Paul S: A Protestant Point of View, in John H Miller, CSC, ed, *Vatican II: An Interfaith Appraisal*, International Theological Conference, University of Notre Dame, March 20–26, 1966 (University of Notre Dame Press, Notre Dame, Indiana) 1966.
57. Murray, John Courtney, SJ: On the Structure of the Church-State Problem, in Waldemar Gurian and M A Fitzsimons, eds, *The Catholic Church in World Affairs* (University of Notre Dame Press, Notre Dame, Indiana) 1954.
58. Neal, Sister Marie Augusta, SND: *Values and Interests in Social Change* (Prentice-Hall, Inc, Englewood Cliffs, New Jersey) 1965.

59. *New Catholic Encyclopedia* (McGraw-Hill, Inc, New York, New York) 1967, vol 12.

60. *New York Times*, July 23, 1967.

61. Newman, Jeremiah: *Change and the Catholic Church* (Helicon Press, Inc, Baltimore, Maryland) 1965.

62. Newman, John Henry: *An Essay on the Development of Christian Doctrine* (Doubleday & Company, Inc, Image Books, Garden City, New York) 1960.

63. Niebuhr, H Richard: *Christ and Culture* (Harper & Brothers, New York, New York) 1951.

64. Northrop, F S C: *The Meeting of East and West* (The Macmillan Company, New York, New York) 1946.

65. O'Dea, Thomas F: The Catholic Immigrant and the American Scene, *Thought*, Fordham University Quarterly, 1956, vol 31, no 121, pp 251–270.

66. O'Dea, Thomas F: Five Dilemmas in the Institutionalization of Religion, *Journal for the Scientific Study of Religion*, 1961, vol 1, no 1, pp 30–39.

67. O'Dea, Thomas F: Sociological Dilemmas: Five Paradoxes of Institutionalization, in Edward A Tiryakian, ed, *Sociological Theory, Values and Sociocultural Change* (The Free Press, New York, New York) 1963, pp 71–89.

68. O'Dea, Thomas F: *The Sociology of Religion* (Prentice-Hall, Inc, Englewood Cliffs, New Jersey) 1966.

69. Otto, Rudolf: *The Idea of the Holy*, J W Harvey, tr (Oxford University Press, London, England) 1950.

70. Outler, Albert C: A Response, in Walter M Abbott, SJ, general ed, and Joseph Gallagher, translation ed, *The Documents of Vatican II* (Guild Press, Inc, America Press, Association Press, New York, New York) 1966.

71. Petre, M D: *Modernism* (T C and E C Jack, Ltd, London, England) 1918.

72. Pius XI: *Non Abbiamo Bisogno* (On Catholic Action) in Gerard F Yates, ed, *Papal Thought on the State* (Appleton-Century-Crofts, Inc, New York, New York) 1958.

73. Pius XII: Encyclical letter *Divino Afflante Spiritu*, quoted from

Anne Fremantle, ed, *The Papal Encyclicals in Their Historical Context*, ptg 5, expanded (The New American Library, Mentor-Omega, New York, New York) 1963.

74. Pius XII: Encyclical letter *Humani Generis*, quoted from Anne Fremantle, ed, *The Papal Encyclicals in Their Historical Context*, ptg 5, expanded (The New American Library, Mentor-Omega, New York, New York) 1963.

75. Pius XII: Encyclical letter *Sacra Virginatas*, quoted from Anne Fremantle, ed, *The Papal Encyclicals in Their Historical Context*, ptg 5, expanded (The New American Library, Mentor-Omega, New York, New York) 1963.

76. Plato: *Phaedrus*, Jowett translation.

77. Rahner, Karl: *The Church After the Council* (Herder and Herder, Inc, New York, New York) 1956.

78. Ryan, John A, and Moorhouse, F X Millar, SJ: *The State and the Church* (The Macmillan Company, New York, New York) 1922.

79. Ryan, John A, and Boland, Francis J: *Catholic Principles of Politics* (The Macmillan Company, New York, New York) 1940.

80. Scheler, Max: *On the Eternal in Man*, Bernard Noble, tr (Harper & Brothers, New York, New York) 1961.

81. Sittler, Joseph: A Protestant Point of View, in John H Miller, CSC, ed, *Vatican II: An Interfaith Appraisal*, International Theological Conference, University of Notre Dame, March 20–26, 1966 (University of Notre Dame Press, Notre Dame, Indiana) 1966.

82. *The Sixteen Documents of Vatican II*, with commentary by the Council Fathers, NCWC translation (Daughters of St Paul, St Paul Editions, Boston, Massachusetts) no date.

83. Smith, Wilfred Cantwell: *The Meaning and End of Religion* (The New American Library, Mentor Books, New York, New York) 1964.

84. Stanley, David Michael, SJ: New Understanding of the Gospels, in John L. McKenzie, SJ, ed, *The Bible in Current Catholic Thought* (Herder and Herder, Inc, New York, New York) 1962

85. Sutcliffe, E F, SJ: Job, in Bernard Orchard, Edmund F Sutcliffe, SJ, Reginald C Fuller, and Ralph Russell, *A Catholic Commentary on Holy Scripture* (Thomas Nelson & Sons, London, England) 1953.

86. Tillich, Paul: *The Religious Situation* (Meridian Books, Inc, New York, New York) 1956. Published in 1932 by Henry Holt & Co, Inc.

87. Troeltsch, Ernst: *Die Absolutheit des Christentums und die Religionsgeschichte*, 2 ed (J C B Mohr, Tübingen) 1912.

88. Troeltsch, Ernst: *Christian Thought: Its History and Application*, Baron F von Hugel, ed (Meridian Books, Inc, Living Age Books, New York, New York) 1957.

89. Troeltsch, Ernst: *Protestantism and Progress: A Historical Study of the Relation of Protestantism to the Modern World*, W Montgomery, tr (Beacon Press, Boston, Massachusetts) 1958.

90. Tucci, Roberto, SJ: Culture, in John H Miller, CSC, ed, *Vatican II: An Interfaith Appraisal*, International Conference, University of Notre Dame, March 20–26, 1966 (University of Notre Dame Press, Notre Dame, Indiana) 1966.

91. Tyrrell, George: *The Church and the Future* (Turnbull and Spears, Edinburgh) 1903.

92. Tyrrell, George: *Medievalism: A Reply to Cardinal Mercier* (Longmans, Green and Company, London, England) 1908.

93. Tyrrell, George: Revelation and Experience, unpublished article quoted in M D Petre, *Modernism* (T C and E C Jack, Ltd, London, England) 1918.

94. Van Bilsen, Bertrand, OFM: *The Changing Church* (Duquesne University Press, Pittsburgh, Pennsylvania) 1966. Éditions E Nauwelaerts, Louvain, adapted by Henry J Koren, CSSp.

95. Van der Leeuw, G: *Religion in Essence and Manifestation*, J E Turner, tr, vols I and II (Harper & Row, Publishers, Harper Torchbooks, New York, New York) 1963.

96. Vidler, Alec R: *The Church in an Age of Revolution* (Penguin Books, Inc, Baltimore, Maryland) 1961.

97. Vidler, Alec R: *The Modernist Movement in the Roman Church* (Cambridge University Press, Cambridge, England) 1934.

98. Ward, Wilfrid: *The Life of John Henry Cardinal Newman* (Longmans, Green and Company, London, England) 1912, vol I.
99. Ward, Wilfrid: *William George Ward and the Catholic Revival* (Macmillan & Co., London, England) 1893.
100. Webb, C C J: *A History of Philosophy* (Henry Holt & Co, Inc, New York, New York) 1915.
101. Weber, Max: *The Protestant Ethic and the Spirit of Capitalism*, Talcott Parsons, tr (Charles Scribner's Sons, New York, New York) 1948.
102. Werner, Martin: *The Formation of Christian Dogma*, S G F Brandon, tr (Beacon Press, Boston, Massachusetts) 1957.

INDEX